BELGRADE

Cities of the Imagination

Cities OF THE IMAGINATION

BELGRADE

A cultural and literary history

David A. Norris

Signal Books
Oxford

First published in 2008 by
Signal Books Limited
36 Minster Road
Oxford OX4 1LY
www.signalbooks.co.uk

A catalogue record for this book is available from the British Library

ISBN 978-1-904955-43-6 Paper

Drawings by Wendy Skinner Smith
Cover Design: Baseline Arts
Production: Devdan Sen
Cover Images: © allOver photography/Alamy
Printed in India

Contents

Foreword

Belgrade is the gateway to the Balkans. It towers over the place where two great rivers meet, the Sava and the Danube. Over the centuries this meeting point has stood for the geographic and political border between the Balkans and the rest of Europe, between East and West. History tells us that this town, lying in the path of all armies who have tried to break in or out of the Balkans, has been destroyed and rebuilt some forty times in the 2,000 years since Christ.

It was bombed the last time in spring 1999, when the government was in the hands of Slobodan Milošević, the only remaining communist leader in south-eastern Europe. NATO's air forces carried out the bombardment during a three-month war with the ruling regime, from which the Serbs freed themselves by a peaceful revolution in October of the following year. The foreign traveller visiting Belgrade in 2007 might not notice the traces of that dramatic campaign unless his attention is turned to the buildings waiting for renovation—of which not many are left. But he may be interested in the narrative behind the buildings bombed by NATO, which now look like new and have become symbols of Belgrade's survival in the period known as "the time of transition".

One of these buildings is the slender, green-blue, glass skyscraper which the visitor cannot fail to see whether taking a bus or taxi from the centre of Belgrade, over Branko Bridge on the Sava toward New Belgrade, or from New Belgrade in the opposite direction toward the centre. It stands alone in apparent supremacy over its surroundings near the crossroads of the two boulevards named after the two scientists, Mihailo Pupin and Nikola Tesla. The skyscraper, now in private ownership, is called the Confluence Business Centre and houses the management boards of several large corporations. It used to be, before it was targeted in April 1999, the hub of Slobodan Milošević's political power and party organization, better known as the Building of the Central Committee.

From his windows facing south-east, the august master had a wonderful view over the junction of the two rivers, over the fortress in Kalemegdan Park on the opposite bank of the Sava, sitting on its rocky outcrop above the confluence as it has done for centuries, and over Belgrade, a modern conurbation astride the remains of ancient settlements put here by Celts, Romans, Bulgars, Magyars, Serbs, Turks and Austrians. From his offices looking north-west, he could watch the whole of New Belgrade, the city's most populous borough, where building began only after the Second World War when Josip Broz Tito began his 35-year presidency of socialist Yugoslavia. This swarming district has been transformed into interwoven strips of modern architectural and urban structures, tall buildings and broad avenues, piled up without any particular order, attractive in their own way, on the level surface of what was once the low-lying Pannonian plains.

New Belgrade has also been witness to the many social and political changes that have occurred in the city during the last sixty years. It was built slowly, over decades, in the spirit of the anonymous architectural style of Socialist Realism, on land which was mostly sand and mire. It was considered a gloomy dormitory for the many thousands of people who came after the Second World War from the regions to the capital city of the new socialist state to be schooled here, to find work and to stay.

But for some time, and especially since October 2000 when Serbia's democratic forces took control of government, those who live here no longer look upon New Belgrade as a dormitory—and with good reason. They now see it as a workshop in which a more modern way of life is being produced, circulated and exchanged in an ever increasing tempo. The transformation has been huge and obvious. Life here teems on the wide and long paths beside the Sava and Danube, on the floating restaurants moored one after the other, especially in the afternoons and evenings. The young and the not-so-young, from New Belgrade and elsewhere, find their favourite meeting points and places for entertainment. The people of New Belgrade have again fallen in love with their rivers, whose banks were empty in the 1990s as they echoed to the sound of shooting, explosions and violent clashes between different political factions, particularly under the night sky. The cost of flats and commercial property in the area is now rising at a dizzy pace year on year. With its broad boulevards, hotels, Serbian and foreign banks, modern shopping centres, boutiques, restaurants, markets, greenbelt space and avenues of trees, sports halls, private universities and clinics, New Belgrade has suddenly become a very desirable place to work, live, mix and socialize.

In young Belgrade slang, you often hear as a mark of respect for a friend's success, "He's living like a king over on New-side!" The word New-side in this complimentary phrase means New Belgrade. And yet it also carries an ambiguous subtext about the part of town where money is quickly made and by means which are not always exactly honest. Your own money and your own flat represent an ideal goal for young people in today's Belgrade; not easy to achieve in a world where employment is difficult to find.

Not long ago, a taxi driver, a man in his early thirties, told me of his experience while driving me to the city centre from New Belgrade. He graduated in medicine over five years ago, he said, and then did the usual things: some voluntary work as a doctor and his military service. After a lot of looking around, replying to adverts and waiting, he finally managed to get a job as a doctor in a small town just over a hundred miles from Belgrade and he was very happy. But his happiness did not last long, for less than a year later he had to leave the job he loved. He was not bothered that he had a long daily commute to and from work, nor that he often worked ten- or twelve-hour shifts. But he could not reconcile himself to his doctor's salary not providing enough for his small family to live on for even ten days in the month. He was forced to make a crucial decision: he left the medical profession for which he had studied eight years, took financial help from his father to buy a new car, and became one of several thousand Belgrade taxi drivers. He was not dissatisfied with his lot, now earning three to four times more than when he was a doctor and with more free time to spend with his family.

I listened to his story, not at all unusual by today's standards in the capital, while the young doctor skilfully squeezed his taxi in and out of the three lanes of modern cars, creeping along in the late afternoon from New Belgrade toward the centre of town. The traffic was thick and almost at a standstill at that time of day, for only three bridges on the Sava link the old part of town, the megalopolis which has remained in the Balkans, with the new part which vaulted over the river and spread out to merge with the former Austro-Hungarian border town of Zemun.

If New Belgrade bears witness to the great changes that have occurred in the decades since the Second World War, old Belgrade nurtures its memory of past centuries and fallen empires in the many layers of earth on which it has survived for over two millennia. The city authorities have paid particular attention to returning to the capital the shine of its former glory, dulled and damaged in the last years of the previous regime.

The Romans put down the first markers at the end of the last century before Christ. The famous fourth Roman legion of Flavius captured the rocky heights above the confluence of the Sava and Danube, and the Celtic settlement which they called Singidunum, the fortress of the Singi. They quickly discovered that it provided a remarkable watchtower over the rivers, marshes and plains to the east and north, and over the hills and forests to the south and west. Unsurpassed builders, as well as excellent soldiers, the Romans established their military camp at today's Kalemegdan Park and built roads leading into the interior of the land to the east and south. They used the roads and the aqueducts they placed alongside them for a full three-and-a-half centuries, for as long as they ruled Singidunum, which became a rich and prosperous provincial town, until the fall of the Roman Empire.

The later conquerors of the Belgrade fortress did not change the lines of those first Roman roads; at least, this is the story that Belgrade's urban planners like to tell. Some historians say that the Turks, in their campaign to drive a wedge into Europe, captured Belgrade in 1521 after many unsuccessful sieges and used the roads that the soldiers and slaves of mighty Rome had cut and paved. The story goes that the line of one such road, probably Singidunum's main street, has been preserved more or less to today. It is the one called in the vocabulary of town planners and other informed citizens the Belgrade ridge and passes through the very centre, dividing the eastern slope which drops down to the Danube from the western slope facing the Sava.

If he likes a walk, our visitor might take in the most important part of the ridge on foot and get to know the centre of contemporary Belgrade. Were I his guide, I would take him first to the plateau of the fortress at Kalemegdan, where the monument to the Victor stands, the symbol of the city and the work of the Croatian sculptor Ivan Meštrović. A most beautiful view unfolds from the plateau over the waters of the great rivers, the Sava and the Danube, which join at the foot of Kalemegdan, over the Great War Island covered in thick undergrowth, over the plains toward Banat and the east, on the left bank of the Danube, and over New Belgrade to the west, on the left bank of the Sava. All the conquerors and rulers of Belgrade have enjoyed this view in both the morning and evening light, as have the people living here over the last 2,000 years, with the occasional chronicler noting down his wonder at the beauty of the sight. New Belgrade, of course, was nowhere on the horizon before the second half of the twentieth century; in its place was a dark and immeasurable marsh above which, so travellers wrote in their journals, the setting sun presented a surreal scene.

Passing through the park from the fortress which the Turks called *Kale-megdan*, the fortress-on-the-battlefield, our visitor would arrive at Knez Mihailo Street, where the ridge begins. While we step along this route, on which the paving stones cover the remains of the Roman settlement buried deep below, I would tell him details from the history of the houses in the street, one of the oldest in Belgrade. Most of them were built in the nineteenth century by wealthy Serbian merchants, many of whom were also public-spirited philanthropists.

Down Knez Mihailo Street we would soon come to Terazije. The name of the street means, in Turkish, an apparatus for measuring water, a kind of oriental water meter. We could stop to catch our breath in the old and respectable Hotel Moskva, built with Russian capital at the turn of the twentieth century, but perhaps not. We would, of course, continue along King Milan Street, once called Marshal Tito Street, past the crossroads "At the London" and on to the new, elegant building of the Yugoslav Drama Theatre. Then, once across Slavija Square, with its throngs of circling traffic, we would climb to the Vračar plateau. There are two churches here, one large and new, the other smaller and older, both dedicated to St. Sava, sharing the space with the National Library. A monument stands in front of them, just as one stands on the Kalemegdan plateau. This memorial is in honour of Karađorđe, leader of the First Serbian Uprising at the beginning of the nineteenth century, when the idea of the modern Serbian state was formed.

The two statues, the Victor and Karađorđe, placed on these two raised sites imbued with almost mythic status in Belgrade eyes, at Kalemegdan and Vračar, mark the beginning and end of the Belgrade ridge. It is the route along which all armies have had to pass for two millennia, as they advanced and retreated, in victory or defeat, preparing for great sieges and battles, from the time of the Romans to the First Uprising, from the barbaric invasion of the Huns in the fifth century to the even more barbaric bombing of Belgrade by the Third Reich in April 1941. Every evening in autumn 1996 and winter 1997 tens of thousands of citizens of Belgrade, young and old, in good health or sick, celebrated their resistance to violence and madness, scorned Milošević's terror and protested by peacefully marching from Kalemegdan to Vračar, and from Vračar to Kalemegdan, from the Victor toward Karađorđe, and from Karađorđe toward the Victor, along the line of the old Roman road.

Our traveller, using his imagination, may even feel this line under his feet as he slowly returns along the Belgrade ridge to his hotel. He will undoubtedly be somewhat bewildered by this whirlwind of past and present times in which he has unexpectedly found himself, but which, now as always, blows with the clouds over the gateway to the Balkans.

Svetlana Velmar-Janković

Introduction

READING THE CITY

A city undoubtedly reflects the mentality of the nation which conceives, and plans, and builds it. Viewed in this light, mere bricks and mortar assume a psychological interest, and are seen as the tangible embodiment of ideas, to be judged according to their practical utility and esthetic value. Thus, the design of a school building, a church, or a house tells its tale more plainly than any words could do.

Despite riches or poverty, the spirit and aspirations of a people are welded into every construction—be it high or low—which meets the eye. This is particularly the case in Belgrade, where the history of the country for several decades back can be traced in the various stages of architecture prevalent in the town.

Lena A. Yovitchitch, *Pages from Here and There in Serbia* (1926)

A city speaks—buildings are its words and streets are its sentences. This is the language in which the community cherishes its hopes and memories. Each road, lane, type of building material or decorative feature can tell us something about the peculiar mix of influences that make up the outward signs of that particular city and the culture which it represents. But it is not a straightforward task to find the key to read these urban texts and reconstruct from them the varied narratives and histories of that place.

Many different stories inhabit the courtyards behind the houses lining the streets. Numerous strands intersect on each corner from which we, as dwellers in our own cities, have absorbed what it is that we need to know in order to go about our daily business. We may not know all the names from the past but we possess a storehouse of knowledge on which we rarely reflect. If we were to stop and think about each detail as we walk down the street, we would be doomed to live life at a reduced pace and probably never reach our destination.

Myths and urban folklore rub alongside the facts of history to produce a virtual cacophony of voices that identify the city. I only become aware of this noise when I go somewhere new and hear only silence. If I go to a city in Britain that I do not know well, there are connections between it and other places and histories with which I am already familiar; these provide some immediate bridge, an initiation into the new sights that helps me make sense of my first impressions. As I pick my way down roads and across squares I can decipher where I am. I recognize the matronly figure of Queen Victoria in front of the town hall and the names of streets recalling distant places in a former Empire. I look at architectural features to pick out the private dwellings from the buildings that are or have been invested with some municipal function. I quickly begin to feel a historical background and establish a relationship with my surroundings based on the general cultural encyclopaedia that I carry around all the time.

Yet in a place further afield, such points, like points of a compass, are absent. It becomes more difficult to discover a basic orientation, to know in which direction to look in order to find north and other points of the compass. In those further fields, where the stories are not mine, I need more in order to appreciate the importance of a house, building, monument, to see how it fits into the larger scheme of that urban pattern, and then to understand the city as a sequence of sentences which have their own internal logic, their own grammar.

SOMEONE ELSE'S MEMORY

The purpose of this book is to facilitate communication with Belgrade, to achieve a fuller understanding of the connections between its different parts and its architectural and urban sights. The journey is akin to entering someone else's memory where there exists a different set of stories underpinning the unity of the city. Chapters contain a description of the buildings and design of a certain area of central Belgrade with other sections that give historical background associated with the district and references to depictions of it in art and literature.

The book opens at the apex of Belgrade, the fortress of Kalemegdan, which overlooks the confluence of the Sava and Danube rivers. In the first chapter I focus on the early history of Belgrade until the nineteenth century when its strategic importance brought many different armies to this place. It was finally taken by the Ottoman Empire in 1521 when Kalemegdan became the seat of a Turkish pasha. In the eighteenth century it fell into Austrian hands only to be returned later to Islamic rule. The Serbian presence in the city was hardly felt during these centuries and change only came with local rebellions against Ottoman government.

The story of the Serbian uprisings and the changes which followed in

Belgrade during the nineteenth century are told in the next two chapters. Particular attention is given to the effects of the rapid social modernization that shaped the city during this period. Modernization was synonymous with Europeanization as Belgrade cast off its oriental look, the legacy of Ottoman rule, and replaced it with western styles and fashions. The arts developed and Belgrade became a cultural centre with writers, artists and critics rubbing shoulders with one another. In these chapters I also present portrayals of life in the city and important political events of the nineteenth century as described in fiction.

In Chapters Four and Five I describe significant episodes from Belgrade in the twentieth century, first as the capital of the new Kingdom of Yugoslavia then of the communist state after the Second World War with the cultural changes reflecting these political transformations. The urban landscape shifted from the ornate style of architecture practised at the beginning of the new era to the more austere principles characteristic of socialist planning after 1945. Novels and films show the experiences of the people who lived under different regimes in the city.

Chapter Six contains an examination of the period at the end of the twentieth century, after the death of President Tito. Yugoslavia began to unravel leading to a bloody civil war that was seen briefly in Slovenia in the summer of 1991 before moving to Croatia and then, finally, to Bosnia 1992-95. Many people had relatives in other parts of Yugoslavia caught up in the conflicts who were forced to flee and turned up in the city as refugees. Some went off to fight as "weekend" soldiers, leaving for short periods as members of paramilitary units to use the opportunity for brutal looting of villages and towns in Bosnia and parts of Croatia. Others, completely against violence, formed opposition groups against the government of the day and stood out as the "Other Belgrade" trying to maintain a sense of order and proportion in the middle of mayhem and confusion.

The government and supporters of Slobodan Milošević formed alliances with criminals in order to keep their positions of power and to make themselves rich. It was a time of utter chaos when international sanctions closed the borders of the country, preventing communication with the outside world and leaving the opposition bereft of support from abroad and the government safe to pursue its own agenda at home. Many commentators have described the break-up of Yugoslavia, its descent into civil war, the activities of political leaders, and the human rights issues which were raised at the time. There is a selection of such works in the bibliography at the end of the book. I focus on how the majority lived through this extreme situation in the city and how their experience has been inscribed in stories told by novelists and film directors.

One of the themes that I introduce in this book concerns the viewpoints of foreign journalists and travel writers who have come to Belgrade and left behind their impressions of the city. In Chapter Seven I look at what seem to be typical perceptions of the city. These tend to see Belgrade through romantic eyes, depicting it either as a primitive world in danger of reverting to some atavistic barbarism, or as overly modern and on the brink of losing its authentic identity. This perspective has influenced internal Serbian views of the city largely because these attitudes have been expressed by representatives from that western world to which a significant part of Belgrade aspires.

The final chapter moves away from the central districts and crosses the River Sava to New Belgrade and Zemun. The history of the relationship between Belgrade and Zemun is important for what it tells us of the cultural position of the city on the border between East and West, the Balkans and Europe. Zemun, now part of Belgrade, used to be the last post of the Central European power of Austria-Hungary before entering the Ottoman Empire at Belgrade. It represented an image of the West just on the other bank of the river.

New Belgrade was built after the Second World War on the marshy land between Zemun and the river. An achievement of socialist urban planning which quickly became a dormitory area, it is now one of the most desirable districts in the city. With its modern architecture, space for new mega-stores and with fewer of the traffic problems encountered in the old centre, people are now beginning to see it with different eyes. The final chapter also looks at NATO's bombing of Belgrade in the Kosovo campaign, the political defeat of Slobodan Milošević in October 2000 and the problems faced by the democratic forces that took over.

From Tito to Milošević

The capital city of Serbia, then Yugoslavia, then Serbia again, has been both praised and reproached by public and governments abroad. The murders of King Alexander Obrenović and his wife Queen Draga in 1903 caused an international outcry and the imposition of the first sanctions against the country when foreign governments withdrew their ambassadors. But a few years later in the First World War Britain and France warmly regarded their Balkan ally as "gallant Serbia". This positive perspective dissolved when the communists came to power in 1945 and generated mistrust in the West where it was thought of as pro-Stalinist.

The writer Lawrence Durrell served as a diplomat in Belgrade for three years from 1949 and he wrote to a friend from there: "Just a brief line to tell you we've arrived safely. Conditions are rather gloomy here—almost mid-war conditions, overcrowding, poverty. As for Communism—my dear Theodore, a short visit here is enough to make one decide that Capitalism is worth fighting for. Black as it may be, with all its bloodstains, it is less gloomy and arid and hopeless than this inert and ghastly police state."

Yugoslavia's reputation as hostile enemy changed dramatically when it became more of an ally under Tito. Standards of living were much higher than elsewhere in Eastern Europe, there was no visible sign of totalitarianism and thousands of foreign tourists holidayed on Adriatic beaches. Fitzroy Maclean's view in his biography of Tito gives an insight into the perception of this western-friendly country, and therefore its people too. He wrote:

> For Yugoslavia Tito's death signified the end of an era, which had started four decades earlier with the epic years of Partisan resistance and continued after the war with thirty-five years of stoutly sustained independence. That Tito's own personality and force of character played a decisive part in the events of these forty years is indisputable. But Tito could not have done what he did without the support of the Yugoslav people. A typical Yugoslav, his indomitable courage, independent spirit, steady nerves, and intense national pride found from the first a ready echo in the ordinary Yugoslav man in the street or on the hillside.

The ordinary person in the West may not have been familiar with the political and historical events which lay behind this changed view, but they knew that Yugoslavia was not like other communist dictatorships in Eastern Europe.

The negative image returned once more with the beginning of civil war in Yugoslavia and the break-up of the country. Belgrade was internationally isolated when the UN imposed an embargo on economic, cultural and political ties, leaving just a few road links as the only way in or out of the country. President Milošević was regarded as the political leader with most responsibility for the conflicts and violence of the 1990s. His style of criminal rule and his government's record on human rights combined to give the country the status of international pariah. He was branded a war criminal during NATO's military campaign directed against him and his government's policies towards Kosovo in 1999. He was finally ousted from power in October 2000 in a largely bloodless coup in favour of the democratic opposition forces under Vojislav Koštunica. Western governments welcomed the change and Milošević was sent for trial at The Hague for his crimes, but he died while in custody before any judgment could be brought. The perspective from abroad seems favourable at the present, and Belgrade may soon be in a position to establish a place for itself in European and other world institutions.

Such discussion concerns a metaphoric Belgrade, a synecdoche for a nation, a state, a government, for which it stands symbolically at the head. The streets, buildings and people of Belgrade are parts of many other stories and memories. I write about architectural and urban developments, influences in art and culture, the historical background to events. I present portraits of the city from the works of its writers and filmmakers. These imaginative works go beyond a picture of Belgrade and narrate the city as an experience in itself. Belgrade is more than the sum total of its buildings and inhabitants; like other large cities, it is a small world in itself. It has its own history and unique identity that set it apart from other places and even acts upon the people who live there, shaping their lives as it is shaped by them.

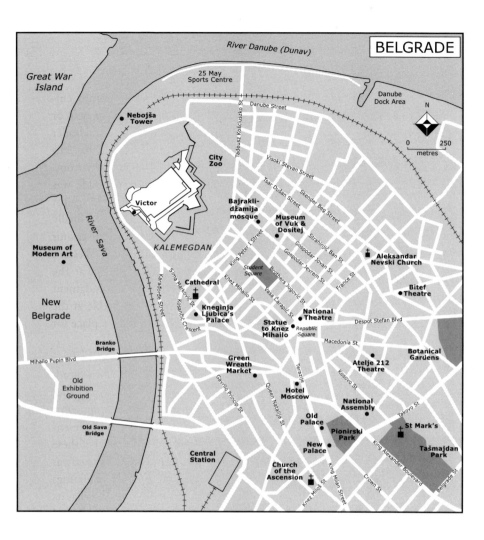

River Danube (Dunav)

BELGRADE

Great War Island

25 May Sports Centre

Danube Dock Area

N

0 250 metres

Nebojša Tower

Danube Street

Tadeusz Kościuszko St

Visoki Stevan Street

City Zoo

Tsar Dušan Street

Skender Beg Street

Bajrakli-džamija mosque

Museum of Vuk & Dositej

Gospodar Jovan St

Gospodar Jevrem St

Strahinjić Ban St

Aleksandar Nevski Church

Victor

KALEMEGDAN

Museum of Modern Art

River Sava

Sima Markovic St

King Peter I Street

Student Square

Vasa Čarapić St

Brother's Jugovic St

France St

Bitef Theatre

Cathedral

Kneginja Ljubica's Palace

Knez Mihailo St

Statue to Knez Mihailo

National Theatre

Republic Square

Despot Stefan Blvd

New Belgrade

Karadorde Street

Kosančić Crescent

Macedonia St

Kosovo St

Botanical Gardens

Branko Bridge

Mihailo Pupin Blvd

Green Wreath Market

Gavrilo Princip St

Atelje 212 Theatre

Old Exhibition Ground

Queen Natalija St

Hotel Moscow

Terazije

National Assembly

Takovo St

St Mark's

Old Sava Bridge

Central Station

Old Palace

New Palace

Pionirski Park

King Alexander Boulevard

Tašmajdan Park

Church of the Ascension

Knez Miloš St

King Milan Street

Crown St

Belgrade St

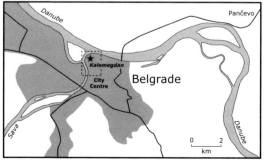

Danube

Pančevo

Kalemegdan

City Centre

Belgrade

Sava

Danube

0 2 km

City on Two Rivers

Chapter One
THE FORTRESS ABOVE THE TWO
RIVERS: THE CITY'S FOUNDATIONS

KALEMEGDAN: POSITION AND PREHISTORY

Belgrade in its Serbian form means White-city (*Beo-grad*), a name vividly evoked by the old fortress as seen from the banks of the two rivers, the Sava and the Danube, which meet below its white walls. The city and its location have often been described in flattering terms by those who have lived here and by visitors from abroad. Miloš Crnjanski, an outstanding figure in twentieth-century Serbian letters, was a poet, novelist and essayist whose work has greatly influenced the literary styles and tastes of modern Belgrade writers. One of his lesser-known books is a travel guide to the city, originally published in French in 1936. He writes about its geographic position in the following terms: "Belgrade sits on a rock rising high over a broad plain. The view encompasses the majestic panorama of the old Serbian provinces of Bačka and Banat, which were also the last to be liberated."

Today we can stand on that rocky outcrop and look out at the view Crnjanski describes from Belgrade's old Turkish fortress of Kalemegdan, now a public park containing many reminders of the city's history. It is here that the story of Belgrade begins in all its incarnations: a city ruled by many different regimes and the capital city of various countries—Serbia, the Kingdom of Yugoslavia, communist Yugoslavia, and most recently of Serbia again.

Kalemegdan crowns the central district of Belgrade's old town. A towering statue of a naked man with a sword grasped in his right hand and a hawk perched on his left stands on the furthest point of this promontory. The monument, fashioned by the famous Croatian sculptor Ivan Meštrović (1883-1962), was placed here in 1928 to commemorate the tenth anniversary of Serbia's victory in the First World War on the side of the Allies. It is appropriately named the Victor (Pobednik) and is often the first port of call for visitors to Belgrade.

The confluence of the rivers Sava and Danube lies immediately below, with the flat expanse of Vojvodina, the lands of Bačka and Banat, stretching northward toward the borders with Croatia, Hungary and Romania. In the distance, overlooking the Danube, the conurbation of Zemun is identifiable by its tall "millennium tower" of 1896 visible on a hilltop. In a different direction, bridges span the Sava to join the old town with the serried rows of tower blocks and wide avenues of New Belgrade, built only after the Second World War. An island occupies the central part of the watery junction giving a staging post from one bank to another. The island was often used by armies laying siege to the town, hence its ominous name of Great War Island (Veliko ratno ostrvo).

All the natural advantages of the city's position are to be seen from the platform around the Victor's base. The fortress walls offer clear lines of sight over comparatively large distances, and the rivers on two sides provide both defensive potential and navigation routes in three directions. Yet such a naturally advantageous location has not saved Belgrade from attack and it has frequently been occupied, then lost and fought over again. Each time a new town has sprung up in place of the old one. Slobodan Glumac offers a telling comment testifying to the city's stormy past in his book *Belgrade*:

> The history books say that Belgrade was razed and put to the torch forty times. This, then, would mean that it was rebuilt forty-one times. Yet different each time, different from the preceding community, almost as if to deny its very existence.

These words from 1989 bear an almost prophetic tone, coinciding with the time when Belgrade was on the verge of another major transformation, as the country of which it was then capital was about to dissolve in the Wars of Yugoslav Succession.

The flat land of Vojvodina to the north was in some very far and distant past covered by a vast tract of water, the Pannonian Sea, which is still yielding occasional examples of prehistoric fossils. Archaeologists have also found plenty of evidence of life from more recent prehistory in the vicinity of Kalemegdan, which reveals that it has been a base for human activity for some eight thousand years. There are two large archaeological sites from the Neolithic period fairly close by. The closer one is to be found at Vinča, about ten miles from the centre of Belgrade. The other is situated further down the Danube at Lepenski Vir in the direction of the Black Sea where the startling remains of a settlement going back to 6000 BC were unearthed. The research undertaken on the very rich and varied finds from these diggings has been of huge significance for international scholarship in deepening our understanding of Neolithic communities, their methods of husbandry, their religious rites and culture generally. Objects from this period of the late Stone Age are on display in the National Museum (Narodni muzej) and the City Museum of Belgrade (Muzej grada Beograda).

Although pickings from Kalemegdan and around the city centre itself have been sparser, there is evidence to support the view that a small settlement was established here in about the same period. Perhaps it functioned as a lookout post, a watchtower for the larger groups downriver. Later, tribes of Illyrians, Thracians and Dacians passed through here in periods of migratory activity during the Bronze Age from about 2000 BC to 800 BC.

Evidence of early knowledge about Belgrade's geographical location comes from the myths and legends passed down from generation to generation. The Homeric world knew that two important rivers met and provided a crossroads at this promontory. The rock overlooking the confluence has been identified as one of the places in the story of Jason and the Argonauts. Returning with the Golden Fleece, Jason and his crew sailed from the Black Sea up the Danube, then turned and steered down the Sava and followed its course in order to find an outlet into the Adriatic Sea before heading south for home. Greek classical authors, including Hesiod, have also left indications that they were aware of this location. From these Greek chroniclers we know that the Celts began to arrive in the area from the fourth century BC during their migration westward. They brought with them the culture and technology of the Iron Age, which they put to good use, soon driving out the Bronze-Age tribes who lived here. One of these Celtish tribes, the Singi, settled on the rock above the Sava and Danube where they built a simple wooden fortification in the third century BC.

There are those, including Miloš Crnjanski, who maintain that some place-names around Belgrade have retained Celtic roots. Looking at the names of rivers, for example, Crnjanski writes that it is a mistake to think that the Sava and the Drava are somehow Slavonic words since they come from the Celtic roots *aw* and *dur* meaning water. (It has to be said that this etymological link has never been conclusively proven.) But whatever the truth of the debate, the site on which Kalemegdan Park now stands has played a significant role in events in the Balkan Peninsula since long before the birth of Christ. Different peoples and cultures from the ancient world have come and gone, each leaving some slight sign of their presence. These traces from archaeological, mythic and textual sources give us some idea of the earliest human activity around this place above the two rivers.

FROM ROMAN CAMP TO SERBIAN CAPITAL

The earliest visible traces of previous occupants at Kalemegdan were left by the Roman legions which fought the Celts and took their settlements along the Danube in order to secure the use of the river by Rome. These military missions were sent over a period of some forty years from 35 BC to AD 6. Having chased out the Celts, they began to build forts of their own in order to hold the ground already taken and prepare the way for further conquest in the region. The fort at Belgrade was home to more than 5,000 legionnaires and was one of a series of similar camps along the Danube. In an expansive and confident mood, the Roman conquerors turned to make a more permanent home for themselves, and around AD 69-80 replaced the wooden walls and structures with ones made of stone. They called their new settlement Singidunum, after the Celtish tribe which had prior ownership over the territory, and they stayed for another three centuries. Excavated finds from Belgrade's Roman period are on display in the National Museum.

As was common practice elsewhere in the empire, Singidunum became more than just a camp with a solely military purpose. On retiring from active service, soldiers would often make a home for themselves in the countryside surrounding their fortress. Meanwhile, Roman power in the region extended in all directions and Singidunum changed from being a frontier outpost to one of the nodal points in the imperial network of roads and river transportation.

The city under Roman management was part of a secure imperial world and enjoyed one of its longest periods of peace and stability. The civilian population of Singidunum continued to grow outside the confines of the sturdy fortress walls, spilling into what is now Belgrade's central district. Emperors passed through the region on their way to defend the imperial borders from marauding bands of outsiders, like Claudius II who marched his army in 268 via Singidunum to defeat the Goths near what is now the southern Serbian town of Niš.

The Roman Emperor Constantine decided on a step that was to have profound consequences for the development of the Balkans and Europe generally, and which echoes down to the present day. He built a new imperial city on the shores of the Black Sea to be named after himself. Gavro Škrivanić of Belgrade's Historical Institute, writing in *An Historical Geography of the Balkans*, comments on this development: "Konstantinopolis emerged from the old Greek town of Byzantium and was built under Constantine the Great in AD 330 and proclaimed as the capital of the Roman Empire. It had an exceptionally strategic position, and became one of the largest mercantile and communication centres of the world." This rival to Rome is better known to the Serbs as Byzantium or Carigrad (City of the Tsar or Emperor); it was later renamed Istanbul after it fell to the Ottoman Empire.

The Roman Empire effectively became two units: a western entity based on the power and the glory of Rome, and an eastern section administered by the new city. The Christian Church took root at the same time, promoted by Constantine who was the first emperor to be baptized, and it too was destined to be divided in two branches. The division was not complete until the Great Schism of 1054 when the leaders of the Church, the Bishop of Rome and the Patriarch in Byzantium, excommunicated one another, thus paving the way for the emergence of the Catholic and Orthodox Churches.

The political and administrative arrangements for the initial partition of the empire led to a weakening of its defences, and Singidunum's years of *Pax Romana* came to an end. The city was sacked by Goths in 378 and then again at the hands of Attila the Hun in 441. The local population was condemned to slavery and for nearly a hundred years the city ceased to exist. The Byzantine Emperor Justinian began a programme to rebuild it in 535, changing the name from the Roman Singidunum to the Hellenized version Singidon. The walls were constructed from the remains of the previous Roman fortress along with new stone and brick—handiwork that has left a confusing legacy for later archaeologists to sift through. Justinian's project was constantly interrupted during the rest of that century by the Avars, another tribe who invaded the Balkans and laid siege to the city three times.

During the sixth and seventh centuries fresh waves of newcomers crossed from the north into the Balkan Peninsula. These latest interlopers were the Slavs who came in search of pasture for their herds and made their way deep into the peninsula. Not much is known of them from this period although they are mentioned by Byzantine chroniclers. They were nomadic peoples who had no form of writing and, consequently, have left behind little evidence about their way of life, customs, rituals or religion. They were converted to Christianity in the ninth century by followers of the monks Cyril and Methodius.

These two brothers were themselves of South Slav origin, from the region of Thessalonica, educated in the Greek rite of the Church, and commissioned by the Byzantine Empire to spread the Gospels among the Slavs. As speakers of a Slavonic dialect, their first task was to develop an alphabet that would make a suitable vehicle for translating the Holy Scriptures into a language comprehensible to all Slavs. The Cyrillic script still bears the name of its inventor who borrowed and adapted Greek letters with numerous additions and modifications in order to accommodate this system of writing to their Slavonic dialect which had some sounds that did not exist in Greek. The Slavs of the ninth century were linguistically much closer than they are today and it was possible to find enough common ground for the brothers' translations to be widely accepted. Some Slavs, like the Slovenes, Croats and Czechs, later accepted the authority of the Church in Rome and abandoned the Cyrillic alphabet, taking up and using Latin as the *lingua franca* of the written word. Meanwhile, each

Slavonic branch of the Orthodox Church, including the Serbs, developed its own liturgical language, influenced by developments in local speech patterns as their dialects evolved into distinct languages with separate although related vocabularies, grammars and pronunciation. The Orthodox Church not only brought the Bible and writing to the Slavs, but it also introduced them to the more sophisticated Byzantine models of social, political, economic and cultural organization which were gradually adopted in secular practices and forms of government.

The terms Serb and Croat were used by Byzantine chroniclers to refer to some of the Slavonic tribes in the Balkans. The Serbs generally lived in the central region while the Croats settled in the west and north. The settlement standing where the Sava and Danube met acquired something of a Serbian population during the ninth century, but they were not a dominant presence. In a letter from Pope John VIII to the Bulgarian ruler Boris written in 878 we find the first mention of the name for the city in its Slavonic form, Beograd. It came under the jurisdiction of Bulgarian emperors, who challenged the supremacy of Byzantium in south-eastern Europe.

Belgrade was recaptured by the Byzantine emperor in 1018, and it then became a bone of contention in the regional power struggle between Byzantium and the Hungarians, or Magyars, who moved into the territory north of the Danube. The city was treated as a commodity in political horse-trading. It was taken by the Hungarian King Solomon in 1072 after a long siege, only to be given back two years later when his son was betrothed to a Byzantine princess. In a similar move, the Hungarian ruler Bela III besieged and destroyed the citadel in 1127, but returned it as part of another marriage contract when he gave the hand of his daughter to the Byzantine emperor. Possession of the city passed rapidly from Bulgarian, to Byzantine, to Hungarian control and back again.

SERBIAN RULE

It may seem a strange thing to say today, as one stands in Kalemegdan in the capital of the modern Republic of Serbia, that Belgrade did not feature in the appearance of the first independent Serbian kingdom. The centre of Serbian power was established further south around the area of Raška. The Serbs were split into disparate clan groups based on extended families. Then, one of their leaders, Stefan Nemanja, managed to win the allegiance of the others so that he could proclaim himself to be local overlord in 1169. Abdicating in 1196, he took holy orders and retired to a life of quiet contemplation in the Serbian monastery of Hilandar on Mount Athos. His dynasty ruled Serbia for the next two hundred years.

His son, also called Stefan, wanted a crown for himself and the status of a kingdom for his country in order to cement its independence. The Byzantine authorities, in whose religious and political sphere Serbia lay, refused his request. Determined to achieve his goal, however, he approached Rome, and the Catholic Church obliged by sending a Papal legate to anoint him in 1217. Having fulfilled his ambition, he proceeded to shift Serbia's allegiance back to Byzantium and secured the right to establish an autocephalous Serbian Orthodox Church. His own brother, Sava, a pious monk from Mount Athos, became the first archbishop of this newly-formed institution. Sava was later canonized and adopted as the patron saint of Serbia.

Dragutin became the first Serbian king to rule from Belgrade in 1284 when he was given the city by the Hungarian King Stephen V whose daughter, Katarina, he married. The city, now linked to the Serbian lands further south and its natural hinterland, was in an advantageous position to expand. Under Dragutin's stewardship the population grew and trade developed. The king paid particular attention to building churches and Serbian influence quickly spread around the city. News of his success in this regard reached Rome and in 1290 provoked a letter of protest from the Pope who was concerned that the Orthodox Church was supplanting the Catholic Hungarian culture of the area. Dragutin died in 1316 and the position of Belgrade again came into question. The city was claimed by Dragutin's successor, his brother King Milutin, and by the Hungarian crown which had given the city as part of a marriage contract. The Hungarians regarded Belgrade as strategically important for their security and, launching an attack in 1319, they captured the city again.

Meanwhile, during the fourteenth century the Serbian kingdom to the south of Belgrade became a powerful empire under Dušan the Mighty (Dušan Silni). The emperor twice took his armies to the very walls of Byzantium and his territory extended over Serbia, Montenegro, Kosovo, northern Greece, Albania and much of Bosnia and Dalmatia. Even so, he was unable to retake Belgrade. His untimely death in 1355 precipitated a power vacuum and left the country in a weakened position. Byzantium, thanks to Serbia's efforts, also lost much of its former influence. Taking advantage of this predicament, the Ottoman Empire, the largest Muslim power in the world, began to expand from its base in Asia and threaten the Balkan Peninsula. Its army under Sultan Murat met a coalition of Serbs and other Christian forces led by the Serbian Prince Lazar at the Battle of Kosovo on 28 June 1389. According to contemporary accounts, neither side won a decisive victory and both withdrew from the field with the loss of their leaders. But in Serbian myth the Battle of Kosovo is considered a defeat and the beginning of the end for Serbian independence. The Serbian nobles quarrelled amongst themselves while Ottoman forces slowly consolidated their presence in the region. With this increasing competition from their enemies the centre of Serbian interests slowly shifted from the southern provinces further north.

A new Serbian ruler, Despot Stefan Lazarević, opened negotiations with the Hungarians and was able to make Belgrade his capital in 1403. By this time the city and its fortress were greatly damaged and depopulated because of frequent attempts to take it by the other powers in the region. Despot Stefan, determined to strengthen the city's fortifications, extended the walls of his citadel down to the Sava and Danube, thus encompassing for the first time the upper reaches of the fortress with the lower area by the rivers in one defensive whole supported by a series of towers. Under his building programme the city was much more resilient to attack both from the river and from land. In his book *The Life of Despot Stefan Lazarević*, Constantine the Philosopher has left many descriptions of Stefan's Belgrade above the rivers "where a gleaming white castle is under construction." (He also tends toward a certain hyperbole in some of his claims: "And who is able to say in writing what is the situation, appearance and beauty of Belgrade!") When Stefan died in 1427, the Hungarians again occupied Belgrade forcing his successor, Đurađ Branković, to move the Serbian capital further down the Danube to Smederevo. From then until the nineteenth century the city was lost to the Serbs.

Taken by the Turks

Ottoman forces besieged Belgrade unsuccessfully in 1456 when the city's defence was led by the Hungarian Janos Hunyadi. Yet the huge military organization of the Ottomans could not be stopped so easily and Belgrade finally fell to Sultan Suleiman the Magnificent in 1521. As the Ottoman armies advanced into the Balkans, cities passed into the hands of the new colonial administrators. Much of the urban Christian population "chose to withdraw to inaccessible mountains where they founded new settlements," explains Nikolai Todorov in his book *The Balkan City 1400-1900*. The cities were significant points in the Ottoman imperial system of communications and security. They existed to maintain authority over the local population and protect trade routes. By the second half of the sixteenth century Muslims formed a majority of the urban population in Serbia. The conquering army drove out the whole civilian population from Belgrade, while a totally new community moved in.

The city duly went through one of its frequent and complete transformations, belonging to a foreign empire, governed by men of a different religion, subject to a radically changed way of life. The Serbs usually referred to their new masters as Turks, or in Serbian *Turci*, although the term is inaccurate as the administrators, soldiers and governors in the service of the Ottoman Empire could come from any part of its vast territories.

The new masters called Belgrade *Dar ul Jihad*, or House of the Holy Wars, giving the name Kalemegdan (from *kale* town and *megdan* battlefield) to the fortified area where previously Celts, Romans, Byzantines, Bulgarians, Hungarians and Serbs took turns to look out over the two rivers. The fort housed a garrison of troops and was the seat of political power for the pasha, or governor, sent by the Sultan to rule the province in his name. Craftsmen and artisans came from the interior of the empire to provide services for them, men who consolidated the oriental look and feel of the place, dominated by Islamic codes of dress, food and social ritual.

Ottoman power spread far beyond Belgrade and into Hungary, Romania, Bosnia, Croatia and Dalmatia, and the city was no longer an outpost of the Ottoman Empire. Rather, it was an important trading, administrative and military centre from which new wars in the West could be supported. Other groups such as Greeks, Armenians and Jews joined the growing community outside the walls, attracted by mercantile interests and the economic potential of the city. Relatively few Serbs continued to live in town and any sporadic attempts to resist Ottoman rule were vigorously crushed.

In 1683 the sultan marched his army to Belgrade from where, after a short rest, they continued their advance into Western Europe under the command of the Grand Vizier Kara-Mustafa. The sultan waited in Kalemegdan while his forces headed towards Vienna. Large areas of countryside were emptied of their population who fled rather than face an uncertain fate at the hands of the Turkish troops. In the end, the Turks again failed to take Vienna and their military capability was severely damaged in the attempt. The Austrians counter-attacked, pushing back the Ottoman forces from their northern provinces in Hungary and Croatia and reaching Belgrade in 1688. Taking the city from the Turks, they continued to press south. The Austrian campaign was supported by local bands of Serbian insurgents hoping for liberation from foreign rule, but it finally came to a halt in Kosovo from where they were forced to retreat, retracing their steps back the way they had come.

Mindful of the very real possibility of Ottoman retaliation, Patriarch Arsenije III Čarnojević led a huge number of Serbs, perhaps as many as 30,000 families, in a great migration out of Kosovo. This event had an irreversible impact on the demographic structure of the region. Serbs left their homes in the south and crossed the Sava into the Habsburg Empire of the Austrians and Hungarians to settle on land that had been deserted because of border fighting in the preceding period. The Turks recaptured Belgrade in 1690 while the Austrian attempt to take the city three years later failed. After so much fierce fighting the fortress of Kalemegdan was changed beyond all recognition. The last of Despot Stefan Lazarević's fortifications disappeared, leaving no sign of the citadel he had constructed. The local population was dispersed far and wide and their homes razed to the ground.

The Peace of Karlovci, signed by the Habsburg and Ottoman Empires in 1699, established a new border between the two warring sides. The frontier now followed the Sava, leaving Bosnia and Serbia to the south in the Islamic state, while the northern and western parts of the Balkan Peninsula in Slavonia and Dalmatia came under Austrian control. The Turkish threat to Europe was over and they were never to advance beyond Belgrade again.

The city acquired a new status; no longer an important point in the system of communication by road and river, it was rather on the northern periphery of the Ottoman domains. The Austrians were firmly entrenched across the two rivers and watched the white walls of Kalemegdan from their vantage-point at Zemun. There was now a Serbian community living to the north of Belgrade as the refugees from the south settled in what had been Hungarian lands. They formed a new orientation for the Serbs living in the small towns of Vojvodina in the sphere of European rather than Ottoman influence. Exhausted by wars and internal problems, the Ottoman Empire went into a period of decline. Austrian forces took advantage of its weakness and attacked Belgrade in 1717. Their commander, Eugene of Savoy, did not make use of the Great War Island to locate his cannon as in previous sieges, instead mounting his main offensive from the east, with his forces crossing the Danube downstream. Control of Belgrade was bounced between competing powers, with the arrival of each new order heralding another time of transition.

BETWEEN TURKS AND AUSTRIANS

Belgrade was a Muslim town for a long period of its history, with an Ottoman garrison, government officials and citizens whose role in the urban scheme of things was determined by their proximity to the pasha. The city that was their home had the appearance and feel of an oriental market town. One seventeenth-century English traveller to Turkish Belgrade, Edward Brown, wrote:

> The street where trade is busiest is covered with a wooden roof as protection from the sun and rain. The shops are small. On a low counter, like tailors in England, sits the shop-keeper selling his goods to the buyer who remains outside, rarely going inside... The covered market is a square, paved with flag stones, a fountain in the centre and rows of various shops at the entrance.

Ottoman rule dictated not only the main functions of Belgrade, from which Christians were largely excluded, but also its architecture and urban design. The skyline was filled with the minarets of the many mosques. Houses consisted of compounds in which the family lived, with blank walls facing the outside world and an inner central courtyard. Life was directed inwards, making urban life an intensely private experience, unlike the domination of public spaces in the cities of Western Europe. The Balkan city in Ottoman times was a place of whispers rather than the declamatory oratory of the West. Life did not happen on the streets, but in the closed world of the family, tightly controlled by social etiquette, both physically and symbolically. Buildings were made of wood and with a single storey, while streets were the random spaces between houses, not a regulated system to ease the flow of traffic. The few western visitors to Belgrade could hardly recognize this collection of buildings as any kind of municipality to which they were used.

In early 1717 Edward Wortley Montagu arrived in Belgrade on his way overland to take up the post of Ambassador to the Court of Turkey. He was accompanied by his wife, Lady Mary, whose correspondence tells a great deal about daily life in the Ottoman Empire. She wrote to her friend Alexander Pope on 12 February 1717 from Belgrade, describing how on entering Serbia they encountered the site of the last battle between Turks and Austrians: "I could not look without horror on such numbers of mangled human bodies, and reflect on the injustice of war that makes murder not only necessary but meritorious." The English visitors, escorted into Belgrade by the pasha's guard, were impressed by the fortifications of Kalemegdan, not knowing that it would soon fall to the Habsburgs before the year was out. Lady Mary's letter confirms that this was an Ottoman city dominated by a cultured and sophisticated ruling class:

> In the meantime, we are lodged in one of the best houses, belonging to a very considerable man amongst them, and have a whole chamber of janissaries to guard us. My only diversion is the conversations of our host, Achmed Bey, a title something like that of count in Germany. His father was a great pasha, and he has been educated in the most polite eastern learning, being perfectly skilled in the Arabic and Persian languages, and is an extraordinary scribe, which they call *effendi*. This accomplishment makes way to the greatest preferments, but he has had the good sense to prefer an easy, quiet, secure life to all the dangerous honours of the Porte. He sups with us every night, and drinks wine very freely. You cannot imagine how much he is delighted with the liberty of conversing with me. He has explained to me many pieces of Arabian poetry which, I observed, are in numbers not unlike ours, generally alternate verse, and of a very musical sound. Their expressions of love are very passionate and lively. I am so much pleased with them, I really believe I should learn to read Arabic, if I was to stay here a few months. He has a very good library of their books of all kinds and, as he tells me, spends the greatest part of his life there.

Under Habsburg administration after 1717, Belgrade quickly acquired the look of a European city. The Austrians added another storey to some of the larger buildings, or simply pulled them down to make way for their own Baroque architectural styles. Mosques were converted into churches or for other uses. Catholic priests and Franciscan monks replaced Muslim clerics and dervishes. The Turkish harems disappeared. The Austrians rebuilt the fortress, such that the overall shape of Kalemegdan today owes much to the efforts of their chief architect, the Swiss Colonel Nicholas Doxat. He strengthened the walls, added more towers and installed a more complex series of inner and outer walls, making it into one of the best defended bastions in Europe.

The population changed again as the Muslims left, and soldiers of fortune, who were prepared to gamble on a quick profit from the new frontier, filled the taverns and trading posts. They were a colourful and highly diverse group from all corners of Europe with representatives of all social classes. Unfortunately, but characteristic for the development of Belgrade, hardly anything remains of this frenetic building activity. It was not long before the Turks recouped their losses when the Austrians returned the city under the terms of the Treaty of Belgrade in 1739. Before leaving, however, they dismantled large parts of their fortifications in order to reduce Kalemegdan's potential as a defensive position.

The Turks made an effort to rebuild the walls of Kalemegdan but not on their previous scale. They tore down the churches and other buildings erected under the Habsburgs and the city quickly reverted to its former appearance. This change in ownership was accompanied by the usual exchange of populations. The Christian townsfolk moved out, with the adventurers taking their chances elsewhere and the Serbs going north to what is now Novi Sad, while Muslim families took up residence once again.

The Austrians occupied Belgrade fifty years later, their war efforts assisted by Serbs fighting on their side, and despite all promises the city was yet again returned to Ottoman rule two years later in 1791. This time the Serbs were at least mentioned in the peace treaty drawn up between the two Great Powers who had spent a century fighting one another across Serbian lands. According to the treaty, the Serbs were to be given amnesty and allowed to remain in Belgrade, while Ottoman troops, principally those known as the janissaries, were to be denied access to the city. These troops were originally recruited from young Christian boys forcibly taken into the service of the empire, removed to Istanbul and brought up as Muslims. They formed an elite guard entirely loyal to the sultan and often used by him as a personal army to defend his interests against those who would try to usurp them. With time they became a powerful force in their own right and were responsible for some of the more draconian measures and oppressive policies against the Serbs. They were increasingly seen as a liability by the imperial authorities who made genuine efforts to build bridges with the local Serbs through the more conciliatory rule of their new pasha, Hadji Mustafa. The janissaries, however, were anxious to re-assert their position and murdered him in 1801 inside Kalemegdan. They then established themselves alongside the powerful local lords, the Dahijas, as undisputed rulers of Serbia. A new chapter was about to open in the fight for control of Belgrade. It was not long before the Serbs rose in revolt against the tyrannical demands of the new regime.

REMINDERS OF THE PAST

There are just a handful of buildings in the centre of town, outside Kalemegdan, which represent Belgrade architecture before the nineteenth century. One of the rare examples of an Ottoman structure is the only remaining mosque in the city, the Bajrakli-džamija on Gospodar Jevrem Street. It was built about 1690 by the Sultan Suleiman II when the Turks retook possession of Belgrade. The name is taken from the word *barjak* meaning a flag or banner that would be flown from the minaret to give the signal to the other mosques that it was time to begin prayers. Jesuits moved in when the city was under Austrian rule 1717-1739 and it was converted into a Catholic church, the minaret serving as a bell tower. Reverting to its original function when the Austrians left, Bajrakli-džamija has reflected the changes of regime that are the hallmark of the city.

The house at 10 Tsar Dušan Street, near the corner with Kalemegdan, is the only surviving example of Habsburg Baroque architecture in a residential dwelling constructed between 1724 and 1727. Changes have been made to the façade and an extra storey was added in the nineteenth century, but its basic structure retains the imprint of the influence of the Austrian occupation of those years. Situated close to the other corner with Kalemegdan straight over the hill from Tsar Dušan Street, is a building originally erected at the end of the eighteenth century at 10 Gračanica

Street. It appears as a family house on a plan of the city from 1789 but was altered by the new owner, Janko Marković, in about 1830. Its classically proportioned simple appearance emphasizes its straight horizontal lines with evenly spaced rectangular windows on the ground and upper floors. The look of the house and its construction in brick covered with plaster are reminiscent of other dwellings in Zemun, Pančevo, Sremski Karlovci and Novi Sad, towns in Habsburg territory. The house and its architecture attest to some continuing cultural influences in the city of European rather than Ottoman origin.

Generally speaking, however, frequent transformations of the cityscape have completely wiped out traces of older architecture. There are records of what were the larger and more important buildings from the pre-nineteenth-century period, but it is not always known exactly where they stood or what became of them. Somewhere close to 10 Tsar Dušan Street was a huge caravanserai, a place for merchants to stay with their carts, horses and camels while transporting goods through the Ottoman Empire. It also incorporated a covered market-place. The structure was erected between 1571 and 1574 by the powerful Ottoman Vizier Mehmed Pasha Sokolović (1505-79). He was, incidentally, one of those Christians taken as a boy from his home in Bosnia who rose to prominence in the imperial service. Some historians place his caravanserai at what is now 13 Tsar Dušan Street, while others locate the same building at the corner of Tsar Dušan and Tadeusz Kościuszko Street (another group even proposes an entirely different location). It is also known that after the Austrian capture of Belgrade in 1717 a headquarters for the new commander was built, the Palace of Eugene of Savoy. Yet it is disputed whether the palace was in fact made by adapting the caravanserai of Mehmed Pasha Sokolović, or a different building in Turkish Belgrade.

There have been many different Belgrades, following one after the other, but with little in common. The earthen huts of Bronze-Age tribes were replaced by a Celtic settlement, then by a Roman military camp, a Byzantine or Bulgarian or Hungarian fort, a Serbian capital, an Ottoman regional centre, even the Baroque outline of a Habsburg city. Each population brought its own language, religion and culture to bear on the territory. Not only has there been a lack of continuity, but the memories of one community have been erased by the next. The site has served as a centre for communications uniting disparate parts of larger administrative units, it has been a lawless frontier town and a lookout post between east and west. Numerous wars, occupations and the ensuing mayhem at each transformation have ensured that its past remains buried under layers of myth. Belgrade's is a complex and at times cruel story. Many poets have written verses about the city trying to express something of this image. Miloš Crnjanski wrote his "Lament over Belgrade" (Lament nad Beogradom, 1956) in which he addresses his home town after many years of living in exile, making an oblique reference to the whiteness of Kalemegdan's walls: "You, however, spread, like a swan its wings,/oblivion over the Danube and the Sava, while they sleep." And he closes that verse with the lines: "And when my head slumps forward and my hours stop,/You will, I know, kiss me like a mother." Vasko Popa in his poem "Belgrade" (Beograd, 1965-71) expresses an altogether more chilling vision:

White bone amongst the clouds

You arise out of your pyre
Out of your ploughed-up barrows
Out of your scattered ashes

You arise out of your disappearance

The sun keeps you
In its golden reliquary
High above the yapping of centuries

And bears you to the marriage
Of the fourth river of Paradise
With the thirty-sixth river of Earth

White bone among the clouds
Bone of our bones

AROUND KALEMEGDAN

One of the main entrances into Kalemegdan Park today is from the pedestrian precinct of Knez Mihailo Street, along which the people of Belgrade come for an evening stroll or to have a drink at one of its many cafés. At the end of the street stands a nineteenth-century building originally designed as a hotel but now containing the City Library. Opposite the doorway into this rather ornate structure is a statue to the poet Milan Rakić (1876-1938). His work stands out among that of the poets from the early Modernist period before the First World War. He was also a career diplomat and served as Serbian consul in Kosovo between 1908 and 1911 when it was still a province of the Ottoman Empire. Across the road and inside the entrance to the park are many more such statues to literary and political figures whose contributions have been significant for Serbian culture and for creating a sense of modern Serbian identity. One of the first monuments is a relief showing Knez Mihailo, one of Serbia's famous rulers, receiving the keys to the city of Belgrade from the Ottoman pasha when the Turks withdrew their last troops and administrators from the country in 1867. On the other side of the path stands a monument to Radoje Domanović (1873-1908), a satirical prose writer whose barbed observations entertained the Serbian reading public at the beginning of the twentieth century. Then come two of the more popular poets from around the same period, Jovan Dučić (1871-1943) and Aleksa Šantić (1868-1924). There is a statue further on, just off a path to the right, to the prose writer Borisav Stanković (1876-1927), who is often credited with introducing the form of the modern novel to Serbia. Close to him is a bust of Miloš Crnjanski (1893-1976), whose importance has already been noted, and not far from him is Jovan Skerlić (1877-1914). Skerlić was one of the dominant figures in Serbian intellectual, cultural and political life in the decade before the First World War, holding several important positions as university professor, literary critic, editor and politician.

From this entrance the path forks and skirts round a fountain, dating from 1906, of a fisherman struggling with a serpent. Sedate dances used to be held on the little square around the fountain in the 1920s and 1930s, giving the young men and women of Belgrade society an opportunity to meet, albeit under the watchful eyes of their chaperones. Straight ahead stretches one of the park's more popular promenades overlooking the River Sava with its port down below and New Belgrade on the other bank. A broad set of stone steps leads down from this path to a small garden area and a monument with the graves of four men from the communist past. The busts displayed here commemorate the lives of Đura Đaković (1886-1929), Ivo Lola Ribar (1916-53), Ivan Milutinović (1901-44) and Moša

Pijade (1890-1957). Đaković was a pre-war activist, Lola Ribar fell as a member of the communist-led Partisan movement resisting enemy occupation during the Second World War, Milutinović was also killed fighting for the Partisans during the battle to liberate Belgrade, and Pijade, besides being a painter, was a member of the Communist Party's executive committee in 1921, arrested and imprisoned for his political activities in 1925, and holder of various high political offices after the Second World War. In the 1990s, when anti-communist feelings ran high, their busts were removed from their pedestals, but are now returned to their original position.

The Victor is clearly visible from the monument to the communist era, just a short walk through the King's Gate (Kralj kapija). There was a gate here from medieval times but the Austrians replaced it in 1725 with a much stronger defensive fortification incorporating a drawbridge. The gate leads to a series of steps, past the Roman Well (Rimski bunar) and up to the main plateau of Kalemegdan. The Roman Well is a complete misnomer as it has nothing to do with anything so far in the past, being sunk by the Austrians in the period 1721-31. The well's shaft is almost 200 feet deep, taking it over thirty feet below the surface of the Sava, since its purpose was to provide the fort's defenders with a plentiful and safe supply of drinking water during a siege. The wall of Kalemegdan stretching away from the Victor is where people sit and take in the view, giving justification to another name by which the Ottomans knew this place: *fećir bajir*, or the hill for contemplation.

The plateau behind, a grassy area crisscrossed by paths with benches and trees, has been the focal point of all the forts built here. This was the Upper Town (Gornji grad), the nerve centre for military and government life in Belgrade and the surrounding region. Stefan Lazarević built his palace on this mound, the Turks had a mosque with quarters for the janissaries, and Austrian soldiers were housed in barracks. It gave the ruling power an inner sanctum, a last redoubt in case of siege. It was securely positioned on top of the hill, while the walls, towers and earthworks tucked behind the Sava and Danube provided the first lines of defence. A small gate built into the white walls of the Upper Town not far along from the Victor is another Austrian improvement from the eighteenth century made on an older structure. It is called Defterdarova kapija, marked by a water fountain at its side erected in 1577 in honour of Mehmed Pasha Sokolović, and from here a path leads down to Kalemegdan's Lower Town (Donji grad). The Lower Town toward the river used to be an integral part of the city's defences and also the site for the quay at which ships would dock to load and unload goods and supplies.

The ruins of a building which it is thought once belonged to the seat of a bishopric are at the bottom of the slope in the Lower Town. Archaeologists found an inscription here relating to the time of Despot Stefan Lazarević. Close to these ruins is a white, oriental structure that used to be one of the seven public Turkish bath-houses, or *amam*, in Belgrade built at the beginning of the nineteenth century, and the only one remaining from Ottoman times. Rebuilt in the first half of the 1960s, it was then used as an observatory. Toward the river from the bath-house is a line of buildings. First is an Austrian gate from 1736 named after the Emperor Charles VI (Kapija Karla VI). Its luxuriously Baroque style serves as a fitting symbol of the extensive modifications and building programme initiated by the Habsburgs. The building next door, from the end of the eighteenth century, has been both a workshop for the production and repair of cannon and an army kitchen. It is now used as a base by the archaeologists who dig and research the area.

The medieval tower that completes this string of buildings, the Nebojša Tower (Kula Nebojša), is from 1460. It was originally intended as a defensive feature but the Turks converted it into a prison in the eighteenth century with a dark reputation as a place from which inmates rarely returned. Another monument stands near Nebojša Tower, by the river, recalling the bravery of the soldiers who defended Belgrade from Austrian assault in 1915. Heavily outnumbered, the Serbian commander, Major Dragutin Gavrilović, ordered his men to defend their position at all costs. His words are etched on the memorial. Addressing them as soldiers and heroes, he went on to say: "The High Command has struck our regiment from its register of active service. Our regiment is sacrificed for the honour of the Fatherland and Belgrade. You do not have to worry for your lives, which exist no longer... So forward, to glory!"

Military functions are long gone and the Lower Town, like the Upper Town, is now a place for recreation where visitors can stroll around what remains of the gates and walls of the old fortress. Members of the sports club Dušan Silni played the first football match in Belgrade close to Nebojša Tower in May 1896. In the 1930s it was suggested that the city

build an Olympic stadium on this large, flat and empty space, but opponents objected that the site was far more important for its historical significance and that it should be left alone. Since then other facilities have been added including moorings for small boats, floating restaurants, a large sports centre, a pedestrian path and a cycle route. In recent years rugby matches have been played here and, it has been rumoured, staff from some of the embassies in town have come out to play cricket. It also now provides the site for the Belgrade Beer Festival held every August. Much of the Upper Town, too, is also given over to sports and other events, with courts for basketball, tennis and five-a-side football, venues for concerts beneath the fortress walls, and space for outdoor theatre performances during BELEF (Belgrade Summer Festival) held annually in July and early August.

The end of this section of Kalemegdan's wall is marked by a stout tower, Dizdareva kula, and two gates, Despotova kapija and Zindan kapija, all from the fifteenth century, while beyond these structures the Austrians built Leopold's Gate (Leopoldova kapija). Another path between Despotova and Zindan kapija also leads down to the Lower Town. On the way it passes by a small church dedicated to the Most Holy Mother of God, but popularly known as the Rose Church (Crkva Ružica). Originally a gunpowder store, it became the garrison chapel after Kalemegdan was handed over by the last Ottoman pasha to the Serbian authorities in 1867. It was ruined during the bombardment of Belgrade in the First World War and rebuilt in the 1920s.

The two statues on either side of the door represent military figures, one a medieval knight and the other a soldier from the First World War. Inside the church is a painting of the Prayer in Gethsemane on which the faces of contemporary figures are to be found: the Serbian king and his son, Peter and Alexander Karađorđević; the Russian Tsar Nicholas II; and the Serbian politician, Nikola Pašić. Two bells inside the church were cast from captured Turkish cannon as were two icons in relief of the Virgin Mary and St. George. Another church, this one to St. Petka, stands just a little further down the slope. It was built in 1937 above a spring from which, it is said, curative waters flow. When digging the foundations of the church, workmen found many skeletons of soldiers who fell defending Belgrade during the First World War which were removed and interred in a special vault close by.

Kalemegdan Zoo is close to Leopold's Gate. It is quite unremarkable except for a monument in its centre to its most famous simian inhabitant. Sami, or Sammy, was a chimpanzee who came to live here in January 1988 until his death in September 1992 and who managed to escape twice. The first time he was soon caught and brought back. He became an urban legend, however, when he broke out for the second time. He was chased into the courtyard at 33 Tsar Dušan Street where he climbed into a cherry tree and then onto a garage. News of his escape spread quickly and over four thousand people turned up to lend him their support. Newspaper reports tell of people holding placards with slogan such as "Sammy, we're with you!" and "Don't give yourself up Sammy!" Eventually he was shot with a drugged dart and recaptured but not before he had become one of Belgrade's foremost heroes.

Besides the zoo, Kalemegdan houses the Institute for the Protection of Cultural Monuments of Belgrade (Zavod za zaštitu spomenika kulture Beograda) situated behind the Victor, the gallery of the Natural History Museum (Galerija prirodnjačkog muzeja) and the Military Museum (Vojni muzej), both near Karađorđe's Gate (Karađorđeva kapija). Up from the zoo and towards the entrance to the park from Knez Mihailo Street stands a grand pavilion named after Cvijeta Zuzorić (1555-1600), a famous Dubrovnik poetess of the Renaissance period. It was built in 1928 and was the first dedicated exhibition space in Belgrade, becoming the centre of artistic life until the Second World War and adding enormously to the city's image as a modern European capital with an active cultural scene. Today it is by no means the only such space but it still hosts regular exhibitions in the spring and autumn, as well as individual and group showings of foreign and Serbian artists.

Back at the entrance to the park, the main path leads to an impressive statue of a female figure, the Monument of Gratitude to France (Spomenik zahvalnosti Francuskoj), erected in 1930 as a symbol of Serbia's recognition of French help in the First World War. Serbia felt culturally close to France, more so than to the Anglo-Saxon countries. Many Belgrade scholars attended French universities in the early twentieth century, and writers and artists would visit and take inspiration from the latest stylistic developments, while French fashions set the tone for Belgrade's high society. Two compositions in relief on the base of the pediment express these feelings. The suffering of Serb and French soldiers is depicted on one side, and a woman with children representing the help given by France to Serbian refugees is on the other side. Behind the statue a path leads in rapid succession through two gates built as part of the Austrian defences in the eighteenth century. The first is Karađorđe's Gate and the second is

the Inner Istanbul Gate (Unutrašnja Stambol kapija). The Clock Tower (Sahat kula) stands further on and it houses a small exhibition of Kalemegdan's development over the centuries.

The writer Sveta Lukić in his 1995 book of memoirs has a description of Belgrade in constant turmoil, but guarded by the fortress of Kalemegdan looking like an armour-plated boat when spied from the confluence below:

> ... its deck is the Upper Town, the Rose Church and Clock Tower are like chimneys, on the bridge stands the Victor, Meštrović's sculpture turned toward his Yugoslav brothers over the Sava. The boat sails on unfalteringly, as if bewitched. There is no other course than across the Pannonian Sea to Europe.

The central plateau of the Upper Town is gained once more on the other side of the Clock Tower where a six-sided Turkish mausoleum or *turbe* made of stone stands on the grass in a fairly central position. Ottoman Belgrade contained about ten of these ornamental graves of which only two remain—this one and another on Student Square. This *turbe* is the burial chamber of Damid Ali Pasha, a successful soldier against the Austrians in the eighteenth century. Two other prominent Turks, Selim Pasha and Hasan Pasha Češmelija, were interred alongside him in the mid-nineteenth century. The *turbe* inspired the author Ivo Andrić to write his short story "The Excursion" (Ekskurzija).

THE EXCURSION

Andrić (1892-1975) is the best-known writer to have lived in Belgrade during the twentieth century. His place as a writer of world renown was affirmed with the award of the Nobel Prize for literature in 1961. His novels and many of his short stories have been translated into English, but not this one. There are very few works of Serbian literature in which Kalemegdan is a major setting. The whole fortress, Upper Town and Lower Town, was closed to the Serbs during the many centuries when it was a centre of colonial power for Turks and Austrians. It was handed over to the Serbs when the Ottoman Empire quit the city in 1867 and although much of it was designated as a public area from the 1870s it continued to be used as a military base until finally demilitarized in 1946, when the last soldiers, including a contingent of Soviet troops, left their barracks. Then, it was truly opened up for all to enjoy.

The park is mentioned in literature from the beginning of the twentieth century as a place where lovers would take a stroll, but Andrić's short story, first published in 1955, marks the first time it receives more than a passing reference. The story gives a vivid impression of the atmosphere of the park and has a ghostly feel with its reference to Damid Ali Pasha's burial chamber.

The story opens with the arrival of a group of children from a school in Vojvodina to the north of Belgrade. Andrić writes:

> The day was very warm, and the column of pupils, led by their teacher, felt a sense of relief when they arrived at Kalemegdan and when they could hide and rest in the shade of the park around the Military Museum. Their teacher sat on a bench and wiped inside his heavy black hat with his handkerchief. The young boys and girls spread themselves out among the uneven shadows of the bushes and trees in a happy throng. Their new surroundings, the glare and greenery of a summer's day, the wide rivers flowing under a tall sky—everything was exciting and goaded them into laughter and movement.

Then the focus falls on two girls, Ana and Olga, who are looking at the *turbe*:

> They, too, together with the rest, stared long at the puzzling letters of the Turkish inscription, then half-aloud they read the translation, written in black letters on a gilded board. (Damid Ali Pasha... conqueror of Morea... Great Vizier, most esteemed follower of the Prophet... Struck down 13 August 1716 at Petrovaradin...). And now, suppressing their giggles, as a piece of fun which they were helpless to stop, its source powerful and overflowing, they shuffled around the locked doors. Then, Olga slowly took the iron ring of the door, knocked twice, and in a changed voice with a theatrical bow solemnly declared, "Lord Great Vizier, arise, your loyal servant is calling you..."
>
> Here, without finishing her sentence, she let the ring go like a naughty, frightened child. (Who can know where that little and unexpected boldness of otherwise calm and restrained creatures comes from

and where it will lead?) And both girls ran off, hand-in-hand and laughing, along the soft path to the very edge of the terrace from which opened up the broad, illuminated view over the meeting place of the Sava and Danube.

The two girls spend the night at the house of Ana's aunt in Belgrade. When they fall asleep Olga has a nightmare in which she is visited by the spirit of Damid Ali Pasha. Scared out of her wits, she is woken by Ana who has heard her whimpering cries. Andrić finishes his story on an altogether different note—that of the resilience of children in the face of their worst fears:

> The girls held one another tightly and both of them at the same time burst into peals of laughter. They laughed so much, so loudly and long, sitting in their white illuminated bed. Their heads were bent towards one another as if they were singing a happy duet. The whole room filled with their clear, carefree laughter.

The girls in their own childish way have caught the spectral echoes that resound softly through the old fortress. Ivo Andrić, like Sveta Lukić and the poets, evokes an image of Kalemegdan both haunting and haunted, captured in the innocent laughter of children.

Chapter Two

FROM REPUBLIC SQUARE TO THE
RIVER SAVA: THE SERBIAN UPRISINGS
AND LATER

ISTANBUL GATE

Republic Square marks the outer limit of Ottoman Belgrade. Here, at a point in front of the equestrian statue to Knez Mihailo and across the road from the National Theatre (Narodno pozorište), stood the massive main gate into the city known as the Istanbul Gate (Stambol-kapija). In Turkish times the road out of town from here took the traveller down through Serbia and to the sultan's court at Istanbul, while inside the city it led to the Inner Istanbul Gate and the Upper Town of the fortress. Always heavily guarded to control traffic entering and leaving Belgrade, it was, according to eye-witness accounts, a most impressive structure. It formed part of a defensive system that ran up the hill from the Danube roughly along the line of what is now France Street, by the National Theatre and into the square. On the other side of the gate, the perimeter defences pushed over the brow of the hill and curved their way down to the bank of the Sava. The city was cradled between the two rivers behind a broad and deep trench further supported by earthworks and on top of them a wooden palisade.

The Istanbul Gate was not the only door into Belgrade through these outer defences. Two other gates gave passage into and out of the town: the Vidin Gate (Vidin-kapija) watched over the entrance on the slope leading down to the Danube, while the Town Gate (Varoš-kapija) guarded the Sava slope. These two structures, however, were overshadowed by the Istanbul Gate. The Austrians gave it its final shape by rebuilding it during their occupation at the beginning of the eighteenth century. The gate had three openings, a wide central way for carts and horses with two smaller ones on either side for pedestrians. Just behind it lay the execution ground where Serbs who threatened the Ottoman order were beheaded and their heads placed on spikes above the gate as a warning to others. Descriptions from the eighteenth and early nineteenth century rarely fail to mention the packs of feral dogs which roamed this gory place, attracted by blood and human remains scattered on the ground. The gate's massive stone blocks were a constant reminder that Belgrade was a seat of colonial power where the pasha had his residence and who, at times, exercised a most cruel and arbitrary authority. The Istanbul Gate in the eyes of the Serbs was an iconic representation of Turkish oppression and became their main target when they launched their attack on the city in 1806.

First Serbian Uprising 1804-13

The First Serbian Uprising began in 1804 and lasted until the insurgents were finally defeated in 1813 and forced to flee. Its causes and the wider circumstances against which it has to be understood go back a little further. The fortunes of the Serbs waxed and waned according to the policies of the Great Powers towards the Balkans. Russia and Austria were always looking for ways to take advantage of the weakness of the Ottoman Empire. In 1774 the Russians concluded the Treaty of Kutchuk Kainardji with the Turks, which gave them the right to represent the interests of the Christians living in the Ottoman Empire, most of whom were members of the Orthodox Church. War between Russia and Turkey broke out again in

1787, and the Habsburg Empire, suspicious of Russian motives in its back-yard, joined in and captured Belgrade, holding it for a brief period between 1788 and 1791. In Serbia this brief conflict is known as Koča's War after the name of the leader, Koča Andjelković, who led the local contingents of Serbs in support of the Austrian forces.

International interest in Serbia was not generally guided by principles of Christian or Slav solidarity. The Russians and Austrians only intended to further their own interests. In 1791 the Austrians made peace with the Ottoman Empire and left their erstwhile allies to the Turks' mercies. The Russians continued to insist on their right to speak on behalf of the Serbians as protectors of the Orthodox Church but actually did very little. Nonetheless the policies of the Great Powers were of fundamental significance for the Serbs who could not hope to defeat the Ottoman Empire on their own. Their next chance came with the rise of Napoleon who invaded Egypt, an Ottoman province, in 1798. The Napoleonic Wars provided the Serbs with the ideal conditions with which to pursue their bid for independence.

The situation closer to home was also changing for the Serbs. The new Sultan Selim III (1789-1807) was a reformer who was anxious to halt the declining influence of his imperial authority. To this end, he introduced certain of the modernizing tendencies in administration and the military that he saw had already brought benefits to the European states that were now threatening him. Recognizing that many of the problems in the border outpost of Serbia were caused by the greed and unruly behaviour of the janissaries, he decided to curb their influence. He installed a new pasha, Hadji Mustafa, who ruled with a benign attitude towards the sultan's subjects, earning him a reputation as a friend of the Serbs. Even so, his enemies were numerous and very strong. In 1801 the janissaries returned to Belgrade, murdered Hadji Mustafa and returned to their previous vicious ways.

The Serbian rebellion began as a reaction against the harsh treatment meted out by the new regime. Intolerable burdens were placed on the local Christian population through taxes and new obligations to the authorities, while any kind of resistance met with the severest penalties. The most powerful men in the province were now those who commanded the janissaries, the Dahijas: Mehmed Aga Fočić, Kučuk Alija Đevrlić, Mula Jusuf and Aganlija. Toward the end of January 1804, Fočić left Belgrade with a retinue of armed men to meet one of the local leaders, Aleksandar Nenadović, at the village of Ljubenino Polje. They were to travel to Valjevo together, but Fočić had received intelligence that Nenadović was planning a rebellion and was importing arms across the River Sava from Habsburg territory. Nenadović was arrested and executed, the first of many to suffer in quick succession as the Dahijas turned on the most important Serbs in the district with the intention of killing them all. The Serb leaders rallied round and nominated as their commander Đorđe Petrović (1752-1817), more popularly known as Karađorđe or Black George. He was a man with military experience who had fought in Koča's War and whose descendants were to derive their surname from him as the royal Karađorđević dynasty.

In February 1804 the rebels met at Orašac, not far from Belgrade, and offered the leadership of their small and rudimentary force to Karađorđe. According to legend, he at first refused the offer on the grounds that he had a hot, at times uncontrollable, temper and could not vouch for his conduct. The Serbs, however, took this as a sign of his resolve to defeat the Turks and continued to clamour for him to accept the commission. He took the proffered office and the insurgents enjoyed initial success against the vast resources of the Ottoman Empire, which was embroiled in the consequences of the Napoleonic Wars.

The rebels laid siege to Belgrade in 1806 with around 25,000 men and forty cannon. Karađorđe put his cannon around the area of today's St. Mark's Church (Crkva svetog Marka) and the adjoining park of Tašmajdan since, from there, his guns were in range of the citadel. He deployed his main camp on the more distant plateau at Vračar. The fighting around the city was fierce, with much at stake on both sides. The defenders resisted as far as they could but the Ottoman Empire could not afford to send them much-needed reinforcements. On the night of the 29 November the Serbs launched their biggest attack on the city. A small force led by Uzun Mirko began the action by taking the Town Gate on the Sava slope. The legend goes that one of his men then climbed on top of the Turkish cannon by the gate and sang out as a signal that the gate was securely in their hands and that the main force led by Vasa Čarapić should strike at the Istanbul Gate. Čarapić was fatally wounded in the offensive, but the attempt was successful and the rebels broke through. The Ottoman commander had no choice but to surrender the city into the hands of the insurgents.

The First Serbian Uprising is pivotal in the development of Serbia and had much wider repercussions for the whole region; Misha Glenny concludes that "the rebellion marked the beginning of modern history on the Balkan peninsula." Another historian, however, is more circumspect in his judgment of these events. While not disregarding the impact which the rebellion was to have on Serbia, Stevan Pavlowitch draws our attention to its original aims: "The First Serbian Rising—as historians would call it—was hardly the outcome of revolutionary ideological thinking or political planning." Instead, he emphasizes the odd alliances that were formed at what was nothing more than a time of national and international chaos. The traditional landowners who supported the rule of Hadji Mustafa were Muslims and not Serbs by origin. They held land which had been granted to them by grateful sultans for their services to the empire. Conversely, the Dahijas were Serbs who had gained powerful positions in the local hierarchy, which they exploited for their own ends. The rebels initially saw their fight to be a struggle against local tyranny imposed by the janissaries and their leaders, not a national rebellion against the authority of the sultan. As time went on they began to change their ultimate goal and began to think of their efforts more as a war for independence.

Local conditions were, moreover, subject to the vagaries of events happening on a much bigger stage. The Napoleonic Wars in Europe were diverting the attention of the Great Powers from any consideration they might have given to Serbian aspirations. The Ottoman Empire was facing pressure on a number of fronts, from the French in North Africa and the Russians around the Black Sea. It suited the Russians to add their encouragement to the rebels in Serbia, although their support was not translated into men and money.

Karađorđe was hence spurred on by international events that seemed detrimental to the Ottoman Empire, and he put his hopes on the Russian connection. Yet when Napoleon invaded Russia in 1812, the Tsar hurriedly made a treaty with Turkey to free his southern flank. The Treaty of Bucharest included mention of Serbia, but only to confirm that Russia agreed that the province be returned to its old position under Ottoman suzerainty, giving the Serbs some limited control of local affairs. The Turks now took their chance to crush the rebellion without outside interference. Three armies entered Serbia in 1813, and Karađorđe was forced to flee across the Sava into Austrian territory. The Uprising was over and a terrible revenge was extracted against the local population by the triumphant

Turks. Nonetheless, the desire for independence from Ottoman rule was kindled and became the central platform of Serbian policy for most of the nineteenth century.

The First Uprising in Serbian National Songs

Ottoman rule over the Balkans excluded the local Christian population from positions of authority and power, leaving them an illiterate peasant society. The achievements of the medieval Serbian state and Church, evident in the art and architecture of churches, monasteries and royal palaces, receded into a distant memory. The writing practised in the administration of the country, in replicating the Holy Scriptures and in recording the lives of the saints of the Orthodox Church was lost and became moribund. Although the continued existence of the Church was an important factor in maintaining a commemorative link with the past, the written language became largely ossified in the form used in the fifteenth century, moving ever further away from the spoken vernacular as it evolved in everyday use. The language of law and government was that of the imperial rulers. In these circumstances, oral literature, songs and stories of different kinds came to represent the most vibrant form of local art.

Serbian national songs, or epic ballads, developed over the centuries along quite sophisticated lines and some have been compared to the achievements of Homer's *Iliad*. These ballads tell stories from Serbian history in the form of heroic myths. They were sung by a bard called a *guslar* to the accompaniment of a simple single-stringed instrument, the *gusle*. He did not know his songs by heart, but as compositions made up of traditional phrases and formulaic expressions on which he could call each time he sang. His repertoire was based on a type of rapid composition recalling these fragments and lines and guiding them into place for each performance. Some of the parts were just phrases: a hero's "black horse" or a maiden's "white throat", in which the adjective barely registers its meaning. Other parts were long descriptions of soldiers arriving at a battlefield, details of the arms they carried, the numbers in each contingent, confrontations between heroes and their enemies. Thus, each song was composed anew at each performance. The narrative outline of a story was well known to the audience, rather like some modern film genres such as the Western. The audience revels in the fulfilment of expectations while taking pleasure in the singer's skill to add a new turn of phrase.

Some of the best-known songs are about the Battle of Kosovo and the legendary hero, Prince Marko (Kraljević Marko). The songs about Kosovo celebrate the battle of 1389 as a tragic Serbian defeat and the beginning of Turkish rule. According to the myth, Prince Lazar is visited by the prophet Elijah who offers him a choice: he can win the day and build an earthly kingdom, or lose but in defeat earn for himself and his people a heavenly kingdom. Lazar, naturally, chooses the latter option. He and his lords meet for a last supper on the eve of battle and with a sense of premonition he accuses his loyal retainer Miloš Obilić of treachery. Greatly hurt, Obilić denies any such thought and declares that he will kill the Ottoman leader, Sultan Murat. The Serbs are indeed betrayed, but by Vuk Branković, who leads his men away from the field when he should support the main army. Both Lazar and Obilić fulfil their epic roles: Lazar dies a martyr, and Obilić is hacked to pieces after killing Murat.

This bare outline is the myth of the famous battle as preserved in the song "The Fall of the Serbian Empire" (Propast carstva srpskoga). The Kosovo cycle contains many other songs that tell of associated events—the fear of the wives of the Serbian lords as they head off for Kosovo, the Kosovo Maiden who gives comfort to the wounded heroes, all telling a narrative with numerous strands and various characters. The Serbs are defeated because of betrayal from within, while preserving the integrity of their heroic demise framed in a strong biblical allegory.

If the Kosovo cycle offers compensation in piety and heroism, the other well-known cycle of epic ballads about Prince Marko offers a different kind of consolation. He is the most highly developed character of all the ballads, an archetypal hero and yet also something of an anti-hero. He is strong and determined in action, but will use tricks and subterfuge in order to win. He shows a comical side: when his mother wants him to get married, he points out that she wants a daughter and he wants a wife, and that these are not compatible aims. He drinks copious amounts of red wine, as does his horse. This mixture of epic and comic elements makes him a more grounded type, someone with whom the peasant society which created him could easily identify.

The legendary prince is based on a real historical figure, Marko, the son of King Vukašin, a Serbian feudal lord. The real Marko was a Turkish vassal who fought for the sultan and paid homage to his authority. The epic Marko is also a servant of the Ottoman Empire, but a servant whom the sultan fears and on whom he has to rely to fight his enemies. Marko can afford to be kind in a cruel world, and very severe when affronted or when he sees dishonesty. He upholds the honour of his family according to the traditional values of a patriarchal code, and at the same time one can laugh with him and at him. In fact, he reflects the very complicated relationship that developed between the Serbs and their Ottoman masters. Not challenging the status quo, the mythic Marko works within its framework, an invention of the colonized imagination, an image of a preferred world.

The epic ballads were not the only form of oral literature. There were other types of songs providing a whole library of material that could cover all occasions while working or celebrating, at harvest time or at a wedding. Yet the large-scale stories and colourful characters in the epics have persisted longer and, perhaps more importantly, they captured the imagination of Europe in the nineteenth century. Goethe and other German Romantics considered these songs to possess an authentic ring which their more sophisticated, modern equivalents had long since lost. The Serbian epics offered a nostalgic glimpse of a purer national soul about which people abroad wanted to know more. Their reputation spread and translations soon appeared in Germany, France and Britain. In Serbia, however, the songs remained very much a daily entertainment, which, like all art, could be enjoyed on many different levels. Although the product of an agrarian and illiterate society, with their place in an urban, educated context limited, they survived within modern Serbian culture as they form a background to later developments.

Belgrade is one of the settings for one of the last great ballads created by the blind bard Filip Višnjić (1767-1834), "The Start of the Revolt against the Dahijas" (Početak bune protiv dahija). The song reworks the story of the First Serbian Uprising using the recognizable formulaic expressions of the traditional ballads and augmenting the historical outline with more dramatic flourishes.

The opening sets the scene for the remainder of the story; the translated lines here are taken from Geoffrey N. W. Locke's *The Serbian Epic Ballads: An Anthology* (in which the translator prefers the spelling Dahiyas):

Dear God, what great and wondrous happenings!
When in the Serbian lands there first swelled up
The tide of change that swept away the Turks,
And saw the realm of Serbia restored.
It was not done by princes waging war,
Nor did the Turkish gluttons wish for it.
The hungry common people of the land
Arose—they could no longer pay the tax,
Nor bear the threefold burden of the Turks.
For all those who were blessed by God were roused—
The blood began to boil up through the earth.
They knew the time had come for waging war,
The time to shed their blood for Christianity,
And to avenge their ancestors at last.

This celebration of the Uprising stresses some elements of the Serbian cause that were absent from the real context. It begins with a reference to God and the hint that this war is a holy crusade, fused with the popular nature of the campaign against the Turks prompted by the "hungry common people". In reality, the Serbian standard was raised at Orašac by local chieftains coming together under Karađorđe's leadership. The song suggests that Serbia will be restored as a consequence of the rebels' action, although it was actually returned as a province to the Ottoman Empire with limited local powers. Blood will be inevitably spilled, since this is a conflict between two diametrically opposed sides, a basic story of good versus evil, in which the downtrodden Serbian peasant will carry the cross of Christ into battle. The final line focuses on vengeance and the demand for retribution for "their ancestors", which the Serbian audience would understand to mean the Battle of Kosovo. Thus, the Uprising is invested with a divine call to arms supported by the cultural memory of the community.

The song, however, continues to tell a rather more complicated story. The Turks themselves are not looking for a fight, which in a roundabout way reflects the historical position of Sultan Selim III, who tried to pursue a more conciliatory policy toward the Serbs. In the ballad the local leaders, the Dahijas, meet by the Istanbul Gate and go to the Danube to fill a bowl with water. They carry it from the banks of the river to the top of the Nebojša Tower at Kalemegdan where, standing round the bowl, they hope to see their futures in the water. What they see disturbs them greatly, as each of them stares at an image of himself without his head. The oldest among them councils that they have wronged the Serbs who will seek their freedom and he recalls the dying words of Sultan Murat after his victory at Kosovo:

> O brother Turks! Vezirs and Generals!
> Now I must die; the empire falls to you.
> Hear what I say; you must obey my words,
> So that your rule may last a thousand years.
> Do not be cruel to the Serbian folk;
> Do right to them, and be considerate.

Sultan Murat is advising his followers to act justly toward the Serbs, but the Dahijas have forgotten these wise words and will pay for their cruelty. The younger hotheads ignore the advice and propose to pool their resources and execute all Serbs who plot against them. Karađorđe is one of their targets but he manages to escape their murderous plans and raises a force to combat them. His rebels come from rural Serbia and go around the villages killing the Turks they find before turning on the towns, the centres of Ottoman power. Karađorđe demands that the Turkish tyrants be handed over to him and his men. The Serbs beat them as they had been beaten, save those who ask for mercy, baptize some, and execute the rest. Those who deserve punishment are punished, justice prevails and Serbia is liberated "from Kosovo to fair Belgrade".

The poem, unlike the Kosovo cycle, does not celebrate defeat but victory. It plays on the edges of historical events; some of its details are quite accurate, and others are clear embellishments. It represents one of the last examples in the national tradition of epic ballads; in fact, it appears on the cusp between two eras as the Serbs begin their return to Belgrade.

SECOND SERBIAN UPRISING AND MILOŠ OBRENOVIĆ

Two years after the defeat of Karađorđe's rebels, the Serbs in the region of Belgrade rose for a second time against intolerable local conditions, this time led by Miloš Obrenović (1780-1860). He was not a revolutionary patriot, nor was he keen to meet the Ottoman Empire in open battle. Rather, he was pragmatic, open to negotiations and ready to compromise.

His situation was helped by the post-Napoleonic international order in which Russia was free once more to meddle in Ottoman affairs. With pressure from Moscow a deal was struck in 1817 that left Miloš as the knez, or prince, of Serbia. The country was not independent but it was invested with more local autonomy on which Miloš could build. Karađorđe returned to Serbia secretly, but his methods and intentions were not what the new leader had in mind. Hearing of his presence in the vicinity, Miloš dispatched some of his men to kill him and, as proof of his loyalty to the sultan, sent his rival's head to Istanbul.

The new knez was not only a brutal despot but also a prosperous businessman. The Serbian economy was by now based on the rearing and export of pigs to the lucrative Habsburg market. Miloš was already successful in this regard and intended to use his position to increase his share of exports and control the frontier. He rapidly grew richer and was able to bribe and buy loyalty, but his enterprise relied on keeping local political power in his hands. The sultan lived far away and it was in Miloš's interests to make himself indispensable to the security of the Ottoman Empire's border with Austria. Such stability also served to stimulate the very trade on which his economic future depended.

Miloš Obrenović was a shrewd ruler whose political ambitions were largely determined by his personal fortune. With Russian support, he won further concessions from the Ottoman Empire enshrined in the *hatti-sherif*, or sultan's edict, of 1830. At a solemn meeting on Tašmajdan this decree was read out to the Serbian leadership. It promised them religious freedom, greater political control over their own affairs and sundry new rights such as their own postal service. It was announced that the Ottoman administration would not interfere in their internal affairs, the territory under Serbian control was enlarged, and Miloš was made hereditary knez. Foreign powers opened consular posts in Belgrade and soon an embryonic diplomatic presence was established with representatives from France,

Austria, Russia and an Englishman, Colonel Hodges. But the new settlement also restricted the ruler's personal power by introducing a council to rule alongside him. This new arrangement did not suit Miloš's autocratic temperament, or his immediate aims. His main opponent was Toma Vučić Perišić, leader of a group calling itself the Constitutionalists who wanted to curb Miloš's dictatorial style of government in order to increase their own share of power. For reasons of their own, members of Miloš's family, his wife, Kneginja Ljubica, and his brother, Gospodar Jevrem, lent their support to the conspiracy. The knez was obliged to accept further limits on his activities until he was finally forced to abdicate in 1839 when he went into exile. He was succeeded by his son Milan, a sickly boy who soon died and who was in turn succeeded by his sixteen-year-old brother Mihailo. Vučić Perišić knew that he was not going to realize his personal ambitions while the Obrenović family remained in Belgrade, so he also ousted Mihailo in 1842 and replaced him as ruler by Karađorđe's son, Alexander, thus furthering the rivalry between Serbia's two royal dynasties.

Building on the Sava Slope

During his rule from 1817 to 1839 Knez Miloš was wary of the pasha and his garrison of troops in Belgrade. The sultan's promises did not fill him with confidence for his own safety since Ottoman actions in the past showed that local officials could easily take matters into their own hands. He preferred to put as great a distance between himself and Kalemegdan as he could afford and spent much of his time in the town of Kragujevac, the centre of the Serbian rebellions and loyal to him. Here he established his court and it remained the Serbian capital until 1842. He could not be entirely absent from Belgrade, however, and during his rule many changes were wrought on the face of the city.

After the Second Serbian Uprising, Belgrade was a settlement dominated by Kalemegdan as the residency of the pasha and the home of the Ottoman garrison. It had a mixed population of some 25,000, mostly Turks but with some Greeks, Vlachs, Jews, gypsies and Serbs. The Turks dominated the population on the slope down to the Danube, while the small Serbian community was concentrated on the Sava slope. The Muslim population, nervous at the extent of the Serbian rebellions and the new status of the province, went into a period of gradual decline. The number of Serbs grew, especially after the increased home rule granted by the decree of 1830.

At the same time, Ottoman styles of dress and architecture continued to act as the dominant models of urban life and the knez himself ruled more in the style of a pasha than a European prince. Fred Singleton wrote of him:

> Miloš was a man nurtured in the old society, and his regime and life style still bore the marks of his origins. In 1830 in his house—or *konak*—there were no tables, chairs or beds. Visitors squatted on the floor or sat on low, Turkish-style divans. Miloš dressed in Turkish clothing. He was unable to read or write and books in Serbian were almost unknown. The main streets of the towns were rough mud tracks. Window glass was not used even in the ruler's *konak*. There were no street lights and at night the streets were deserted.

Singleton calls the knez's main residence a *konak*, a palace. The word can also refer to a place for an overnight stay whether an inn or quarters for guests as part of a monastery complex. Miloš's Belgrade residence was over the hill at Topčider and out of sight of Kalemegdan, and more importantly beyond the range of the pasha's guns. The main site of Serbian development, however, was in the area where they were already a majority around the Town Gate. The Serbian quarter stretched roughly from the brow of the hill and Knez Mihailo Street, down past the corner where the Cathedral, or Saborna crkva, stands to the River Sava, and over to the market now called Zeleni venac, the Green Wreath. A number of buildings from this early period survive, helping to give a picture of the style and taste of the time.

The road by the Sava now called Karađorđe Street runs from a point just below Kalemegdan as far as the main railway and bus stations. It formed a district called Savamala, inhabited by impoverished gypsies whom Miloš, in a typical display of ruthlessness, moved to the other side of town to a district called Palilula, on the Danube slope, just outside the trench marking the town limits. The area was open to river traffic and as such was developed for its trading potential. At the end of the street, where the Hotel Bristol stands today, there used to be the Little Market (Mala pijaca) to which traders from Bosnia would traditionally come arriving by boat at the wharf on the Sava.

Merchants from Belgrade's Serbian community were among the first to build homes for themselves here. Their houses typically contained commercial premises on the ground floor with the upper storey used as living accommodation. No. 29 Karađorđe Street was built in 1828 by the Žujović family, and close by no. 37 was built in 1832 by Jakov Jakšić who served in Miloš Obrenović's Ministry of Finance. Along the same street other houses were constructed, often with commercial intentions in mind, and also kafanas with rooms for visitors bringing their goods to sell or coming to buy in Belgrade (a *kafana* is a typical café serving food and drink). A new customs house was erected in 1835 by the Sava called the Đumrukana, of which there is no trace remaining but it had the distinctive honour of hosting Belgrade's first theatre performance in 1841.

The street now looks rundown but it was the financial centre of nineteenth-century Belgrade. Situated by the river and prone to flooding, the land was marshy, but after the draining programme of 1867 it became more suitable for large construction projects, allowing proper hotels, the first stock exchange and apartment buildings to make their appearance. The opening of the main railway station in 1884 linked Belgrade with Vienna to the west and Istanbul to the east, establishing the city once again as an important point in the arteries of modern communication crossing the region.

Kosančić Crescent is a street further up the hill from Karađorđe Street. It contains hardly any traces from the time of Miloš Obrenović, but its development was of great symbolic significance. The trench, which was the city's first line of defence, used to follow its course as it wound down to the Sava. The oldest building on the street is at no. 18, the house of Vitomir Marković erected in the middle of the nineteenth century, although there are some older dwellings on adjoining streets.

Some of these older houses are easily identifiable by their distinctive Balkan style of architecture. The Balkan style was common in nineteenth-century Belgrade and exhibits many influences from Ottoman architecture, although it later adapted to include more European influences. Slobodan Bogunović in his encyclopaedia of Belgrade architecture describes some of its typical attributes: "The outer appearance of a house in the architecture of the Balkan style gives a picturesque impression with its overhanging, deep and shady eaves, jutting bay-windows, white-washed walls, garden verandas, tiled and gently sloping roofs, windows level with the façade and opening outward, and tall chimneys imaginatively decorated at the top." The bay-windows are on the first floor and in some cases run the entire length of the façade. Otherwise, they may be oval or rectangular in shape, facing the street, with windows at the front and often at the sides to let in maximum light. Rooms in such a house were usually organized in a symmetrical pattern around a central hall that served to emphasize their externally balanced proportions. In poorer examples, the shape of the roof combined with low ceilings can give a somewhat squat appearance. There are a few examples of this Balkan style around Zadar Street, off Kosančić Crescent, as well as others of a later date with more classical or Baroque European features.

An architecturally interesting example is to be found at 6 Zadar Street, designed in 1928 by the architect Branislav Kojić, who was also responsible for the "Cvijeta Zuzorić" pavilion in Kalemegdan. Intending the house to be his family home, he fused traditional Balkan style with Modernist trends to produce a façade that combines both national and international elements.

Kosančić Crescent was known as the district of choice for Belgrade's wealthier families in the nineteenth century. The view of it today is spoiled by the large empty plot between nos. 12 and 16, a result of the German air-raid on 6 April 1941 that brought Yugoslavia into the Second World War. The National Library of Serbia moved into a very elegant building here in 1925, only to be bombed and gutted by fire sixteen years later, an event which destroyed hundreds of thousands of volumes, rare books, maps, medieval manuscripts and donations left by private collectors. Almost the entire national cultural heritage existing in print form disappeared overnight. Great efforts have been made to repair the loss, but it is not unknown even now for a request for some item in the new building of the National Library to meet with the reply that it has not been in the collection since 1941.

Some other notable architectural landmarks can be found close by. No. 10 Gračanica Street is one of the oldest houses in the city, even predating the time of Miloš Obrenović, while 5 Gavrilo Princip Street, called Manak's House (Manakova kuća),on the corner with Prince Marko Street, is constructed in typical Balkan style. The original building on this site contained the harem of a Turkish *aga* who found himself dispossessed of his property when the Serbs won greater independence. It was bought in 1830 by a Greek called Manojlo Manak who built the present house with a bakery and kafana. It was renovated in the 1960s and is now part of Belgrade's museum complex.

The Green Wreath Market is at the top of Prince Marko Street, an area once covered by a large pond where people would come for a day out and boating. In 1840 a German lady opened a kafana here, but instead of putting a name over the door she displayed a piece of green tin representing a wreath—from which the modern name for the area is derived.

The Konak kneginje Ljubice, Kneginja Ljubica's Palace, stands opposite the Cathedral on the corner of Knez Sima Marković and King Peter I Streets. Miloš, the kneginja's (princess's) husband, originally intended the house for himself as a symbol of his wealth, but it was too close to Kalemegdan for him to make much use of it. His wife then moved in with their two sons, Milan and Mihailo. The exterior expresses strong echoes of the traditional Balkan style, simply designed but larger than usual. The interior is of quite a different character, with a pattern of rooms and furnishings showing a distinctly European taste, probably due to the influence of the kneginja.

Over the years the building has fulfilled many different functions, reflecting Belgrade's turbulent history. Ljubica was forced to leave in 1842 after the coup which brought the Karađorđević family back into power. It then housed the Belgrade Lycée, a school founded at Kragujevac but which was moved to the new capital. It was then given to the Ministry of Justice in 1863 and became a school for deaf and dumb children in 1918. When the communists took power in 1945 it became the Republic Bureau for the Protection of Monuments of Culture. During the 1970s it was completely renovated to house a museum collection displaying interiors of Belgrade homes from the nineteenth century.

Across the road at 5-9 Knez Sima Marković Street is another large and architecturally impressive apartment building, but constructed in a completely different style at the turn of the twentieth century. Building work began in 1880, but was only completed following a second phase of activity in 1910. It has a richly decorated façade sporting small balconies with wrought-iron fencing. Its long frontage has a distinctive Central European feel in complete contrast to Kneginja Ljubica's Palace across the road. The differences between the two buildings are a visible record of how far the city shifted in its cultural orbit in a period of eighty years.

KAFANA AND CATHEDRAL

Around the corner from here and across the road from the Cathedral is the well-known Belgrade kafana The Question Mark (Znak pitanja), represented outside by the simple sign "?" The story goes that when the first kafana opened here, the priests from the Cathedral, aghast that a drinking establishment could stand opposite a house of prayer, stole out one night and painted out the name. No-one could remember what it was actually called, so it became "?" The truth is not quite so fanciful. The building dates from the early 1820s, when it was built by one of Miloš's functionaries, Naum Ičko, from whom the knez bought it in 1824. He gave the property to Ećim-Toma Kostić, the doctor who cured him when he was wounded in 1807 at the attack on the town of Užice during the First Serbian Uprising. The new owner opened a kafana under his own name Ećim-Tomina. Records show that he introduced a billiard table in 1834, one of the few available in the Balkans and a very popular attraction. In 1878 the kafana was renamed At the Shepherd's (Kod pastira), and later At the Cathedral (Kod Saborne crkve). It was bought in 1884 by Ivan

Pavlović, an enterprising businessman who added an extra dimension to the kafana by selling priests' robes and other church paraphernalia. Much of what he sold was cheap trinkets, but it is not entirely clear which aspect of his trade offended the church authorities more—the sale of inferior icons or the name of his establishment, At the Cathedral. Eventually they decided that things had gone too far and threatened legal action unless Pavlović changed the name of his kafana. Not knowing what to do, he decided to put a "?" over the door and wait for the affair to quieten down. His temporary solution became the name that stuck.

The Cathedral was a symbol of the new freedoms granted by the *hatti-sherif* of 1830. It replaced an earlier church erected in 1728 but which had fallen into disrepair. At first the knez thought he might renovate the old church, but this was too expensive and the decision was taken to demolish it and build a new one. Work began on the new church in 1836 and was not completed until after Miloš went into exile. It has two particularly striking features. First, its Baroque style represented a fresh approach to church architecture in Serbia and did not meet with universal approval. Orthodox churches were traditionally constructed according to a different design with cupolas instead of tall spires, as can be seen in the Church of St. Mark in Tašmajdan. Second, it is closed on all sides and there is no point from which it can be viewed as a whole, whereas one might expect such an impressive icon of the national Orthodox Church to have an open perspective from at least one angle, like the new Church of St. Sava near the National Library.

The Cathedral became the place for coronations, royal weddings and funerals. Both Miloš Obrenović and his son Mihailo are buried in the church, while the remains of several medieval monarchs were also interred here. Just outside the main door are the graves of two of Serbia's most important men of letters, without whom it is difficult to imagine the modern Serbian language ever existing: Dositej Obradović and Vuk Stefanović Karadžić.

DOSITEJ OBRADOVIĆ

Dositej Obradović (1739-1811) was the foremost representative of Serbian culture in the eighteenth century. He was born in Vojvodina, among the community of Serbs who made their homes in the southern province of the Habsburg Empire following the great migration of families in the wake of the Austrian withdrawal at the end of the seventeenth century. The Austrians allowed the Serbs to settle in the area on condition that they provided the frontier regiments to protect the empire from the Turks across the river at Belgrade. The Serbs here lived in completely different social and cultural circumstances from their cousins in Serbia proper where people were rooted in small villages with little experience outside their locality. The Vojvodina Serbs lived in small towns and, more importantly, were granted a certain amount of local autonomy, which left them running their own affairs. They traded along the Danube and their communities became quite wealthy, opening schools and founding municipal institutions. They enjoyed a greater degree of religious freedom and were able to build new churches and monasteries, activities frowned on by the Muslim leadership to the south.

The Serbian Church in Vojvodina opened important links with the Russian Orthodox Church, and sent priests to train in Russian seminaries. They brought back books printed in the liturgical language of the Russian Church. Over the centuries the Slavonic languages drifted further apart and the form used in the Church, although retaining many older linguistic features, followed some of these local changes. The Russian and Serbian Church Slavonic languages met and fused together in Vojvodina to produce a new, hybrid variety sharing elements of both. This new form was called Slaveno-serbski and was adopted as the liturgical language of the Orthodox Church in Vojvodina. It bore little resemblance to the vernacular language, but it emerged as the written form of Serbian in the eighteenth century. Children attended church schools in order to learn Slaveno-serbski as if it were a foreign language.

Born in Čakov, Dositej Obradović was orphaned at an early age and brought up in Timişoara. His real name was Dimitrije, Dositej being a monastic name he received when he entered the Monastery of Hopovo in 1757, intending to train for holy orders. He never completed the required period and three years later left the cloisters and embarked on a remarkable series of journeys. These experiences were to influence his thinking and transform his outlook on the world. He initially planned to go to Russia to continue his monastic education but instead went to Croatia, Dalmatia, Corfu, southern Greece, Mount Athos—where he stayed at the Serbian monastery of Hilandar—and Smyrna. He lived in Vienna for five years between 1771 and 1776, stayed for varying lengths of time in

Germany, Prague, Italy and Paris, and in 1784-85 had a six-month sojourn in London. He attended lectures at famous universities, absorbing the fresh concepts and theories sweeping across Europe with their emphasis on education, the power of rational thought, practical advances in science and learning—everything that was opposed to precepts built on blind faith and superstition. He was an accomplished linguist and would learn the language spoken in his place of residence, adding it to his repertoire. He sought out the company of like-minded people, taught their children as a private tutor of foreign languages including Latin and Classical Greek, and managed to earn for himself a living in this way. In 1783 he published his memoirs, *Life and Adventures* (Život i priključenija), detailing what happened to him during his journeys. He writes in a completely cosmopolitan spirit, as a European who realizes that he is from a country on the periphery of the modern age. His writing is didactic. He openly states that his intention is to teach his fellow-countrymen about the wonders he has seen abroad. In short, Dositej Obradović introduced the Serbs to the principles of the European Enlightenment.

Intending to extend literacy and education at home, Obradović saw that the people around him were using one language for everyday communication and another as a written form. He himself tried to write in a way more closely resembling the spoken language, but there were many obstacles to be overcome, both linguistic and political. The letters of the Cyrillic alphabet were adapted for the use of Slaveno-serbski. It contained some signs redundant for the vernacular and lacked others to represent all the sounds of contemporary Serbian. Words for abstract notions, more used in writing than speech, were founded on principles common to the Church Slavonic forms but not applicable to the spoken language. Furthermore, Obradović could not simply ignore the practices of writing which had developed and how he himself had been taught to read and write. He continued to write using phrases and grammar patterns that showed Slaveno-serbski roots while at the same time trying to break through these imposed norms and create a new expression. He succeeded in introducing some element of reform into the language but it was a difficult task for which he could count on few supporters. The Church was a conservative institution with little interest in change and was slow to adopt new ideas. Its social position was to some extent guaranteed by its status as the provider of education, which included its role in the teaching of

Slaveno-serbski. This was the language of the Holy Scriptures, a sacred speech, intoned at all important rituals to celebrate life and death in the community. It was the language of commemoration and celebration for which Obradović's vernacular seemed a poor substitute. His name was associated with education and learning and known to all Serbs, for good or ill. In 1802 Obradović was invited to Trieste where there was a substantial community of wealthy Serbian merchants originally from Dalmatia. He stayed there until 1806, when he was invited by the rebels in Serbia to join them in Belgrade. Although elderly by now, he answered their call and arrived in the city the following year. He worked tirelessly for Karađorđe's government as an adviser on various issues, his wide experience abroad earning him much respect. He acted as the first Minister of Education in Serbia and opened a school, the Velika škola or Great School, intended for the illiterate leaders of the rebellion. He died in Belgrade in 1811. There is a statue to him in the park opposite the Faculty of Philology (Filološki fakultet) on Student Square. His monument shows him dressed in the manner of a European gentleman of the eighteenth century, very different from the Ottoman styles prevailing in the Belgrade of his time.

VUK STEFANOVIĆ KARADŽIĆ

Karadžić (1787-1864) represents a continuation of the work begun by Obradović and a break with tradition. He was born in Tršić, in western Serbia near the border with Bosnia. Being lame he could not work on the land, so was sent to school where he was taught his letters. As one of the few literate people at the time he served in the first Uprising as a clerk in Karađorđe's government in Belgrade, where he also attended the Great School. With the defeat of the rebels in 1813, he fled with the main force into Habsburg territory and made his way to Vienna. There he made the acquaintance of a Slovene, Jernej Kopitar, a linguist who worked in the Vienna Court Library and also as a censor of Slavonic and Greek books.

Kopitar was interested in helping promote the transformation of the various Slavonic languages spoken in the Habsburg Empire into more modern forms of communication. Since German or Hungarian were the official languages of government and the courts, the other languages had not enjoyed the same advantages that such status bestows. Kopitar was encouraging the Czechs, for example, to reform their alphabet, and was keen to pursue a similar plan for Serbian. With his support, Vuk Karadžić began a series of tasks which were to become his life's work.

Unlike Dositej Obradović, Karadžić knew that change could only come about by a wholesale shift in thinking about the standard form of Serbian. He adopted the principle of "write as you speak"—that is, words should be spelt as they are pronounced, as phonetically as possible. He was not going to reform the written language, but rather take the vernacular as the model for the written form. To this end, he set about devising a Cyrillic alphabet appropriate to the task for which he intended it. He discarded letters for which there was no sound in the modern spoken language, and introduced new ones to represent sounds for which there were no signs. He used his own native dialect and pronunciation as a base from which to begin his work, which caused some teething problems. For example, in his region people did not use the sound "h" and would often omit it from words where it should etymologically be employed. Gradually, he produced an orthography that was a compromise among different local variations and which could function across the territories where the Serbs lived.

Besides the alphabet, he worked on a dictionary and grammar books in order to codify the rules of the vernacular language. For the first time, the spoken Serbian language was made into an instrument fit for all the tasks required in the modern world. Today's standard Serbian is the legacy of Karadžić's programme of reforms and he is widely regarded as the father of the language.

He is equally well known as the first person to begin a systematic collection of Serbian folk songs. This aspect of his work was linked to his linguistic project, as songs provided him with examples of the usage and meanings of words and phrases that acted as models. It was also part of his ethnographic aims to produce a record of Serbian customs and traditions. He began by writing out the songs he could remember from childhood. He published later volumes by visiting Serbian villages, where he would sit and listen to local singers with pen and paper in hand. He knew and recorded some of the more celebrated bards of the time, both men and women. For example, he noted down the song about the First Serbian Uprising, "The Start of the Revolt against the Dahijas", from Filip Višnjić himself. This aspect of his work met with great success. His collections were celebrated in Europe where he was rewarded with an honorary doctorate from the University of Leipzig while receiving a pension from the Russian Tsar.

There was also a reading public thirsty for such poetry brought from the margins of Europe, a kind of exotic fancy for the educated imagination of an audience that had long forgotten its own origins in oral culture. This reception of Serbian epic ballads was really the response of a western public anxious to know more about a primitive culture. The figures from these narratives represented heroes lost in the mists of battles fought long before, in a land existing more in the realms of a fairy tale than a real place with real people. In their poetry the Serbs appeared as warlike children, not quite ready for civilized society. These images of Serbian society have survived in the negative traits associated with the Balkans today. Karadžić brought a Serbian cultural presence into the wider European mainstream but at the risk of a twisted interpretation.

It was not possible to promote reforms that would encourage the modernizing tendencies in Serbian society without making enemies. The Orthodox Church was opposed to Karadžić's objectives for the written language. It mounted a campaign to protect the dominant position of the liturgical language as the standard written form, and also in defence of its social prestige and political position as the foremost national cultural institution. The Church's response to his translation of the New Testament in 1847 was swift and sharp, condemning it as inappropriate to the scriptures. Karadžić was called a crypto-Catholic, and proof was offered in his alphabet when he added the letter "j" as a Serbian Cyrillic letter to represent the sound "y" (as in "yes"). The letter was adopted from non-Slavonic languages, but combined with the fact that his wife was herself Austrian and a Catholic only served to support the Church's argument that his reforms were undermining the authentic origins of Serbian culture.

His other opponent was Miloš Obrenović, suspicious of the motives of this man who had once been loyal to his rival, Karađorđe. As time passed, however, more people began to appreciate the sense of his proposals, and the principles he advocated for the new orthography gradually found acceptance even in official circles. By the time of his death in Vienna in 1864, his reforms had achieved widespread approval as the modern norm for use in schools and in publishing. There is a statue to Vuk Karadžić today on King Alexander Boulevard near the Library of the University of Belgrade.

Miloš's Belgrade in Literature

Serbian society possessed a rich oral culture at the time of Miloš Obrenović, but relatively little in the form of written literature. Vojvodina was the main source of literature in the eighteenth and first half of the nineteenth centuries. Educated Serbs came from the north to serve in Miloš's administration, to record the laws and teach in the first schools. Jovan Sterija Popović (1806-56) was one such writer, who lived for some ten years in the city. Vuk Karadžić himself attracted a small circle of Serbs studying in Vienna who supported his attempts, and some of that number wrote poetry fusing elements from the spirit of traditional folk songs with more modern Romantic poetry like Branko Radičević (1824-53). Although not numerous, these writers represented a beginning for modern Serbian literature.

Belgrade, however, hardly featured in the Serbian cultural imagination. The Vojvodina Serbs set their works almost exclusively in their own home towns, while the presence of the folk tradition with its rural ambience far outweighed the emerging urban experience. Belgrade was still half-foreign, not fully internalized as a national environment during Miloš's rule.

Yet despite its conspicuous absence in the cultural expression of the age, Belgrade and its early history have inspired writers in more recent times—in stories, for example, by the authors Slobodan Selenić, Svetlana Velmar-Janković, and Miroslav Josić Višnjić, all three of whom are major figures of modern Serbian literature.

Selenić (1933-95) spent a year as a postgraduate student at the University of Bristol in the 1950s before returning to Belgrade and, following an academic career, teaching drama. He published numerous novels and plays that met with wide acclaim by critics and the general reading public. He was also an active figure in cultural politics as president of the Union of Writers of Yugoslavia in the late 1980s. During the turbulent years of the early 1990s he was a founding member of one of the first coalition groups, the Democratic Movement of Serbia, to oppose the government of the ruling Socialist Party of Slobodan Milošević.

Selenić's literary career began with the 1968 publication of his novel *The Memoirs of Pera the Cripple* (Memoari Pere Bogalja), followed in 1980 by *The Friends from Kosančić Crescent 7* (Prijatelji sa Kosančićevog venca 7). This second story is about the relationship between a sophisticated citizen of Belgrade, Vladan Hadžislavković, and an Albanian from Kosovo and newcomer to the city, Istref Veri. The major part of the novel takes the form of a manuscript sent by Vladan to Istref in the 1970s, in which he attempts to make sense of the strange relationship that has developed between the two of them since they met in 1945. He includes the story of his family and their house at 7 Kosančić Crescent, in which he and Istref lived together for a while.

At one point the manuscript describes how an ancestor, Milić, a loyal supporter of Miloš Obrenović, is planning a new house for himself. Initially intending to construct a traditional dwelling, he sees one of the new European-style houses then coming into fashion:

> He walked around its unfinished walls as if it were a strange woman, stared at its large windows, pillars, entrance with stone steps, the baked bricks with their dazzling red colour, all the while his Turkish house with its foundations just completed paled in his eyes. He stopped work on it, left the cleared ground to be covered by the snow, stacked up the fallen beams, sold off the clay bricks, settled his accounts and began to imagine his new residence. With his Turkish pipe on his lips, legs crossed sitting on a silk sofa, immobile, Milić went on building and reconstructing his invisible house behind the dark, slanting slits below his eyelids. He removed the overhanging bay window from the first floor, made the windows bigger, moved the rooms about then returned them to their original order, building his fairy-tale house with great difficulty. When spring arrived and the snow melted, his new dwelling stood clearly in his mind's eye in almost every detail.

The house ends by being both European and Ottoman, what Vladan calls "a Moslem wife in a rococo hat!" With its blending and clashing of different cultures, European and Ottoman, the architectural monument to the Hadžislavković family represents the history of Belgrade in microcosm.

At the end of the novel, Istref drives over to Kosančić Crescent. He arrives in the dark of night and looks for the house, but it is no longer there. There is no space between numbers 5 and 9. The ending is a ghostly conclusion, with the disappearance of the house symbolically representing the past slipping from view.

Velmar-Janković has written novels and stories which taken together encompass different districts of Belgrade and much of its history. She has won numerous literary prizes, including one specifically for her life's work relating the narrative of Belgrade in her fiction. In her 1981 collection of short stories, *Dorćol*, she takes the names of some of the streets in central Belgrade, called after heroes who fought in the Serbian Uprisings such as Vasa Čarapić and Uzun Mirko, as titles. She imagines these historical personages to be spectral figures who still walk in Belgrade, but fixed to the length of the street which bears their name. In one of her tales, she includes the story of Knez Miloš and Kneginja Ljubica, adding her own stamp to Selenić's theme of a complex and uncanny Belgrade by bringing her ghostly apparitions to street level. Ljubica ponders on her past, her marriage to Miloš, their stormy relationship and the historical times in which they lived. Velmar-Janković remarks that few people today realize that the street was named after her, and that there are "even fewer of them who can recall who, in truth, was the Kneginja".

Josić Višnjić, born in Stapar, Vojvodina, is recognized as one of the most talented authors of his generation. After several years of difficulties with the communist authorities, he made a dramatic comeback in 1990 with his novel *The Defence and Fall of Bodrog in Seven Turbulent Seasons* (Odbrana i propast Bodroga u sedam burnih godišnjih doba). The book concerns the 1848 uprising of Serbs in Vojvodina at the fictional town of Bodrog, against Hungarian attempts to take away their autonomy. Some of the rebels go to Belgrade in order to raise support for their cause, where they meet with or hear about important people in the city such as Toma Vučić Perišić, the minister of foreign affairs Ilija Garašanin, and cultural figures like Jovan Sterija Popović.

One of the characters in Josić's novel writes down in a diary his impressions of what he sees in the city. Recalling the adventure many years later, he remembers the excitement he and his friends felt journeying back to Serbia, which their families had left generations before. He writes, "Then, when we were young, we were all setting foot for the first time in the southern region, the motherland of our grandfathers and distant ancestors, and so we added everything that we knew from stories and books to that which our eyes saw, our ears heard, our mouths said and our fingers touched." They arrive at the Sava quay and set about looking for somewhere to stay in the district around Karađorđe Street. Later, the diarist recalls some of what he saw in Belgrade:

Here is a list of some that kept my eyes transfixed for hours: the Prince's Palace, the New Residence, the Customs Office, the Cathedral, the Old Hospital, the Department of State, the Great Barracks... then the Bajram Bey and the Bajrakli mosques... the Lycée, the Palilula Church, the Military Hospital, the Library, the Prussian Consulate, the District Court, the Serbian Crown Tavern and the Turkish Inn... well, there's no end, none at all... and I can't write them all down here.

Some of the buildings Josić Višnjić mentions still survive, while others have long since disappeared. In a world in which memory and amnesia co-exist, Belgrade appears as a city which refuses to be fixed, vanishing just as it appears to be coming into tantalizing reach. In the literary imagination the urban landscape is always on the brink of being transformed into something else, of taking a new form, and adopting a new beginning.

Chapter Three

FROM KNEZ MIHAILO STREET TO THE RIVER DANUBE: THE ROAD TO MODERNIZATION

RETURN OF THE OBRENOVIĆ DYNASTY

Belgrade was the official capital of Serbia and the site of Knez Alexander Karađorđević's court from 1842. He continued the building programme initiated by Miloš, paying particular attention to development further away from the city and the fortress of Kalemegdan. The new regime remained in place until 1858 when Vučić Perišić was ousted, imprisoned with the same minimum of ceremonies that he showed to his rivals, and died while in prison, presumably poisoned. Miloš became Knez of Serbia for a second time in 1859, and although elderly quickly resumed his active participation in affairs of state.

Of all Serbia's nineteenth-century rulers Miloš was among the most ruthless. He also accomplished a great deal for the young semi-autonomous state, maintaining an admirable *modus vivendi* with the Ottoman government that held sovereign power, extending the borders of his territory when able to do so, and encouraging internal developments. His many faces make him something of a paradoxical figure. He died the following year when he was succeeded by his son, Mihailo. From the time of the First Serbian Uprising to the First World War, for over a hundred years the rulers of Serbia were either forced to abdicate or were assassinated, except for Miloš who died peacefully while in office.

Mihailo, like his father, was ruler for a second time. Spending many years in exile, he was the first leader of Serbia to be educated in the West. He brought to his poor country a desire to modernize all areas of government, establish the rule of law, introduce a proper tax system, and having established secure government funding, to form a standing army and to attend to the infrastructure of his country, which demanded an ever increasing supply of educated and professional citizens: lawyers, doctors, teachers and engineers. Belgrade was the centre of his political plans for the future of Serbia. He was acutely aware of the backward nature of the society he was to govern, and of the elements within that society that were resisting the kind of progress for which he stood. The old way of life in village communities grouped around extended family systems was dying out as the state evolved. The rhythms of daily life in Belgrade were dictated by the need to be able to reach work and schools, and by the general requirements of municipal life. Belgrade was fast becoming an urban centre of modern Europe, but linked to a hinterland more used to traditional customs.

One of the fundamental aims of Mihailo's government was to rid the capital city of the Ottoman presence. His hands were in part tied by the continuing presence of the pasha and his military garrison at Kalemegdan. Large numbers of Muslims had already left, unhappy at the way things were going. Serbs were becoming more and more important in social, economic, cultural and political affairs. When Mihailo became knez, relations were already strained between the different communities in Belgrade. The Turkish quarter was stagnating due to outward migration, while the Serbs were busy developing areas away from the old heart of the city towards Palilula, Savamala and Vračar.

Matters came to a head in 1862 when a quarrel broke out between Serbs and Turks at a water fountain not far from the Istanbul Gate where a queue of people were waiting to fill water jugs. A brawl followed in which a young Serbian boy was seriously wounded. A patrol of Serbian police went to the Ottoman police station to try to resolve the problem. The Turkish gendarmes fired shots and killed two members of the delegation, claiming that there was a large crowd behaving in a threatening manner. The Ottoman governor ordered the Istanbul Gate to be closed and his cannon opened fire on the town.

The situation was critical and negotiations began immediately with the foreign consuls based in Belgrade acting as intermediaries. The Great Powers in Europe, fearing that the Ottoman action was potentially destabilizing for the whole region, forced the sultan eventually to agree terms including the removal of the pasha and his troops from Serbia. The pasha ceremoniously handed over the keys of Belgrade to Knez Mihailo in 1867 at the spot where the commemorative stone stands today at the entrance to Kalemegdan Park. He and all his troops left Belgrade and Serbia for

good, although a few more years were
to elapse before the country enjoyed
complete independence.

Despite this spectacular success,
Mihailo also made many enemies.
The knez was in intense negotiation
with the other peoples of the Balkan
Peninsula. In geopolitical terms these
countries had much in common,
principally their hostility to the
Ottoman presence in their region,
but also because they were all under
the influence of the Great Powers
over which they themselves had no
control. His outlook was simple: the
Balkan countries together would be

better able to defend their own interests rather than allow outside forces
to dictate the terms of regional relations. He was quite successful in the
initial stages of his plans and reached agreements with the Romanians,
Greeks and Bulgarians for mutual support. He also managed to persuade
some Croats who were in favour of greater autonomy from the Austrian
and Hungarian presence on their territory that their best hopes for independence in the future lay in a union with Serbia.

These foreign policy successes did not earn Milhailo any friends
among the Great Powers, especially as the situation in Bosnia was looking
more uncertain. Taking a lead from Serbia, the local Christian population
was showing increasing dissatisfaction with Ottoman rule and likely to
rebel. An uprising in any of the Turkish provinces could have unforesee-
able consequences. Mihailo was also alienating previous sources of
support at home. Perhaps it was the price of his political success, perhaps
because he was not a natural democrat and often resorted to the kinds of
authoritarianism for which his father was better known, but Mihailo did
not enjoy universal popularity in Serbia. Conservative opinion was not
happy with the speed of his reforms and the kind of social transformation
taking place. An established way of life was disappearing with little chance
to absorb the new manners and customs. Many people felt lost in this
state of transition and very uneasy at what the future might hold. For the

more radical sections of this new Serbia, change was not happening fast enough and the knez appeared more like an oriental despot than the ruler of a modern European state. Little progress was made toward parliamentary rule, with political power wielded by a small group around Mihailo's court.

There were many important actors who wished Mihailo out of the way and he was warned that there was a plot against his life, to which he is said to have replied, "If I have not done good by the Serbs, I certainly have done no evil, thus if they kill me they will kill only Mihailo, and not the Serbian knez." He was assassinated while out walking with his aunt, her daughter and granddaughter on 29 May 1868. The Serbian government claimed that Alexander Karađorđević was involved, in an attempt to regain the position from which he had been forced to abdicate ten years earlier when the Obrenović family returned to power. The event was, in fact, the result of a personal vendetta. If Alexander was hoping to make a comeback in the chaos following the royal murder, he was to be disappointed as there was no coup.

For all his faults, Knez Mihailo is regarded as one of those figures whose contribution to the development of Serbia was of the utmost significance for its future. Mihailo did not have any children, which left the immediate question of the succession to be resolved. The grandson of Gospodar Jevrem Obrenović, the son of Mihailo's cousin, was the only remaining Obrenović male and he was duly appointed the next knez. He was a fourteen-year-old boy, by the name of Milan, attending a school in Paris.

A regency conducted affairs of state for the next few years, but when Milan took on the mantle of ruler he soon faced criticism. He was profoundly opposed to all attempts to extend parliamentary rule, which earned him the hostility of some of the political lobby at the time. In 1878, following popular uprisings in Bosnia, the European Powers again intervened in the Balkans. At the Congress of Berlin they created a new Bulgarian state and Austria took over the administration of Bosnia from the Turks.

Clearly nothing could be done without outside support from one of the major states and Milan set about courting the Austrians. They eventually gave him what he wanted: a royal title and final recognition of full independence from the Ottoman Empire. In 1882 he was crowned king (*kralj* in Serbian), although the price he had to pay was to put himself and his country under direct Austrian influence. Ostensibly recognized internationally as the sovereign King of Serbia, Milan found himself entirely dependent upon Austrian support, and the Austrians insisted that he take no initiatives in foreign policy without their agreement.

Milan displayed all the weaknesses of the Obrenović family with none of the successes for which Miloš and Mihailo were famous. His wife, Queen Natalija (1859-1941), was a very forceful personality with whom he was rarely seen to be on good terms, and whose popularity increased as his declined. It was said by the twentieth-century statesman Slobodan Jovanović (1869-1958) that during the short and disastrous Serbian war against Bulgaria in 1885 the king displayed all female weaknesses, while Queen Natalija displayed all typical male virtues. In the face of continuing opposition in the country and plots at court King Milan was forced to abdicate in 1889.

END OF THE OBRENOVIĆ DYNASTY

Milan was succeeded by his son Alexander whose policies, private actions and autocratic mode of government contributed to making him much despised in Serbia. In fact, it became difficult to pinpoint who were his real friends. While he manipulated the country's fragile democratic institutions in order to maintain his personal authority, Belgrade society was shocked at his infatuation with a widow, Draga Mašin, who was one of his mother's ladies-in-waiting. She was generally regarded as a gold-digger, a woman with a colourful past who was entirely inappropriate to the position of queen. The Orthodox Church took the matter very seriously and advised against marriage. Political circles were concerned not only by the influence she had over the king, but also at her promoting the interests of her two brothers. Their wedding was hastened at the news that Draga was expecting Alexander's child, although this was later shown to be a phantom pregnancy and increased doubt regarding her intentions. It was not clear after their marriage in 1900 which decisions were his and which were the result of her interference. The situation in the palace was providing huge amusement abroad and Serbia was becoming a joke state with a king showing all the excesses of intrigue and passion that foreigners thought characteristic of the Balkans.

Draga could not have children, and as Alexander was Milan's only child and there was no other Obrenović male heir, the royal couple began to turn their thoughts to securing the succession through the female line. Suspicions were immediately aroused that this was one of Draga's ploys in the interests of her own family. The king and queen sensed the danger posed by their enemies and decided to strike first by purging the army's officer corps. Their move was to be disastrous as a group of disaffected officers decided that their only solution was a coup that would include the deaths of Alexander and Draga and the prompt return of the Karađorđević dynasty. One of the leaders of the conspiracy was a certain Colonel Dragutin Dimitrijević-Apis, who was to play a part in the assassination of the Archduke Franz Ferdinand during his tour of Bosnia in 1914.

The plotters set out from the Dom oficira, a club for army officers but now the Student Cultural Centre, in the early hours of 11 June 1903. They broke into the royal palace and overcame the guards loyal to the king before searching the building for their victims. They were eventually found hiding in a secret chamber where they were attacked with great ferocity, their corpses hacked by swords and then thrown from the window into the park below. The Russian consul discovered their mutilated bodies when out for a walk the following morning.

Their murder was in many ways a turning point for Belgrade and Serbia. Domestic reaction was not unpleasantly surprised when news of the regicide spread, and the elderly Peter Karađorđević was immediately invited to assume the throne. Alexander and Draga had abandoned their legitimacy in a series of acts that showed no regard for the rights of the citizens of Serbia to participate in the running of the country without fear and intimidation. They used the power at their disposal to deprive others of access to channels of government and to rule as if Belgrade and the whole country existed for their personal benefit.

Abroad, however, news of the event was received with great consternation. The Serbian royal couple were not regarded with any particular respect, but the general consensus was that even if their behaviour might be considered scandalous they did not deserve such an ignoble and barbaric end. Furthermore, established foreign governments felt a twinge of empathy in that Alexander was the rightful king and in possession of correct legal authority. A shudder of collective fear must have run up the spines of European statesmen at how easily the assassination had occurred. Equally, it may have been the absence of public anguish and apparent impunity for the killers that caused foreign governments to seek retribution from Serbia. Many governments recalled their representatives home and the country was left in a state of international isolation.

NAMES OF PLACES AND DISTRICTS IN BELGRADE

The Serbian word for street is *ulica*, which is sometimes shortened to *ul.* in writing. It may come either at the beginning of the name of the street or at the end; for example, Ulica kneza Mihaila (literally Street of Knez Mihailo) or Francuska ulica (France Street). The first pattern usually refers to a street named after someone: Ulica kneza Miloša (Street of Knez Miloš), Ulica kralja Milana (Street of King Milan). In these circumstances the word ulica is often omitted. When the word *ulica* follows the name of the street it is usually because the first word is being used as an adjective: Pariska ulica (Parisian, or Paris, Street), Karađorđeva ulica (Karađorđe's Street).

The word *venac* usually means a wreath, but when used in town refers to a curved street like a crescent in Britain, such as Kosančićev venac (Kosančić Crescent) or Obilićev venac (Obilić Crescent). A wide main road may be called a *bulevar* (boulevard): Bulevar kralja Aleksandra (Boulevard of King Alexander). The word for a square is *trg*: Trg Republike (Square of the Republic, or Republic Square).

Street names are written in the Cyrillic alphabet on a blue plaque. It is quite usual to find that a street has an old and a new name on two different plaques. Changes of regime and political circumstances in the twentieth century have led to the renaming of roads and squares to reflect the new order. Major causes of these transformations were the victory of the Communist Party at the end of the Second World War and the collapse of communism at the end of the 1990s. Thus, at the end of the war Krunska ulica (Crown Street) was rechristened Ulica proleterskih brigada (Street of Proletarian Brigades), while Bulevar kralja Aleksandra became Bulevar revolucije (Boulevard of the Revolution). The aim was to eradicate the last traces of the previous regime by writing out references to the royal families, dynastic offspring and other unwanted historical baggage.

The main street King Milan Street, as another example, became Ulica Maršala Tita (Street of Marshal Tito), as it was common for the main street in the towns and cities of Yugoslavia to bear the name of the president. With the end of communism the pre-war nomenclature was revived in an effort to wipe out the remnants of that regime. Thus, the examples above have all reverted to their old name.

Some streets have a history with a complicated series of changes. At the bottom of what is again called King Peter I Street, near to the corner with Kosančić Crescent, is a plaque detailing the different names under which this particular thoroughfare has been known. Translated into English, it reads:

Earlier Names of Streets
Dubrovnik Street 1872-1904
King Peter Street 1904-1946
7th July Street 1946-1997

This series of changes charts the historical importance of the street. Being near the river it used to be associated with merchants coming from Dubrovnik to Belgrade. Then, in 1904, the coronation of King Peter took place in the Cathedral signalling the restoration of the Karađorđević family. When the communists came to power it was named after the date on which the uprising against the Germans began in Serbia during the Second World War. This is not even the full list of different names applied to this street. Even before taking the name Dubrovnik Street, it was known for part of its length as Glavna Čaršija, corresponding to something like Main Town or Town Head Street. For a brief period from 1916 to 1918, when Belgrade was occupied by the Austrians, the new authorities preferred to omit reference to the king and it was called Saborna ulica (Cathedral Street).

The right to give a name to the city space is not only about giving it an address for the delivery of post. It also evokes historical associations that tie the place to a particular sense of history. It emphasizes certain events over others, marking what is worth commemorating and committing to public memory. The unity of the space is devoted towards one understanding of the past that has contributed most to contemporary identities. It is a visual and textual representation of the community that helps to explain how it has arrived at this point in present time. Folk memory is not only inscribed but also created on these plaques.

After the fall in 2000 of the unpopular President Milošević (1941-2006), whose name is associated with the Wars of Yugoslav Succession and the decline of Serbia in the 1990s, the new government appointed a committee to look into fresh names for streets and squares. Many have reverted to their pre-war status, while others have been rechristened after a historical figure not previously regarded as appropriate for public commemoration. In this situation city plans quickly go out of date and most people carry in their heads two sets of names. It is not uncommon to ask a taxi-driver to go to an address and for him to cross-check with an alternative name for the same place, making doubly sure that it really is where he thinks it is.

While the names of individual streets have been reclassified over the generations, it is not so easy to control in the same way the names of larger districts. The area of a city quarter may expand or contract with time, but their markers are longer lasting. The names of places in and around Belgrade often refer to events long since forgotten or which have lost their relevance. Reference has already been made to the Turkish etymology for Kalemegdan. Tašmajdan comes from the same language for *taš* (stone) and *majdan* (a mine or digging place), since from early times stone has been quarried from here to be used as building material.

Dorćol is the general name applied to the area of central Belgrade on the slope leading down to the Danube and also has a Turkish origin in *dort-jol* (four ways or crossroads). It was first given to the point where King Peter I Street meets Tsar Dušan Street when, in Ottoman Belgrade, it was unusual to have such a clearly defined and rectangular crossing. It is thought that this intersection first emerged during the time of Roman Singidunum. Topčider, or Topčidersko brdo (Topčider Hill), is now a favoured parkland area for short excursions just beyond the smart part of town where many embassies have their residences. Its name is derived from the word *top* (cannon) and refers to the fact that during their siege of the city in 1521 the invading Ottoman army used this place to cast heavy guns because it lies at a safe distance from the city and has a supply of fuel and water.

Ada Ciganlija is another popular place for recreation close to the city on the River Sava. An *ada* is an island in the river, *ciganin* in Serbian means a Romany, and a Romany community used to live on the marshy land opposite the island at a place called Ciganska Bara. The district of Palilula, on the other hand, has two competing derivations. The name comes from the Serbian phrase *paliti lulu*—to light a pipe. One possible origin is that an artisan famed for his clay pipes lived and worked in this area. The other is that this area was situated just outside the city precinct of Ottoman

Belgrade in which smoking on the streets was prohibited because of the large amount of wood used as building material and the consequent danger of fire. So, as people came out of town this was the first place where a man could light his pipe.

KNEZ MIHAILO STREET

There are not many buildings in the centre of the old town dating further back than 1867. The first wave of demolition came with the Belgrade town plan proposed by Emilijan Josimović in that year, when the Turks left the city. Architects and the Serbian government wanted to create a modern town with monumental buildings to announce that the new state had finally arrived and that it was European in its cultural and political orientation. Their practical aim was to produce an urban environment to satisfy contemporary demands for housing with a speedy and efficient transport system. Ottoman Belgrade may have had many pretty gardens, but its houses were mainly constructed of wood and other lightweight materials that did not allow for buildings of more than one storey. It was dusty in summer, muddy when it rained, and without proper drainage and sewerage. Roads were narrow and unsurfaced with no street lighting to allow movement at night.

This haphazard collection of houses and pathways was replaced by public buildings and a network of streets laid out in a geometric pattern to ease the flow of people, vehicles and goods. Some of the more recent buildings were spared and remained as a base on which to construct the vision of the future. Knez Mihailo Street was intended as the spine of the old town on Josimović's plan of 1867. It has been known by that name since 1870 and is one of the few to have kept its original form untouched through all these years.

The street runs along the ridge separating the two slopes of the old town. Excavations have revealed that the same route provided the central road from the time of the Roman civilian settlement at Singidunum leading to the military base overlooking the rivers. The Belgrade City Library is at the head of the street, opposite the entrance to Kalemegdan. It was originally built as the first European hotel in Belgrade, the Hotel at the Serbian Crown (Gostionica kod srpske krune), opening in 1870 and constructed with a central courtyard following the basic design of a traditional Turkish *han* or inn, but with grand contemporary façades. After the

Second World War the building was used as a substitute for the National Library on Kosančić Crescent, which burnt down in 1941. The Faculty of Fine Arts (Fakultet likovnih umetnosti) stands across the road and a little way down the street away from the park. It housed the Austrian Consulate at the beginning of the twentieth century before adopting its present occupation in 1937. Further down the street is the restaurant called the Greek Queen (Grčka kraljica), the oldest building on Knez Mihailo Street. It was constructed sometime before 1867 with elements combining the traditional Balkan style and more modern features. It first went by the name of the Despot's Inn (Despotov han), a reference to the Serbian lords who ruled from Belgrade in the Middle Ages, until the communists changed it to the more acceptable Blue Adriatic (Plavi Jadran).

Across from the Greek Queen at no. 52 is a building from 1878 constructed in the classical style. The central balcony facing the street is supported by figures of Atlas, leader of the Titans in Greek mythology, condemned to hold the sky on his shoulders after an unsuccessful revolt against Zeus. Many buildings here reveal the abrupt change in architectural taste that swept through Belgrade during the 1860s. The European design and highly ornate balconies on the upper storeys of many of the houses represent a complete contrast to the older Balkan style.

The house at no. 48 is from 1869 and was built by the brothers Krstić as a restaurant and hotel known as Krsta's Inn (Krstina mehana). This

building was also used by the Serbian Assembly to meet on the first floor until its own premises were ready in 1882. Next door, no. 46, was built by Veljko Savić and had commercial premises at street level with living accommodation above; it is now the popular Kolarac kafana.

Further along on the other side of the street is the imposing Serbian Academy of Sciences and Arts (Srpska akademija nauka i umetnosti) at no. 35. Constructed in 1923-24, it was designed to front onto three streets with its highly decorated façades. The figure at the top of the building over the central doorway is a statue to the Greek goddess of Victory, Nike, attended on either side by allegories of industry and commerce, and then further out statues of women with children representing the future. The Academy Gallery is included within the complex on the ground floor and often has exhibitions of Serbian painters and foreign collections. In addition, the street offers another gallery space next door in the Gallery of the Society of Visual Artists of Serbia (Galerija Udruženja likovnih umetnika Srbije). The Delijska fountain stands in front of the Academy. The word *delija* refers to an Ottoman horse-soldier and the water here was intended for the sultan's cavalry in Ottoman Belgrade. This is the third such fountain on this spot, erected in 1987 when the whole street was given its most recent face-lift. On the corner with Obilić Crescent is the restaurant and kafana the Russian Tsar (Ruski car) built just a couple of years after the Academy. The very ornate ground floor is topped with balconies on the first floor made to look as if from stone, while the ones higher up are of wrought iron. The buildings on the rest of the street down to the corner with Terazije are more modern and replaced a line of small shops and coffee houses.

The street contains many of Belgrade's better stocked bookshops. At the corner with Terazije is a short and narrow street with a pedestrian exit to the Green Wreath Market and a bookshop over four floors called Mammoth (Mamut). The skeleton of a mammoth was discovered when the foundations for the Albania (Albanija) building at the end of Knez Mihailo Street were being excavated. Further down toward Kalemegdan is the bookshop belonging to the Prosveta publishing company. Geca Kon was the owner of these premises before the Second World War. Born in Vojvodina in 1873, he came to Belgrade to open his bookshop in 1901 and later developed his business interests to include publishing. He was very successful, giving encouragement to and printing the work of some of the most famous names in Serbian literature of the time. As a Jew, he and his family suffered like many of Belgrade's Jews during the German occupation in the Second World War, meeting their end in a concentration camp. There is another bookshop on the ground floor of the building of the Serbian Academy, while further along the street others include Dereta, Narodna Knjiga and Plato. This last company has another bookshop in the same complex as the Faculty of Philosophy (Filozofski fakultet) overlooking Student Square. The publishing company Stubovi Kulture has its own bookshop also nearby on Republic Square. These last two bookshops also include internet cafés and are among the best for foreign books, including those useful to visitors to Belgrade.

Knez Mihailo Street has remained the main shopping street in Belgrade, offering the latest fashions and designs. Over the decades traffic has been restricted or banned and pavements widened until the decision to make it a completely pedestrian precinct in the late 1980s. It has always been the place to meet friends, have a coffee, chat, stroll on a little further, stop again and look in the shop windows. The following is a description of that walking habit, the Corso, as experienced in the early years of the twentieth century by a contemporary observer:

> The Corso, the artery of Belgrade, was never more lively. It was an everyday spontaneous review of fashion and elegance. Twice daily, in the morning and evening, it was full of young people and the main meeting point for all Belgraders. Here everyone could meet or at least see everyone else. They did not only exchange pleasantries, but also opinions. For walking was not just an opportunity for flirtation, but also for debate and news, for analyzing in detail the latest political and cultural events.

Little has changed today, underlining the street's social significance.

REPUBLIC SQUARE

The central square is of symbolic importance in all cities, a fitting site for monumental buildings to reflect the growing confidence and prestige of the state. The statue to Knez Mihailo was placed in Belgrade's Republic Square in 1882, with the names of the towns liberated from Ottoman garrisons in 1867 inscribed around the pediment. The prince is pointing south, in the direction of those parts of the country still under Turkish rule, an indication that the state was not going to rest until the final unification of Serbia. The square was formerly known as Theatre Square (Pozorišni trg), appropriately enough as the National Theatre is one of its dominant buildings. When the project to build a theatre for the city was first discussed in the middle of the nineteenth century, the Green Wreath marketplace was suggested for the site. Work on foundations began, but the ground proved too marshy to support the size of the edifice. Knez Mihailo gave his approval to the idea that the theatre be built on the new square just a few days before his death. It was opened the following year and since then has provided the main space for the production of plays, opera, ballet, and major musical events. The façade has been reconstructed a few times, not least because of bomb damage during the two major wars of the twentieth century.

The other large structure fronting the square, the National Museum, was originally built as a bank although it, too, is on a grand scale. It was erected on the site of one of Belgrade's most popular kafanas, the Dardanelles (Dardaneli), demolished in 1901 to make way for the new look of the main square. The kafana was frequented by many of the actors from the nearby theatre, and the day before its demolition patrons gathered in front, some seventy or more of them, to have their photograph taken at the place they had spent so many of their happy hours. The photograph is a telling social document with people from different classes and callings, and in their midst the most famous actors of Belgrade theatre of the day: Milorad Gavrilović and Čiča Ilija Stanojević. The communists turned the bank building into the National Museum after the Second World War.

The square has become one of the focal points for city transport with seven roads intersecting, either by directly flowing into the square or running close by. It was dotted around with imposing stone façades but remained an open public space, the whole giving a sense of serenity rather than bustle. Since the Second World War it has also been a place for celebration. When the Partisans, supported by the Soviet Red Army, liberated Belgrade in October 1944 the square famously filled with people dancing the kind of folk dances favoured by the liberating troops, many of whom came from rural areas. A huge popular demonstration of support to celebrate the formation of the first post-war government gathered here on 27 March 1945, and on 29 November of the same year the name of the square

was changed. In the early years the government orchestrated large meetings on the square for which the balcony on the front of the National Theatre provided a useful podium.

After the fall of communism, however, such events have not always been to the advantage of the ruling regime. A huge opposition rally converged on the square on 9 March 1991, forcing the government to impose a crackdown by bringing in water cannon to disperse the crowds. Large anti-Milošević demonstrations met here again during the popular daily protests between November 1996 and February 1997. During the NATO bombing campaign against Serbia in 1999 there were daily concerts by the country's most popular artists, keeping up citizens' morale during daylight hours before the sirens warned of air raids in the evening. In more peaceful times it is used to stage many events and performances for BELEF, the Belgrade Summer Festival in July and early August, and for a massive New Year's Eve party.

STUDENT SQUARE

Student Square is at the end of Vasa Čarapić Street and is the terminus for public transport running past Republic Square. In Ottoman Belgrade this was the site of the main graveyard, with numerous mosques and other Muslim religious institutions in the vicinity. A trace of this graveyard is evident in the mausoleum on the corner of Višnjić and Brothers Jugović Streets, built in 1784 for the burial of Šejh-Mustafa Bagdađanin. From 1824 the Big Market (Velika pijaca) was moved here, linked by a straight road to the Istanbul Gate. By 1839 the market had grown so large that police had to regulate the positions of stalls and banned the sale of live pigs. It continued to function during the whole of the nineteenth century but was increasingly out of place. The market was a busy place for the sale of fresh fruit and vegetables, some of which would inevitably fall to the ground and rot. The unpleasant smells and dirtiness did not sit well with the elegant buildings going up in Knez Mihailo Street and the main square with the National Theatre. It also outlived its usefulness, as the new main residential areas were at some distance in Vračar and Palilula. In 1926 a convenient fire broke out destroying the market and providing the city government with the opportunity to transfer its business to the Green Wreath Market and to Kalenić Market (Kalenićeva pijaca) at the end of Crown Street in Vračar, both of which are still lively and operating today.

With the disappearance of the Big Market, the area was planted as a park, with ornamental walls, gates and statues.

The Big Market was also known as the Market by the Main Police (Pijaca kod Glavne policije), as both the local Serbian and Turkish police were stationed along the lower road of the square, roughly on the corner with Višnjić Street. The Serbian gendarmes were moved a little way to the so-called Glavnjača during the 1850s. Their building no longer exists, having being pulled down to make way for the Faculty of Mathematics (Prirodno-matematički fakultet) in 1954. The Glavnjača was the main police headquarters with a prison in Belgrade where many suspects under different regimes were interrogated. It was used by the Obrenovićes, then taken over by the new authorities and before the Second World War often housed political prisoners; the Gestapo took it over during the war, then the communists for a brief period.

A number of important figures from the nineteenth century had their homes in or around Student Square. Alexander Karađorđević lodged for a time in a house where the Faculty of Philology now stands and where his son, Peter, was born in 1844. Gospodar Jevrem, the brother of Miloš Obrenović, and Toma Vučić Perišić were near neighbours here, while Ilija Garašanin, Knez Alexander Karađorđević's foreign affairs minister, lived at the end of Uzun Mirko Street.

In keeping with the intention to create a city centre fitting for a European capital, the old buildings around the square were demolished and replaced by grander constructions. In 1863 Captain Miša's House (Kapetan Mišino zdanje) was constructed and given to the city in a philanthropic gesture by a rich merchant, Captain Miša Anastasijević, to house many of Belgrade's cultural institutions. Dositej Obradović's Great School was moved here and joined by the forerunners of the National Museum and the National Library. In 1905 the school became the University of Belgrade, which continued to keep its premises in Captain Miša's House. One of the tallest buildings in the centre, a cabin sat on its roof serving as a lookout point for fires in the city. It was damaged by Austrian guns in the First World War since an antenna was fixed on the roof as part of an experiment in wireless telegraphy. The main administrative offices of the University and some academic Departments are still here at 1 Student Square. The Faculty of Philology was built next door in 1922 and the Stock Exchange in 1934, which became the Ethnographic Musuem (Etnografski muzej) when the communists took power. The square has been renamed a few times. It was called the Great Square (Veliki trg) from 1872 to 1896, when it became the Royal Square (Kraljev trg) from 1896 to 1946, and finally Student Square.

DORĆOL

Dorćol extends down the slope from Student Square to the Danube although most places of interest are contained between the square and Tsar Dušan Street, and from France Street to Kalemegdan. In Ottoman Belgrade this was the main residential area for wealthier merchants and officials of the pasha's administration. It was often referred to as either the Lower Town (Donja varoš) or the Turkish Town (Turska varoš) to reflect its geographic position spreading down the slope or its demographic structure. The part of town down the slope on the other side of the hill towards the Sava, for the same reason, was called the Serbian Town (Srpska varoš).

Dorćol resembled a typical oriental settlement of the Ottoman Empire. It appealed to foreign visitors, with gardens hidden behind high walls, winding streets and open-fronted shops with goods spilling outside. One Polish visitor, the writer Roman Zmorski (1822-67), described it as "a wonderful view of the East thrown within a hand's reach of Europe". During the Austrian occupation of 1717-39 Dorćol's appearance changed considerably as the Muslim population moved out and some houses were demolished to be replaced by buildings in the baroque European style. The only house surviving from that period is at 10 Tsar Dušan Street, although it has gone through much refurbishment.

The Turks restored the oriental look of the area after 1740 when it again became an elite part of their town. The houses of the richest and most powerful Turks were then taken over by the leaders of the First Serbian Uprising. Karađorđe moved into the palatial premises formerly belonging to one of the Dahijas, Mula Jusuf, and his lieutenants chose similar accommodation for themselves. The area never really recovered its former glory after 1813 and Dorćol became rather neglected. The Jewish quarter was an exception to this general rule as it maintained its opulent appearance during the nineteenth century in the area below Kalemegdan around today's Jewish Street.

The city's Jewish community came to Belgrade at the end of the fifteenth century from Spain bringing with them their own language,

Ladino. They were a solid community of merchants and artisans who comprised the third largest such enclave in the Balkans, after Istanbul and Thessalonica. There is plenty of evidence of good relations between the Serbian and Jewish communities in Belgrade; the first state printing press founded by Knez Miloš printed books both in Serbian and in Hebrew, while many Jews regarded themselves as Serbs of the faith of Moses. They were nearly all wiped out when the city was occupied by the Germans during the Second World War.

One or two examples of earlier architecture remain such as the mosque at 11 Gospodar Jevrem Street and the two museums on the same street, the Museum of Theatrical Arts (Muzej pozorišne umetnosti) at no. 19 and the Museum of Vuk and Dositej (Muzej Vuka i Dositeja) next door. The Museum of Theatrical Arts was built as the house of the Belgrade merchant family Božić in 1836. The Museum of Vuk and Dositej belonged to one of the secretaries for finance in the pasha's administration before being taken over by Dositej Obradović during the First Serbian Uprising to house the Great School from 1808 to 1813. It has served other functions in its long existence, being used as the French Consulate for a time. It was restored after the Second World War when it was decided to make it into a memorial centre to celebrate the two most prominent representatives of Serbian letters.

There are other museums in the area: the Jewish Historical Museum (Jevrejski istorijski muzej) at 71 King Peter I Street and the Gallery of Frescos (Galerija fresaka) at 20 Tsar Uroš Street. The latter offers exhibitions of copies of medieval church art, painting and sculpture from Serbia. There is a monument on Gospodar Jevrem Street marking the spot where the young boy was wounded during a fight between Turkish soldiers and Serbian youths, eventually leading to the freedom of the city in 1867.

The liberation of Belgrade from the Turks that year gave an opportunity to a new generation of architects and planners trained in the West to put into action the proposals drawn up by Emilijan Josimović for the redevelopment of the centre of Belgrade. Dorćol was completely transformed. The old Ottoman quarter was pulled down and replaced by the present geometric shape; a set of streets runs down the slope toward the Danube with intersecting ones across in the direction of Kalemegdan. The Sava slope descends over the brow at the top of the hill. The central feature in this area is formed by the three connecting sweeps of the crescents called

Obilić, Toplica and Kosančić. These three roads curve over the old trench that marked the city limits of Ottoman Belgrade. They are, appropriately enough given their position, named after three legendary heroes who fought the Turks (Miloš Obilić, Milan Toplica, Ivan Kosančić).

Opinions vary regarding these changes to the city centre. Some see the result as too planned to the extent that it seems artificial. Angles, widths and heights are too carefully measured and inhibit any sense of organic growth. Others differ and point to the elegance that these proportions lend to the overall effect of the central district. And, they argue, construction has continued to add new textures and contours to the urban skyline. No doubt, the debates will continue and constantly expand the dialogue between the urban setting and the people who inhabit it.

SKADARLIJA

Skadar Street, known to all as Skadarlija, has long been famous for its kafanas, nightlife and bohemian atmosphere. It is positioned just outside the old town, parallel to France Street. In the early nineteenth century it was a Romany district with a reputation for hard drinking, where both Serbian and Turkish young men would come beyond the reach of their parents and "civilization". Houses were poor and flimsy, looking rather like a shanty town. From the middle of the century more solid houses were built following traditional Balkan designs, the street was cobbled and in 1872 received its official title as Skadar Street. A large number of kafanas remained but the street's reputation was transformed from a den of iniquity to a place for a respectable evening out. It particularly attracted customers from the arts, actors, writers and painters.

About 1890 Skadar Street boasted the greatest concentration of restaurants and drinking houses in Belgrade, some of which remain today: the Golden Jug (Zlatni bokal), the Three Hats (Tri šešira) and the Two Stags (Dva jelena). At no. 34 is the house of Đura Jakšić (1832-78), a poet and painter who had a reputation for falling out with the authorities. Many of his paintings hang in the National Museum and his house is often used as an exhibition centre or for literary evenings where writers read from or discuss their work. His poetry, and the work of others such as Jovan Jovanović-Zmaj (1833-1904) and Vojislav Ilić (1860-94), was typical of later Serbian Romanticism. Zmaj is also well known as a poet for children. His verses are still read to them, and it is not unusual for adults remembering their earliest contacts with literature to be able to quote at length from his work.

The Three Hats is about half-way down on the corner with Gospodar Jevrem Street. Opened in 1864, it took over from the Dardanelles when that establishment was pulled down and its artist customers needed a new local. Branislav Nušić (1864-1938), a writer of plays and short stories, also penned many witty and satirical articles, one of his favourite subjects being the city's kafanas. Writing about one in Skadar Street, he noted:

> The Three Hats is today the most popular kafana in Skadarlija. It has been in its time the seat of Belgrade's bohemians, but another kind of public has joined them... It used to be the house of the father of Ðoka Dimović who ran the Imperial. The father was a milliner repairing and applying dye to old hats. His house, in which he lived and worked, had a sign on which were painted three hats, each of a different style. The kafana has taken its name from that sign.

His article offers a fascinating introduction to this Belgrade social institution. The term comes from a combination of two Turkish words, *kafa* and *han*, a place for drinking coffee. The Serbs introduced alcohol but there is no evidence that the move was resisted by the Turkish inhabitants of the city. Most also serve food, tending towards traditional Serbian dishes rather than international cooking. Nušić analyzes the names of kafanas. The early ones were simply named after their owner, then later by reference to their location or to historical events or figures. The latest craze in the city centre in Nušić's time was to adopt foreign names such as Union, Splendid, Excelsior and Palace—a trend of which he disapproved as they often replaced older names. He writes scathingly of one called the New Age (Novi vek) which had undergone what he clearly regarded as needless "modern refurbishment", with—of all things—a jazz band and dancing. Obviously for him a kafana was not intended for such frivolous amusements, but a place for drinking, cards and conversation.

A public water fountain, a copy of one in the centre of Sarajevo and a gift from that town to Belgrade in 1989, stands at the bottom of Skadarlija. The Bajloni brewery used to function here, next to the restaurant Skadarlija, built by a Czech immigrant Ignjat Bajloni on the site of a fresh spring of mineral water—an important ingredient in his beer. The brewery has recently been sold and is waiting for redevelopment. The current look of the street, with cobbles, fountains and refurbished restaurants, was completed in the 1960s. The work was the project of the Belgrade architect Uglješa Bogunović, a labour of love one suspects as much as for financial gain, in which he was enormously assisted by his wife, Milica Ribnikar, herself an accomplished sculptress.

Across the road from Skadarlija is a market named after the founder of the brewery. Behind the market, a former evangelical church has been used for BITEF, the Belgrade International Theatre Festival, since 1989. The festival was founded in 1967 and has grown into a large showcase for contemporary performance, with theatre companies coming from all over the world to take part.

EDUCATION IN NINETEENTH-CENTURY BELGRADE

Knez Miloš Obrenović laid the foundations for the development of culture in Belgrade by his founding of and support for various institutions during the 1830s. He established the state printing press in 1831, a year later Gligorije Vozarević opened the city's first bookshop in the new Serbian district around the Town Gate, and the first newspaper the *Serbian News* (Novine Srbske) appeared in 1834. The knez recognized that the new state would need to train its young people although there were precious few facilities at home. Consequently, at his initiative, the Serbian authorities began to make grants available for young people to study at universities abroad from 1835. In 1838 he built the Lycée in Kragujevac, which was transferred to the Konak kneginje Ljubice four years later. The Lycée was intended in these early years to provide the kind of pragmatic education needed for civil servants in the growing administration; in 1815 there were just 24 government officials, but this number grew to 672 by 1839. Its first teachers were Atanasije Teodorović and Petar Radovanović, later joined by Jovan Sterija Popović when he came to Belgrade in 1840. Sterija wrote textbooks for schools as well as working on his own plays and novels during his eight years in Belgrade.

The number of schools and pupils enrolled increased dramatically during the second half of the nineteenth century. The figures also show a changing view of the role of women in society as the old traditions of Serbia came under pressure. In the school year 1879/80 there were 558 primary schools for boys and 56 for girls, with 817 teachers of whom just

56 were women. This disproportionate distribution of school places was not reflected in Belgrade where there was an equal division of eight schools for boys and eight for girls. Twenty years later the country could boast 936 schools for boys and 165 for girls, with 1,940 teachers of whom 916 were women; all had the right to a full pension after 35 years employment in the profession. The larger towns also had premises for a *gimnazija*, or grammar school, for more advanced education, and training colleges for teachers. The first leaders of nineteenth-century Serbia were themselves often without education but they valued its development and encouraged its growth, so that by the end of the century the country was in a position to offer almost universal schooling for all.

Alongside basic education, it was recognized from an early stage that a modern state also needed a system of higher learning. The Society of Serbian Literary Education (Društvo srpske slovesnosti) was founded in 1841 to promote the codification of the modern Serbian language and to spread literacy and teaching throughout the country. Knez Mihailo suspended the activity of the society in 1864 as he suspected some of its members of using its offices to spread ideas politically too liberal for his taste. He replaced it with the Serbian Learned Society (Srpsko učeno društvo), which moved beyond the limited expectations of the former society and began to develop as an independent institution dedicated to the development of critical thinking, a fully-fledged learned society. King Milan took the step in 1886 of founding the Royal Serbian Academy (Kraljevska srpska akademija), which eventually absorbed the Learned Society. The Great School was reformed as the University of Belgrade in 1905 with four faculties: Philosophy for languages and the humanities; Law, including economics and politics; Technical Faculty for engineering and architecture; and finally there was a Medical Faculty.

The university could boast an international scholarly reputation. During the First World War some of its professors lived in exile and were invited to join academies abroad while Serbia was under Austrian occupation. The geographer and anthropologist Jovan Cvijić (1865-1927) spent the war years in Paris where he published in French his book on the Balkans, *La Péninsule balkanique: géographie humaine* (1918). Pavle Popović (1868-1939), a literary scholar, was in Britain when he published his major study of the history of Yugoslav literature as a combination of Serbian, Croatian and Slovenian literatures, *Yugoslav Literature* (Jugoslavenska književnost, 1918). Belgrade was no longer a Turkish city on the periphery of the Ottoman Empire but becoming a sophisticated centre of European learning.

PAINTING AND PAINTERS IN THE NINETEENTH CENTURY

Changes were also evident in Belgrade's nineteenth-century visual arts. At the beginning painting was restricted to decorating the walls of churches, producing icons and other religious objects, and conditions were not really conducive for the development of visual arts in the first half of the nineteenth century. Infrastructure for the provision of materials was lacking, as were studios for working, space for exhibiting and a circle of patrons willing to buy the finished article. There were some Serbian painters outside Serbia, including the successful female artist Katarina Ivanović (1817-82) in Vienna, and a handful of painters from Vojvodina came to Belgrade in the wake of the general movement of educated Serbs going south to offer their services to the new principality. Two of the better known among these migrants are Uroš Knežević (1812-72) and Jovan Popović (1820-64). They have left behind many portraits of Belgrade's more prominent citizens, merchants, politicians and participants in the two rebellions. They also worked on canvases with motifs taken from folk epics and Serbian history. Many of their paintings can be seen in the National Museum.

The generation of painters in the second half of the nineteenth century continued the development of portraits and also themes from the legends and myths of the past. Greater sophistication in their use of colour and range of expression is evident in the works of Đura Jakšić, Steva Todorović (1832-1925), Mina Vukomanović (1828-94), who was the daughter of Vuk Karadžić, Uroš Predić (1857-1953) and Paja Jovanović (1859-1957).

There are two factors of particular interest in the work of these painters. The first is the way in which they chart social changes. In the early portraits the sitters are dressed in clothes corresponding to Ottoman styles, revealing the Turkish role model that dominated in Belgrade. Knez Miloš and other leading members of Serbian society at this time would wear a fez or turban, and this practice continued more or less to the 1860s. The newcomers from Vojvodina were the exception in Belgrade, since they all wore western clothes, the Sava and Danube marking the division between two different cultural worlds. The clothing of the men from Vojvodina led the Serbs of the south to refer to them as *Švabe*, a derogatory term for Germans. Knez Mihailo brought with him ideas to transform Serbia politically, but also a sense of western dress and taste. Pictures of him in frock coat, wing collar, bow tie and leather shoes are in sharp contrast to the Ottoman style of the previous generation.

The second significant factor in the work of these painters is their treatment of Serbian history into which they would embroider visual effects based on legendary sources and stories in the epic ballads. Predić and Jovanović both trained in Vienna, but many of their paintings reflect such scenes. Predić's canvas of the *Kosovo Maiden* (Kosovka devojka) giving comfort to fallen Serbian heroes on the battlefield of Kosovo has become an iconic representation of the tragedy of the famous battle. His *Bosnian Refugees* (Bosanski begunci) was based on the rebellions in Bosnia and the consequences for those who resisted Ottoman oppression in the 1870s, but given in a similarly idealized setting. In his *Dušan's Coronation* (Krunisanje Dušanovo) Jovanović painted the Serbian knights greeting the new Emperor Dušan in highly stylized suits of armour, looking like Hollywood actors preparing for a scene of medieval jousting. Yet some of their depictions were highly effective, such as the same artist's *Migration of the Serbs* (Seoba Srba), showing the departure of the Serbs for Vojvodina in 1691 led by their patriarch on horseback. The stoical attitude of the figures represented on the canvas is a moving declaration of the meaning of the event. These painters were drawing and fixing images for a revived collective memory of the new urban middle classes. They were transforming a folk memory into a more modern vehicle for the invention of a new national ideology based on the Serbian struggle for freedom from foreign domination.

Photography also made its appearance in Serbia in the nineteenth century with Anastas Jovanović (1817-99) as its first representative. His talent was recognized at an early age by no less than Knez Miloš who sponsored him to study in Vienna. During his studies, and like many other young Serbs in the Austrian capital in the 1840s, Jovanović met Vuk Karadžić who encouraged him in his work. He was one of the pioneers in this new field and experimented with different methods for producing images. He has left behind a vast number of pictures representing a catalogue of nineteenth-century Serbia with his scenes from Belgrade, Novi

Sad, Kragujevac and elsewhere.

Special praise is usually reserved for his portraits, however. His sitters included not only public figures from the world of culture and politics, but also anonymous men and women from all walks of life. His work has value both as a series of social documents and as a collection of images of people who, by their expression and the manner in which they pose, reveal something of themselves. His famous picture of Toma Vučić Perišić shows a man of the old school, an Ottoman urban type with a fez and clothing to match. At the same time, his face expresses the cautious reserve of a cruel man who does not easily trust people, with a firm mouth and one eye slightly squinting.

Conversely, Jovanović's many portraits of Knez Mihailo reveal a different individual, not only through his fashionable European attire, but also in the intelligence and inquisitive nature visible in his open countenance. Jovanović was loyal to the family of his first benefactor, and when Mihailo became knez in 1860, he was not only his photographer but also worked as his secretary, managing the day-to-day running of the court. After Mihailo's murder in 1868, he retired from life at the palace and devoted more of his time to photography.

NINETEENTH-CENTURY LITERATURE

As with education and painting, literature underwent many changes and developments. Belgrade was no longer an environment for singers of epic songs. Filip Višnjić might have celebrated the First Uprising in song, but there was little room for him in the mid-century city. Young people who went abroad to study not only brought back their professional qualifications and diplomas, but also new styles and tastes in literature. The first influences of modern European literature came from the Romantics, especially German and Hungarian models. Branko Radičević first combined these more sophisticated verse forms with elements from folk lyrics to forge a new poetic style with a much broader thematic base. He was followed by Đura Jakšić and Jovan Jovanović-Zmaj, both born in Vojvodina but who also settled in Belgrade. Jakšić took part in the Serbian rebellion of 1848 against the Hungarians which ended in failure and left him for most of his life a disappointed and frustrated figure. His favourite themes of nature and the national cause show a clear Byronic influence. Jovanović-Zmaj was a more prolific writer whose poetry was more lyrical than Jakšić's tendency to heroic reflection. Later Romanticism, promoted by Laza Kostić (1841-1910), went further in adapting foreign poetic models to the Serbian language, and Kostić's poetry took the Belgrade reading public much closer to a modern feeling for rhythms and symbolic expression.

The last three decades of the nineteenth century were dominated by prose and Realist literary trends, although poetry in a late Romantic style continued to find a space for itself. The period of prose, mainly short stories, coincided with that of greatest political and social change. Most of this generation of writers were born in Serbia and received at least their grammar-school education in Belgrade, although like the Romantic poets many of them had university training abroad.

Svetozar Marković (1846-75) was not so much a writer himself, but he promoted many of the ideas that influenced his generation. At university in Russia he read the works of radical Russian thinkers and brought their ideas of social progress with him back to Belgrade where he founded the movement of United Youth. He and his followers were early socialists, opponents of the alienating effect of modern capitalism on the fabric of society. Idealistic and uncompromising they were often at odds with the authorities. Milovan Glišić (1847-1908), one of the writers influenced by Marković's ideas, wrote short stories often based on village settings, reflecting traditional patriarchal values contrary to the dehumanizing effect of rapid urbanization and early industrialization.

Laza Lazarević (1851-91) was an advocate for the progressive United Youth, but later in life adopted a more conservative political position. He studied medicine in Berlin before returning home to practise as a doctor, eventually becoming personal physician to the king. He was also a writer, although his main profession took up much of his time and he only completed some nine stories, but each is a small masterpiece of its genre, style and theme. Critics have often drawn attention to his sentimental attitude toward the past and the disappearing traditions of the countryside. Lazarević saw the world in which he grew up dissolving under the demands of modern society, his work hovering between nostalgia and a harsh picture of inevitable transformation.

Lazarević includes Belgrade in one of his short stories, "The First Morning Service with Father" ("Prvi put s ocem na jutrenje"), set in a small Serbian town and narrated as a childhood recollection. The narrator tells us about his family, dominated by his father, a silent man occasionally very generous and sometimes inexplicably absent. It turns out that he has a passion for gambling. One night, he returns home with his cronies and they begin to play cards. The atmosphere in the house becomes more and more oppressive as the night progresses, and the child, unsure of what is happening, feels a rising sense of fear and panic. The family loses everything through the gambling and the father is prepared to commit suicide for the disgrace he has brought on them. He is stopped by the boy's mother who points out that they began their married life with nothing and can begin again. The father, as an act of repentance, takes his son to church that morning.

What is not clear from the story is why the narrator remembers these events from so long ago. Then, in a final sentence, he tells us that he has seen again the man whom he blames for leading his father too far in his gambling obsession, a character called Zelembać. "When I went to Belgrade last year to buy some goods I saw Pera Zelembać in Topčider, in convicts' clothes: he was breaking stones!" It is significant that the narrator travels from his village to Belgrade, which has negative moral associations opposed to traditional rural values. Lazarević shows us a modern interpretation of the city in a society, which in the space of one hundred years, from the beginning to the end of the nineteenth century, moved a distance of some four centuries in terms of its cultural trajectory.

DORĆOL AND KNEZ MIHAILO IN MODERN FICTION

In her collection of stories *Dorćol* Svetlana Velmar-Janković offers images of figures taken from Serbian history, characters involved in creating a sense of cultural identity: Vasa Čarapić, Uzun Mirko, Dositej Obradović, Vuk Karadžić, Captain Miša, Jovan Jovanović-Zmaj and others. The name of each character is also the name of a street in the district of Dorćol. The stories are organized around a rough geographical pattern, so that as the reader reads each one he is taken on a journey.

The first story, "Francuska ulica", is named after France Street, which borders the district. The next few tales refer to streets at the top and bottom of the slope as it faces the Danube, while the remainder cut across them in an east-west direction. Their order in the text gradually leads deeper into the district until the last story, "Stara čaršija", a name for the central part of the district and the crossroads of King Peter I and Tsar Dušan

Streets. The name of the whole quarter is taken from this crossroads, or in Turkish *dort jol*.

Each story begins by introducing the eponymous historical figure after whom the street is named. They are spectral images who invisibly tread their eternal paths down their street, every day the same, observing the life of the city, reflecting on their historical roles and looking out for the ghosts of others who used to live on their streets. Their individual reflections coincide and conflict, building up a complex picture of Serbian culture. There is a fundamental distinction between the figures of Karađorđe and Knez Miloš Obrenović. The former is a heroic figure finally defeated by the greater numbers of the Ottoman forces, forced into exile, betrayed by Miloš and then murdered by him. Miloš Obrenović uses cunning and stealth to achieve his political ambitions, even turning against Serbs when he suspects them of not supporting his tyrannical rule. This is the source of cycles of success, deceit and failure typifying the representation of Serbian history in her fiction.

There are numerous other details in Velmar-Janković's work that draw attention to the constant return of destructive forces. In the story about the brawl around the water fountain leading to the Ottoman withdrawal from Belgrade, there is a description of the 1862 Turkish cannonade on the city, immediately followed by reference to later bombardments in the First and Second World Wars: "The bombs exploded, truly at intervals, yet nevertheless one after the other (it is still not 1915, nor 1941, nor 1944, but it is a beginning)." The narrator remarks on such coincidences by simply commenting "that some dates are repeated". History is not governed by relationships of cause and effect, but by coincidence and accident, the result of the contiguity of events.

Isolation is another dominant theme in Velmar-Janković's work. The characters seek out other historical figures where their streets intersect or yet others whose lives are associated with their streets. Gospodar Jevrem, brother to Miloš Obrenović, waits in vain each day for Vuk Karadžić and Dositej Obradović on their respective corners but he never meets them. They try to speak to each other but their voices do not carry from one to another. Individuals and historical eras appear as so many unconnected moments, with each character trapped in the age in which he lived. The statue of Vasa Čarapić watches from his vantage point people crossing the road in front of the National Theatre to Republic Square. He notes a connection between the alternating green, red and yellow traffic lights and the movement of the pedestrians from which he concludes that the people are somehow dependent on the lights. All that remains is a series of haphazard links based on inexplicable parallels.

Velmar-Janković's image of Belgrade is one of a sinister ambiguity. The last story focuses on the crossroads from which Dorćol derives its name. We are told that executions used to be carried out on this spot in a most peculiar manner. The condemned man would be led out to the centre of the place and then decapitated while still standing. His head, the narrator observes, flies from his shoulders and his body "already dead, still alive staggers toward oblivion". The transformation from life to death is the passing of a frontier in which, for a brief moment, opposites co-exist.

The city is never permitted to develop and emerge fully whole before its evolution is arrested again by another war or other dramatic event. Belgrade's history is a narrative of different identities which co-exist in a confusing pattern expressing the simultaneous existence of opposites.

In one of her later novels, *The Abyss* (Bezdno, 1995), Velmar-Janković offers a fictional account of the last years of Knez Mihailo. It is written in the form of personal diaries and letters left behind by him, his wife Kneginja Julija and the manager of the court's affairs, the artist and photographer Anastas Jovanović. It is a historical novel in the best sense of the word. The image and atmosphere of the age in which the action is set is captured and expressed.

The first part of the work is a diary written by Mihailo during his exile abroad in 1858. He is happy living with his wife on their estates in Hungary and mixing in fashionable circles in Vienna, Paris and London. The following year, turbulent times return to Serbia, and his father, Miloš, is invited back to Belgrade to rule again. Mihailo's peaceful existence is about to change when he becomes knez on his father's death. His diary is now accompanied by notes written without dates by his friend, Jovanović, in whom he entrusts the running of his court. These two voices tell in tandem the pressures on the new state, relations with the foreign consuls who are constantly implicated in plots and intrigues, and the activities of the pasha in Kalemegdan. We are now in a position to be told not only what the knez is thinking and feeling in the confessional tones of his diary, but also the changes in the man as observed by someone who knew him well.

The transformation in Mihailo's new life as knez is most vividly seen in the relationship between him and his Hungarian wife, Julija. By 1862 the prince's voice is rarely heard in the book. Instead, Jovanović's notes and comments are joined by letters from Julija to her family. In her loneliness and incomprehension at the transformation of her husband into someone she barely recognizes she has begun an affair with a foreign aristocrat. Her family admonish her for the scandal she is causing, while she defends herself by blaming circumstances: Mihailo is abandoning her for affairs of state, the court treats her as a potential enemy, the city to which she has been brought is alien and in complete contrast to the sophistication to which she has been accustomed. Mihailo's return from exile becomes for her a form of banishment.

Julija describes the troubles of 1862, which began around the water fountain with a trivial incident:

> On that Sunday afternoon in June, while I was reading and sipping my tea, and Belgrade's good families were out taking a stroll in the countryside, a few young Serbs, boys really, servants in nearby houses, came to the Čukur fountain to fetch water. At the same time and with the same intention, several officers from the Turkish police arrived. As the Turkish authorities had become arrogant recently, so the officers began to behave in an overbearing manner. They would not wait their turn for water but shoved the Serbian boys aside. In the ensuing mêlée an earthenware jug, which one of the soldiers was carrying, broke. He struck the nearest boy about the head with the shattered remains. Covered in blood he began to wail, his friends began to call for help, Serbs and Turks flew from the surrounding houses, a Serbian constable turned up with some gendarmes, and a fight broke out. The Turkish soldiers who provoked it tried to flee but were prevented by the Serbian gendarmes.

Her depiction of events introduces a note of incredulity to the unfolding drama in the city. After Turkish soldiers shoot and kill the interpreter sent to help with negotiations and another Serbian representative, a mob attacks the gates leading into the Turkish part of town and the pasha orders his cannon to fire on the city. She comments: "I had already learnt that, here, one death invokes revenge, and that revenge is followed by another killing. In the Orient, that tragic sequence can be a very protracted affair, multiplied hundredfold or even thousandfold. And Serbia is still the Orient, although Mihailo will not allow himself to say so."

The meaning of this "Orient" in Velmar-Janković's fictional world of 1860s Belgrade is evident on multiple levels. The city's oldest quarter, Dorćol, is exotic with its colourful gardens, mosques and meandering streets that lead nowhere but can lure an unsuspecting foreigner into danger. It presents a mixed face to the outsider, both demure and gaudy. It is a spectacle offering fascination and fear, the promise of hope and the betrayal of expectations. Belgrade, in Velmar-Janković's fictional universe, represents both a bridge between different cultures and, in her words, an abyss into which its inhabitants may fall.

Chapter Four

TERAZIJE AND KING MILAN STREET: CAPITAL OF SERBIA AND YUGOSLAVIA

BELGRADE SOCIETY BEFORE THE FIRST WORLD WAR

After the assassination of King Alexander Obrenović, Peter Karađorđević was invited to take the throne. He was modest, unassuming and diplomatic, a man with a completely different nature to his predecessor. Trained as a soldier, he appreciated the need for an *esprit de corps* and held a high sense of duty.

But what kind of a country was Serbia? The established view of the decade leading to the First World War is of a Serbian Golden Age. Belgrade was emerging as the capital city of a modern state with institutions that could support a functioning, democratic, parliamentary monarchy. Great changes had taken place in the last quarter of the nineteenth century. Belgrade was now a beacon for all Croats, Slovenes, Bosnians and Macedonians who sought freedom from Vienna or Istanbul.

Yet this view has been called into question, both at home and abroad, with the hindsight of the 1990s when the country disintegrated through a series of bloody wars. Some historians now question the idealized myth of Yugoslav solidarity. Serbia, in the first decade of the twentieth century, was still caught between a European future and the lingering legacy of its Ottoman past.

When Peter was crowned in 1904, Serbia had a population of about three million, a land area of 18,725 square miles and a border stretching for 825 miles, of which 580 miles was shared with the Austro-Hungarian and Ottoman Empires. The population was expanding at the rate of 190,000 per year as a result of increased birth rate and immigration. The size of the country increased dramatically after the Balkan Wars of 1912 and 1913 when Turkey was driven out of the region by an alliance of Serbia, Montenegro, Greece, Bulgaria and Romania. Serbia now included the southern provinces of Macedonia and Kosovo, the number of inhabitants grew by another 1.5 million and the land area by 12,355 square

miles. About 87 per cent of the population was comprised of peasant farmers with a small plot of land producing barely enough food to feed the family who worked it. Most people made their own clothes, shoes and tools when possible. Consequently, the vast majority of the population played no role in the money economy of the state and paid no taxes.

Serbia had very little industry, hardly any banking facilities, poor infrastructure in roads and communication links, and worst of all it had little prospect of being able to improve its position in the short term. Literacy rates in the villages were as low as 23 per cent, but higher in the towns at about 55 per cent. Most Serbian towns numbered between 5,000 and 10,000 inhabitants, with a few larger ones: Vranje (pop. 10,600), Šabac (12,000), Požarevac (12,500), Leskovac (13,500), Kragujevac (14,500), Niš (25,000) and Belgrade.

The capital city's population grew from 70,000 in 1900 to 90,000 by 1910, although, in comparison to neighbouring countries, it was fairly small alongside Bucharest's 287,000 inhabitants and Athens with 122,000. The occupations of Belgrade's inhabitants reflected its position at the centre of political, economic and administrative life: civil servants (24 per cent), artisans (23 per cent), professional groups (21 per cent) and merchants (13 per cent). The architectural space they created attests to their cosmopolitan taste and their promotion of cultural and social activity.

After the death of King Alexander, new opportunities opened up for public debate. An independent newspaper, *Politika*, began publication in 1904, founded by Vladislav Ribnikar (1871-1914), which today still has the largest circulation in Serbia and has become the longest-running daily paper in the Balkans. Coming as a breath of fresh air, it appeared as a sign of change in Belgrade's cultural, intellectual and political life. The city's elite, educated in the best European universities, was aware of the immediate need for a constitution defining the rights and responsibilities of the crown, ministers, the National Assembly and courts of justice. This circle of leading citizens was able to discuss the relative merits of the British and French political systems, and to debate the principles of freedom and justice to be applied via the institutions of government. However, the political culture in which these polemics were conducted at the beginning of the twentieth century remained highly specific to Belgrade, quite unlike the context of London and Paris from which the models were taken.

An important factor in the city's social structure was the small number of people in these upper echelons and the consequent trend for individuals to appear across a broad range of functions. It was not unusual for professors from the University of Belgrade to sit alongside professional politicians as deputies in the Assembly drafting legislation. Such people were very much aware that they needed to play an active role in order to provide a lead for the country. But where in the West there was a greater tendency toward the atomization and professionalization of institutional processes, in Belgrade there emerged a single elite group to perform the different functions normally divided among different sub-groups. This personal touch tended to distort the emergence of political parties in Serbia, giving public debates the appearance of family feuds.

Belgrade was not a natural capital city for Serbia. The medieval centre of the state was further south, while Knez Miloš, wary of the pasha, made Kragujevac his capital. Belgrade was perched above the meeting-point of the two rivers in the north-west corner of the country, its geographic position symbolic of its western leanings. Its architectural appearance from Miloš's time and later was influenced by the West, as were its models of government. But Serbia was a fragile entity, in constant danger of losing its independence and its identity. These fears were heightened in the decade before the First World War as the Austro-Hungarian Empire began to realize its plans to extend its territory in the region. It formally annexed Bosnia in 1908, having held administrative control since the Berlin Congress of 1878. From 1906 to 1911 Vienna closed its borders and refused to allow Serbia to export goods across its territory to the West.

These developments no doubt influenced the Belgrade elite's thinking about political priorities. The first step was national liberation, while the rights and freedom of the individual would follow once the safety of the collective was assured. The historian Dubravka Stojanović recognizes the weight of traditional patriarchal values in her judgment on Belgrade's political culture. She observes that the elite were happiest when discussing the principles of democracy that they studied and experienced in the West but that they "added to these ideas local colours, translating them from the abstract utopias to the older, better-known models, much closer to the Serbian tradition". The times, however, were difficult; and time did not appear to be on Belgrade's side.

THE FIRST WORLD WAR AND THE CREATION OF YUGOSLAVIA
In 1914 the Austrian Archduke Franz Ferdinand visited Sarajevo, the principal town of the newly-acquired province of Bosnia. His stay happened to coincide with the anniversary of the Battle of Kosovo. A small band of conspirators planned his assassination, led by Gavrilo Princip who at seventeen was one of the oldest among them. They were helped by a secret society in Belgrade called "Unification or Death", or sometimes the "Black Hand", which provided arms and money. One of the leading figures in the society was the same Colonel Dragutin Dimitrijević-Apis who had been active in the plot against Alexander in 1903. Both Princip and the colonel met their ends in 1917; Princip died in jail and Apis was put on trial before a military tribunal engineered by his many enemies and shot for treason in Greece. After the death of the archduke and his wife in Sarajevo, Vienna demanded that Serbia take responsibility for the assassination. The Austrian demands, however, were formulated in such a way that Belgrade was bound to reject them, since acceptance would require Serbia to surrender its sovereignty.

The first shell of the war was aimed at Belgrade on 29 July 1914. Much to everyone's surprise, the first Austrian invasion was repulsed, but after a renewed attack the country was occupied by enemy forces the following year. The city suffered greatly in the bombardment of 1915 with great loss of life and much damage to its infrastructure. The Austrian authorities, once in control, were determined to eradicate as far as possible all outward forms of Serbian identity. The Cyrillic alphabet was banned from public use, printing presses were smashed, street signs and destination boards on trams were changed into the Latin alphabet, and history books in schools were rewritten to downplay national achievements.

Belgrade became a cultural desert with most of its pre-war intelligentsia retreating with the army and taking refuge on Corfu from where the government-in-exile continued its work. The poor health of King Peter forced his retirement from an active role and his son, Alexander, was made prince-regent. After the Allied victory in 1918, Serbia was joined by Slovenia, Croatia, Bosnia, Montenegro and Vojvodina in an enlarged state of South Slavs. The creation of this first Yugoslavia, known officially as the Kingdom of Serbs, Croats and Slovenes, was announced by Prince Alexander in Belgrade on 1 December 1918.

In the immediate post-war period, Belgrade suffered all the problems common to other urban societies in the aftermath of large-scale conflict. The old town families suddenly found themselves surrounded by thousands of newcomers. Some of them were poor, dispossessed refugees, while others lived by their wits taking advantage of the anarchic conditions into which Belgrade was plunged at the end of the war. It was the capital of a country without internationally recognized borders, not even a name. The author Ivo Andrić describes the atmosphere in the city in his novel *Gospodica* (1945), translated into English under the title *The Woman from Sarajevo*:

> Life in Belgrade in the year 1920 was gaudy, lusty, unusually complex, and full of contrasts. Countless diverse vital forces flowed parallel with obscure weaknesses and failings; old methods of work and the strict discipline of patriarchal life existed side by side with a motley jigsaw of new and still unformed habits and chaos of all kinds; apathy side by side with intensity, modesty and every kind of moral beauty with vices and ugliness. The panting and reckless bustle of various profiteers and speculators took place alongside games of intelligence and the dreaming of visionaries and bold ideologists.
>
> Down the worn and partially destroyed streets came this foaming and swelling flood of people, for each day hundreds of newcomers dived into it head first, like pearl fishers into the deep sea. Here came the man who wanted to achieve distinction and the man bent on hiding himself. Here mingled those who had to defend their possessions and their status, threatened by the changing conditions. Here were many young people from all parts of a state that was still in the process of formation, who looked forward to the next day and expected great things of the changed circumstances, and also a number of older people who looked for a means of adjustment and for salvation in this very flood, hiding the fears and the loathing which it inspired in them. There were many of those whom war had thrown up to the surface and made successful, as well as those it had rocked to their foundations and changed, who now groped for some balance and for something to lean on.

The new country was greeted enthusiastically by almost all, although initial euphoria was soon replaced by disappointment. Croats especially had been hoping for a greater degree of autonomy than the government in Belgrade was prepared to allow. Following their political traditions, Belgrade's politicians assumed that the new state would be a parliamentary monarchy with centralized institutions in the capital city. Unfortunately, neither the Karađorđević dynasty nor Belgrade held the same emotional resonance for all the population. The Croat deputies were mostly elected from the ranks of the Croat Peasant Party under the leadership of Stjepan Radić. Denied their home rule, the Croats initially boycotted the National Assembly, but eventually agreed to take up their seats. Shortly afterwards, however, in the summer of 1928 Radić was shot and killed during a debate in the Assembly by a Montenegrin deputy, Puniša Račić. All possibility of compromise was now gone and the ordinary operation of government proved impossible. Faced with an extreme situation, King Alexander dissolved parliament and took power in his own hands on 6 January 1929. In the same year, he renamed the country the Kingdom of Yugoslavia in preference to the title that had emphasized the presence of three different and by then reluctant partners.

Opinion is divided over Alexander's actions. Was he genuine in his stated aim to reunite the country, or was he another Serbian public figure who could not understand the nature of the political problems facing the enlarged country? The question was never answered as he was assassinated during a state visit to France in 1934 after landing in Marseille. Both internal and external enemies were implicated in the plot, in particular the Croatian fascist movement the Ustaše, banned in Yugoslavia, which was in turn supported by Mussolini's Italy. Alexander's son, Peter, was still a schoolboy and too young to take the throne so the late king's cousin, Prince Paul (or Knez Pavle), became regent. The prince never expected nor wanted to be a political figure. He was a connoisseur of art, an Anglophile whose brother-in-law was the Duke of Kent, and clearly was not prepared for the huge task ahead.

TERAZIJE

The street leading from the end of the pedestrian-only Knez Mihailo Street to the Slavija Square is a long straight road actually made up of two parts: Terazije and King Milan Street. In Ottoman times the main water supply to Belgrade flowed under here toward Kalemegdan. At certain intervals stood tall towers made of wooden boards marking little reservoirs for drawing water. These towers were called *terazije* in Turkish and one was placed in front of where the Hotel Moskva now stands—hence this street's name.

In the 1830s this area just beyond the city perimeter was marshland with a reputation as a good spot for hunting wild ducks. The only sign of human activity was the road that curved up from the Istanbul Gate and divided here, one route leading down what is now King Alexander Boulevard for Smederevo and ultimately Istanbul, the other following King Milan Street and the road to Kragujevac and central Serbia. The land formed a small plateau with a view down to the River Sava and the first Serbian district of Belgrade around the Town Gate.

The first development on Terazije was at the initiative of Knez Miloš to expand beyond the confines of the Ottoman town. He had the idea of giving free parcels of land to Serbs living further down the slope on condition that they build homes and workshops on the plateau above. Priority was given to craftsmen like blacksmiths and wheelwrights since these trades would be useful on the highways for travellers, merchants and their caravans arriving or leaving with their goods. In time it became a busy stopping point with people plying their trade, repairing carts, fixing horseshoes and other businesses. It was also possible to link this new development directly with the Town Gate without going through Belgrade's Turkish quarter.

Terazije has always raised many issues for urban planners. The problem can be boiled down to one question: is it a thoroughfare or a city square? Its shape is marked by its original purpose, with space for carts to pull off the roads to be repaired. Rather than having straight sides, Terazije is actually egg-shaped with bulging curves, adding to the sense that this is more than a space for traffic to pass through. Its width gives the feeling that it is waiting to be filled with a greater purpose. Knez Alexander Karađorđević decided that the old Turkish water tower was no longer a fitting marker for the new district and planned to replace it with a fountain. But he lost power before the monument was finished and the project was taken over by Miloš who completed it in 1860. The fountain is inscribed on all four sides with Miloš's initials and the year of his second inauguration.

Terazije was given a face-lift in 1911 when a more decorative water feature was installed. The original was moved to Topčider and put next to the church and Miloš's residence there, before being returned to its present position in 1975. As part of the same renovations the middle of the road was laid with lawns and flower beds, surrounded by an ornamental fence with elegant street lamps. It was, in effect, treated as a square with traffic allowed to pass down either side. Much thought was also given to the space between the two hotels, the Moskva and the Balkan, and how best to set off the view down to the Sava. After the First World War it was proposed that the gap be filled with a series of statues to celebrate the victory and commemorate those who fell in the conflict. Unfortunately, the sculptor produced an effigy of a naked man holding a sword and a hawk as the centrepiece of the arrangement, forcing a quick change of mind; the Victor was placed in its present position in Kalemegdan facing away from the centre of town.

After the Second World War the new regime introduced a different solution to the Terazije issue. They removed all the pre-war non-functional decorations, widened the pavements, pulled up the tram lines and replaced them with an overhead power supply for trolleybuses, turning it into the practical thoroughfare of today. The street now became an important point in the route of the annual May Day parade. This was a significant highlight in the calendar of communist Yugoslavia, an opportunity to put on display the latest technological developments, military hardware, and the support of the masses for the Party. Terazije maintained the theatrical purpose of a grand square, but without its stage props and scenery.

Terazije is now one of the city's main traffic arteries connecting the central part of the old town to residential areas beyond. At the gap between the Moskva and the Balkan hotels is a junction of two roads. One goes to the right and down to the main bridge across the Sava to New Belgrade. This direction also links to the underpass that takes vehicles under Terazije and helps avoid congestion in the city centre. The other road is a steep hill, Balkan Street, leading to the railway and bus stations. The other side of Terazije has been closed off by the later addition of more modern buildings, reducing the sense of its open space. A little further down, the broad and imposing King Alexander Boulevard sweeps round and away from the main street.

At the crossroads is the Monument to the Patriots (Spomenik rodoljupcima) commemorating the Serbs who were hanged here by the German Army in 1941. The sight of the bodies swinging from the lamp posts was meant as a warning to others not to resist the armed occupation of the country. In the distance, above Slavija Square at the end of King Milan Street, rises the cupola of the massive St. Sava's Church (Hram svetog Save), which stands on the plateau at Vračar, offering a towering presence visible down the length of both streets.

From "Albania" to "Moscow"

The twelve-storey building known as the Albania Palace (Palata "Albanija") dominates the bottom of Terazije. Before, a kafana with the name Albanija, built in typical Balkan style, occupied the site from the nineteenth century. It may not have been pretty to look at, but it was a firm favourite of its clientele. The playwright Branislav Nušić said of it in 1929:

> There stands even today, as a reminder of old Belgrade, and will continue it seems for centuries, the kafana Albanija, a blot on the face of Belgrade, but El dorado to all its customers. There isn't a kafana which spends less on its comforts and has more trade; nor is there one which has such a varied and mixed public.

Unfortunately, this view of its attractions was not shared by all, and for some years there was pressure on the city authorities to pull it down and replace it with something more appropriate. Urban planners and architects wanted a modern showpiece, which led to the Modernist design of the new Albania Palace in 1938. It was the tallest building in Yugoslavia and the iconic image of Belgrade, but stories circulated about the dangers were it to fall down. In fact, during the Allied bombing of the city in 1944 it was hit and damaged but was quickly and successfully repaired with no hint of it collapsing.

Between the Albania Palace and the Hotel Balkan is a fairly new block of shops and commercial premises built in 1964. No. 12 Terazije was the site of an old kafana, the Golden Cross (Zlatni krst), in which the first moving picture show was screened in Belgrade. A film industry appeared and grew very soon after this event. The Hotel Balkan on the corner is also a twentieth-century construction, from 1935, although there was an older hotel of the same name here for decades before. Across the road, the Hotel Moskva, or Moscow, was constructed in its monumental style between 1905 and 1907. Unfortunately, the house next door is not of the same distinctive architectural style and reduces the overall effect provided by the grandeur of the hotel.

Lena Jovičić, brought up in a bilingual home with her Serbian father and Scottish mother, describes Belgrade in the early part of the twentieth century in her book *Pages from Here and There in Serbia* (1926). She writes of the modernity of the Hotel Moskva:

> The Belgrade of to-day is an agglomeration of Easter and Western ideas moulded and adapted to meet the requirements of this corner of the world. The contrast between the old and the new town is thus accentuated. Buildings of more than two or three stories high were few and far between in the beginning of this century, when the Hotel Moskva—so obviously Russian in design—seemed like a pelican in the wilderness. Twenty years have brought about many changes in Belgrade.
>
> The progress that has been made since the work of reconstruction began in 1919 is little less than marvellous. In a remarkable short space of time new, modern buildings have been erected to take the place of those destroyed by the bombardment. On every hand there is evidence that Belgrade has risen like a Phoenix from her ashes.

The literary Phoenix involved the Moskva where, after the First World War, a group of artists, musicians, writers, poets and sundry bohemians began to meet in the kafana of the hotel. They did not form a coherent school or movement, but their meetings, discussions and polemics over the nature of art provided an engaging and stimulating atmosphere for a younger generation of Modernist writers amidst the Belgrade ruins. Miloš Crnjanski, Rastko Petrović, Momčilo Nastasijević and others cut their first literary teeth in this company.

A group of buildings on the wide pavement of Terazije beyond the Hotel Moskva are representative of Belgrade's trajectory from a small Balkan town to a major European city. The Athens Palace (Palata "Atina"), at 28 Terazije, was built in 1902 as the family home of Đorđe Vučo, with commercial premises on the ground floor and living accommodation on the upper two storeys. It is an example of balance and harmony in an architectural design with features of the Italian neo-Renaissance set off by the two small cupolas on either side.

A somewhat earlier house, Krsmanovićeva palata, is at 34 Terazije, constructed about 1885 by Joca M. Marković but which he soon had to surrender to Aleksa Krsmanović because of a debt. Krsmanović lived here until his death in 1914. The front of the building facing Terazije is not in itself particularly remarkable, but behind the house is a large semi-circular terrace overlooking a family garden. Built on a slope, the house actually has two floors at the back—a feature not evident from street level. It has had many different owners and functions. At the end of the First World War, because of the extensive damage to both royal palaces, Alexander Karađorđević took up residence here. He proclaimed the unification of Serbs, Croats and Slovenes in one state in the large reception room facing Terazije after which he gave a speech from the window to the crowd gathered outside. Between the two world wars the house was used by the Yugoslav Autoclub while the ground floor at the back was an exclusive shop selling oriental carpets. During the Second World War it became a canteen for officers of the German administration in Belgrade. After the war it was nationalized and used in turn as a youth centre, a diplomatic club, the offices for the government protocol section, and a bank.

The small but elegant structure at 40 Terazije was built in 1911 as a studio for the photographer Milan Jovanović (1863-1944), with his initials in relief above the entrance. His studio was on the first floor, the wall of which and most of the roof were all in glass, offering a very distinctive appearance from the main street at the time. Jovanović trained in Vienna and Paris before practising in Belgrade where he photographed a large number of famous people from the worlds of culture and politics.

Across the road, the Ministry of Justice at 41 Terazije is an imposing administrative building from the 1880s, although the house next door at no. 39 is perhaps more interesting. This is the Smederevo Bank (Smederevska banka) from 1910 and offers the most distinctive design features in Terazije. It has a highly decorative façade in which the vertical lines in particular are emphasized. The eye moves naturally up this narrow three-storey house whose height is extended by the central cupola at the top. The balconies give a sense of greater depth, which fills out the vertical proportions of the design.

On the corner with King Alexander Boulevard rises the Igumanovljeva palata, named after Sime Andrejević Igumanov. Born in the southern town of Prizren, he founded a school in his home town which was to be supported by the rent from this building. He established other philanthropic foundations for education and children, and on the top of this building was placed a tall statue of him with children representing his legacy. The statue was removed in the 1960s when the city was more interested in updating its image and it was replaced by a neon advertising sign.

KING MILAN STREET

Terazije and King Milan Street together form a seamless flow, with the border between them marked by the colourful and highly decorated frontage of the Vuk Karadžić Foundation (Vukova zadužbina). The road was first known as the Kragujevac Highway (Kragujevački drum) when it was not much more than an elaborate and large cart track, muddy in winter and dusty in summer, until it was cobbled and planted with an avenue of chestnut trees. In 1872 it was called Knez Milan Street (Ulica kneza Milana), only to be re-christened in its present slightly different form in 1888 after Serbia's recognition as a kingdom. The communists changed the street in 1946 to Marshal Tito Street (Ulica Maršala Tita), which it stayed until the end of the communist system when it received the title Street of Serbian Rulers (Ulica srpskih vladara) in 1991. The new name, however, lacked the kind of commemorative or memorable ring expected of a capital city's central thoroughfare. It was felt that the old name offered a specific historical reference and a complement to the other monarchs' monikers in the city centre, so it reverted back in 1997.

At the beginning of King Milan Street is the red and white façade of the Vuk Karadžić Foundation. The house was constructed in 1871-72 for the judge Dimitrije Golubović but did not remain long in his possession as it was used as the Russian Consulate prior to being bought by the Ministry of Education in 1879. It remained in the ministry's hands for over a hundred years until it became the office for the Vuk Karadžić Foundation, an organization which continues to promote his name and to work for the development of the Serbian language. The building also houses the Institute for Literature and Art (Institut za književnost i umetnost) funded by the government to conduct research in these areas. The building was given its distinctive exterior during renovations in 1912, with a heavy wooden door, dark red decoration and elongated windows on the first floor as a modern interpretation of a traditional Byzantine church design. Further down and across the street, next to the palace complex, is a small side street with a water cascade down the centre. This is Andrić Crescent, named after the winner of the Nobel Prize for literature Ivo Andrić, where there is a statue to the writer. There is now a museum at no. 8 in the flat where he lived for the last years of his life.

King Milan Street was refurbished after the First World War and many new buildings were planned for it, all finished in a few short years. The consequent transformation produced a central avenue in the style of other European capitals fronted by tall buildings of impressive design and dimensions. The House of the Serbo-American Bank (Dom Srpsko-amerikanske banke) went up in 1931 at no. 10. The Hotel London was built on the corner with Knez Miloš Street, and the name of the crossroads is still known to all as "At the London" (Kod Londona). Construction after the Second World War has produced many more newer buildings that may individually have their merits, but which rarely blend with the earlier architecture. The street has hence lost something of its coherency.

Across the road from the palace complex is the Serbian Assembly, built 1953-54 in a modern design unlike the classical proportions of the buildings opposite. In 1963 the Chamber of Commerce (Privredna komora Beograda) was constructed on the site of the old Hotel London with little thought to the appearance of surrounding buildings. From 1969 to 1974 the city's tallest skyscraper was constructed on the street, the Belgrade Palace (Beogradska palata)—more frequently and affectionately called the Belgrade Lady (Beograđanka). It can be seen from all over the city and defines the central skyline and, although impressive in its own way, hardly blends with the surrounding architecture. It is spread over 23 storeys with a supermarket in the basement, a department store on the first few floors, office space on the upper floors and the studios of a TV and radio company on the very top floors.

The area around the Beograđanka was first developed by Knez Miloš as part of a military district including barracks and a powder magazine. Across the road, the Student Cultural Centre (Studentski kulturni centar) was originally built as the Officers' Club (Oficirski dom) in 1895, part of the facilities for the army. The small statues of knights on the front betray its earlier incarnation, and it was from here that the conspirators set out on their errand to murder King Alexander and Queen Draga in 1903. Behind the cultural centre is a park bearing the name Manjež, from the French word *manège*, meaning both the art of horsemanship and a place for training horses. This was the site of a riding academy that Knez Mihailo added to the military complex in the 1860s as a training ground for the cavalry of the Serbian army which he was keen to develop. The need for the facilities declined after the First World War for two reasons. First, the war saw the introduction of certain technological advances which, while not doing away with the use of cavalry altogether, at least reduced their military effectiveness. Second, the National Theatre in the centre of town was damaged during the war and was not fit for staging performances. In these circumstances, it was decided that the adaptation of the Manjež, the large hall intended for cavalry drills, as a new theatre would solve one of the city's temporary problems. This building fronted the park on King Milan Street and eventually became the home of the Yugoslav Drama Theatre (Jugoslovensko dramsko pozorište). Its most recent facelift came about following a catastrophic fire in 1997 when the whole building was reconstructed with a modern façade and interior. The theatre has an active company producing plays by modern Serbian and foreign playwrights, while the National on Republic Square tends more towards a classical repertoire.

Across the road from the theatre are Flower Square and the beginning of Njegoš Street. This plot was designated as a parcel of land to be developed as a market in 1843 when the first steps were taken to extend Belgrade further beyond Terazije and into the district of Vračar. In the last quarter of the nineteenth century and particularly after the announcement of Serbia's transformation into a kingdom this district became the elite residential area. The new middle classes of merchants, professional groups, army officers and state officials moved here and built large town houses. The area bordered by King Alexander Boulevard and King Milan Street as far as St. Sava's Church provides many examples of rapid urban development.

The people who moved into the district proved to be the kind of articulate middle class who would get things done for themselves. They formed the Society for the Beautification of Vračar (Društvo za ulepšavanje Vračara) in 1884, and one of the amenities they pressed for was a covered market at Flower Square of the kind beginning to appear in western towns. They got their wish, and the first stand for fiacres in Belgrade was also put here in 1886 in order to help speed up the journey time to the city centre. The bottom of Njegoš Street by Flower Square was used as a taxi rank for more modern vehicles until the beginning of the twenty-first century when the area was pedestrianized.

The house at 1 Njegoš Street has the name of the society dedicated to improving Vračar inscribed at the top, and in the hallway, just inside the front door, are four plaques on the wall listing the names of honoured (and deceased) members. It is a list of people from a wide variety of professions giving a sociological insight into that new elite: café owners, retired generals, a butcher, civil servants, a judge and many others. Many of the houses at the beginning of the street have recently been converted into small bars with outside seating, or expensive boutiques. Even so, there are still traces of the previous atmosphere. The house at no. 11 is highly decorated with many original figures in relief on the front. Behind the modern appearance at ground level facing the street, the small workshops of some craftsmen are still to be found in the back courtyards, indicated by old signs above the entrances advertising a cobbler, watch mender, or bag repairer.

Flower Square itself has gone through various transformations and eventually became an enclosed supermarket with some flower stalls in front. The supermarket was the first self-service outlet in Belgrade, introduced by the communists during the period when the country was going through radical reform and moving away from the Soviet model of state socialism, and a sign of the gradual westernization of Yugoslavia from the early 1960s. In the early twenty-first century the supermarket became a showroom for expensive cars. There has, however, remained one constant on this little square. In front of the car showroom stands an oak tree, under the protection of the state, which has been here on this spot as a witness to all change since the time of Knez Miloš.

PALACE COMPLEX

There are two palaces standing side by side on King Milan Street. The first residence on this site was built by the leader of the State Council under Knez Miloš, Stojan Simić, in the 1830s, as Terazije was going through its initial building programme. His house stood just behind the palaces visible today, further back from the line of the road in the park. Knez Alexander Karađorđević bought Simić's house in 1846 for his own use.

In moving here, the new knez made a symbolic gesture by leaving Ottoman Belgrade for the site of the new development. The building, known as the Stari konak or the Old Residence, was used as private accommodation by all the nineteenth-century rulers of Serbia and housed administrative offices. It also was the place where princes and kings hosted

celebrations and official gatherings, entertaining foreign guests and Belgrade's elite society. It was decorated in an entirely European style with parquet floors and brightly-lit candelabras quite unlike more traditional tastes in furnishing.

Slobodan Bogunović remarks on the modernizing influence it had on the city:

> The running of the Old Residence in terms of palace protocol, internal furnishings and organization of rooms, represented a complete contrast with those of Miloš Obrenović in the ruler's first Belgrade residence. It was the result of social evolution and was used to encourage the adoption of cultural models other than the national. The ruling family introduced completely new types of social amusement and concepts of behaviour, which were passed on to the more prominent citizens through their required attendance at palace balls, official receptions, tea parties, concerts and other celebrations. These new forms of social ritual representing European influences slowly spread from the palace through Belgrade society.

Not all events in the Old Residence were to be pleasurable. In 1903 King Alexander Obrenović and Queen Draga were assassinated here, and Peter Karađorđević had it demolished the following year.

Milan thought the Old Residence inappropriate for official occasions when he became king, so he built a new palace in 1884. Having decided that a more impressive building was required, Milan hired the services of the architect who had built the National Theatre a few years before. The result was a stage on which to play his role. The grandiose palace provided offices and reception rooms, while he and his family continued to live in the smaller building behind. More modern public and government buildings were opened around the palace, giving the district an air of importance compared to the earlier and smaller constructions around the Town Gate—which lost its place as the focal point of the Serbian capital.

King Peter Karađorđević began work on another palace just across the park from the one built for King Milan. The result is a more sombre but statesman-like design. Construction began in 1911 but was interrupted by the war during which the unfinished building was damaged. His successor, King Alexander, finally moved into the new royal residence in

1922, where he remained until his death in 1934. Afterwards, with Alexander's son still a minor, Prince Paul ruled as regent, but rather than live in the palace he used it for different purposes and from 1936 it was the Museum of Prince Paul (Muzej Kneza Pavla).

The royal residences have since become known as the Old Palace (Stari dvor), situated toward Terazije, and New Palace (Novi dvor), next to Andrić Crescent. After the Second World War Yugoslavia was declared a republic from which the former royal family was banned and their property nationalized. The Old Palace has become the building for the Council of the City of Belgrade, while the New Palace is the office of the President of Serbia.

PERFORMING ARTS

Two types of early music and theatre had developed in medieval Serbia, one in the life of village communities and another in the life of religious orders. In villages the performers of oral ballads formed a troubadour class, singing and playing in public places and on other occasions to smaller audiences. The performances were centred on the single player for whom no special building, stage or any kind of infrastructure was needed. There was also an embryonic secular theatre, but like most other public manifestations of Serbian culture it disappeared with the conquest of the region by the Ottoman Empire.

Church art was not entirely cut off from secular activities. Yet the Church held a position of social and moral authority, which it exercised partly through its special rituals that maintained some distance from the everyday experience of the bulk of the population. This distance was an integral part of the mechanism that perpetuated its authority, allowing the Church and its representatives to minister to their flock but not be absorbed by them. The Church fostered what might be regarded as its own theatre of heavenly beauty, pageantry and splendour in divine service, which was accompanied by its own kind of music and chanting originating in the traditions of the Byzantine Empire.

Devotional music played an important part in the early Church but did not survive as performance art in public. Developments in these fields became possible again for those Serbs who fled north at the end of the seventeenth century and established small semi-autonomous communities in the borderlands of the Habsburg Empire. Sremski Karlovci was the centre of the Serbian Church and, therefore, of cultural life among the Serbs of Vojvodina. The Byzantine traditions of church singing and music were practised here and later exported south over the border into Serbia. Secular music as performance art, on the other hand, was slow to develop. The centres of European music were in the West or Russia, and their influence could only spread through foreigners who were attracted to work in Belgrade, or by sending students to be educated abroad.

One of the first promoters of music in Belgrade was Davorin Jenko (1835-1914) from Slovenia who was responsible for musical arrangements at the National Theatre for some thirty years. Stevan Stojanović Mokranjac (1856-1914) played a highly important role as a composer, an arranger of music and in particular as one of the founders of the Belgrade Choral Society of which he was director. Blending the traditions of both folk and church music, he enjoyed much success at home and abroad with tours of Bulgaria, Croatia, Montenegro, Turkey, Russia and in 1899 Berlin, Dresden and Leipzig. The Belgrade Opera was founded in 1920 and the Belgrade Philharmonic in 1923.

Stefan Hristić (1885-1958) studied in Leipzig, Paris, Moscow and Rome before taking a leading part in promoting the musical life of the city as a director of the Opera, a conductor and composer. The efforts of people like him received an unexpected boost after the Russian Revolution of 1917 since Belgrade was one of the destinations for many fleeing the Bolsheviks. The refugees included singers and musicians who were only too willing to contribute their talents to the benefit of the host community. Performances of ballets, operas and concerts were supported in the city, staged by permanent companies and with frequent touring groups from abroad. It was common practice among the new middle class to hire private tutors for learning foreign languages and playing musical instruments. These activities were regarded as simply part of what every child should receive in order to be fit for adult life. A Czech pianist and teacher of music, Emil Hajek (1886-1974), came to Belgrade to work in the Stanković Music School, and in the 1930s was one of the founders of the city's Academy of Music (Muzička akademija), which offered higher level instruction in all areas of playing, singing and composing and helped to bring musical arts to an international level.

The beginning of modern Serbian theatre, like music, emerged from Sremski Karlovci in the eighteenth century. The freedom of Serbia in the first half of the nineteenth century encouraged theatre people to cross the border into the principality ruled by Knez Miloš. Joakim Vujić (1772-1847) founded the first theatre in Kragujevac in 1835 of which he was manager, producer, actor, translator and director of dramatic works, staging plays by mostly foreign playwrights.

The premiere of the first public dramatic performance in Belgrade was in late October 1841, attended by the young Knez Mihailo Obrenović. The event was an entertainment with acting and singing based on the folk ballad "Prince Marko and the Arab" (Kraljević Marko i Arapin) held in one of the ground-floor warehouses of the Đumrukana, the customs warehouse on the Sava quayside. This was Belgrade's first professional company and only lasted one year but in that time performed some 55 plays, including one by the most accomplished Serbian dramatist of his day, Jovan Sterija Popović.

Popović was born in Vršac, and attended grammar schools in Sremski Karlovci, Timişoara and Pest before studying law. He returned to his home town where he first taught Latin and then opened a law practice. Like many intellectuals from Vojvodina, driven by patriotic feelings, he decided to work in Serbia. Spending the years 1840-48 in Belgrade, he taught in the newly opened Lycée and then transferred to the Ministry of Education. He was active in the cultural life of the principality, supporting among other projects the founding of the Society for Serbian Literary Education. He was recognized as one of the leading educated Serbs of his day, following in the footsteps of Dositej Obradović, and remained in contact with all other major figures involved in the cultural development of the young country such as Vuk Karadžić. He wrote textbooks for the first generation of pupils in grammar school, essays, literary criticism, poems, stories, novels and plays. He also wrote historical tragedies with more than a hint of Shakespearean influence in his combination of court intrigues and struggle for power with familial rivalries. Many of these works were based on figures from Serbian medieval history such as his *The Death of Stefan Dečanski* (Smrt Stefana Dečanskog), first performed in the Đumrukana in 1841.

The critics welcomed each of his serious works, but were less enthusiastic about his comedies, although they are the part of his repertoire that has remained popular today. He had a talent for spotting the comic element in human failings and placing this in a context where a tragic undercurrent flowed just below the surface. He clearly owes a debt to Molière, many of whose plays he translated into Serbian. The topicality of his vain, ambitious, self-serving, characters in a society beset with great historical changes has kept returning to the Belgrade stage, each generation finding in his bitter-sweet portrayals elements of contemporary life.

In one of his later plays, *The Patriots* (Rodoljupci), he turns to the attempt by the Serbs of Vojvodina to come out from under the shadow of their more powerful Hungarian neighbours in 1848. He depicted the failure of the revolution to be a result of false patriotism, political lies and the manipulation of the national ideal by men greedy for wealth and power. He was rational and satirical in equal measure, showing both the farcical and tragic features of his own time.

Belgrade's theatre-going public had to wait a long time for another singular talent like Popović, until the arrival of Branislav Nušić. He dominated the Belgrade stage for much of his life, and his work is still in demand by theatre audiences. He was born in Belgrade and began writing before he reached his twentieth birthday. In his youth he was not only a prolific writer but also earned himself a reputation as a political dissident, a supporter of radical reform. The authorities took exception to some of his writing and he spent a short period behind bars. On his release he was sent out of the way, as consul for Serbia in Macedonia and Kosovo, still provinces of the Ottoman Empire. He worked in these offices for some ten years before returning to the capital, no longer a man of the opposition but transformed into a supporter of the establishment. He found it easier to get his work published and performed, and to find employment such as dramatist and assistant to the Director of the National Theatre in Belgrade, Director of the National Theatre in Novi Sad, and librarian in the National Assembly.

Nušić's early work was noted for its satirical social comment and criticism of the establishment, largely absent from his later phase. He also wrote humorous stories and comments on daily life in the capital as a columnist for the daily press. Such writing probably only served to reinforce the views of the official critics that he was, in fact, a superficial talent. During the First World War he retreated with the army on their dangerous route through Albania to reach Corfu, as did many intellectuals from the capital who did not wish to remain in an occupied city.

After the war he returned a broken man, having lost his only son in the fighting. This sense of loss moved him to retire from public life for much of the 1920s but he bounced back and again followed a writing career toward the end of his life. In 1933 he became a member of the Serbian Academy of Sciences and Arts where in his acceptance speech he spoke mainly about the work of his predecessor Jovan Sterija Popović, acknowledging his debt to the great man.

In Nušić's best plays humour and comedy are always mixed with some satirical feature, as is often the case in Popović's works. One of his first plays was *The Member of the National Assembly* (Narodni poslanik, 1883) in which a candidate for the government and a candidate for the opposition find themselves not only under the same roof but also about to be joined through marriage as father-in-law and son-in-law. The election campaign and wedding plans proceed apace, interfering one with the other. Another of his more famous plays is *Mrs. Minister* (Gospođa Ministarka, 1929). The plot concerns Živka Popović whose husband unexpectedly becomes a minister in a rapid change of government. She is not used to the high life and most of the comedy comes from her making a fool of herself.

Nušić provided a preface to this work in which he describes his dramatic intentions, and which is included in the English edition of his plays *Three Comedies*. He wrote that there is a line cutting across society that marks the limits of normal behaviour. Some people rise above this line and contribute great things to the social good, while some fall below the line and commit crimes against the general interest. Those who rise above the norm or fall below its expectations live life in a heightened state of emotion and excitement, and it is these people who usually generate dramatic form. The majority of us, however, live in the middle ground, hovering around the line where not much happens to stir the blood. He finishes by saying, "Well, I have taken by the hand a good wife and housekeeper from this middle ground, Mrs Živka Popović, and led her suddenly and unexpectedly above her normal way of life. For such people, altering the weights in the scales of their normal lives can cause them to lose their balance so badly that they can hardly stay upright on their feet. Therein lies the content of *Mrs. Minister* and the whole simple reason for the problems it reveals."

THE EVOLUTION OF FILM

While theatre came late to Belgrade, film arrived relatively quickly. It was only a matter of months after the first moving picture show in Paris by the Lumière brothers that one of their representatives, André Carré, arranged the first screenings in Belgrade in 1896. One of his evenings was attended by the king himself, Alexander Obrenović, and his mother, Queen Natalija. Carré returned to Belgrade a year later where he made the first films in the Balkans. These films were not made as dramatic enactments but simply by putting a camera in front of people moving in the street and capturing them going about their everyday business. The whole idea of being able to watch oneself, or one's fellow-citizens, on a screen was in itself a sufficient novelty. Carré's films were of people walking in Kalemegdan, of trams on Terazije, and of workers coming out of a tobacco factory. Unfortunately, none of these has survived down the years. His films were screened in kafanas and in tents like at a fairground, with the first permanent cinema opening in 1909 soon followed by others.

The oldest surviving film from Belgrade in the early twentieth century is of King Peter's coronation in 1904. It was made by two Englishmen from Sheffield: Arnold M. Wilson and Frank Mottershow. Wilson was a solicitor and the honorary Serbian consul in the northern steel town. He was invited to the coronation and took with him a local cameraman. Mottershow was one of the founders of English cinema as a dramatic art, but at this stage of his career he was, like most of his contemporaries in the early world of films, a maker of documentaries. No filming took place inside the Cathedral where the coronation took place, but there are many images of the parade before and after the event with the great and good of the military, Church and government winding their way through the city streets on foot, on horseback and in carriages. The short documentary concludes with a military display where Peter appears very regal astride an imposing white horse observing a mock cavalry charge.

The film provides a valuable visual record of Belgrade at the time. It opens with a long panning shot over the district of Savamala, looking over the Sava and following its course towards the confluence with the Danube. Then, interspersed with the parade, Mottershow captures images of ordinary people as they walk through the streets to attend and watch the spectacle. Curious passers-by stop and stare into the camera, doff a hat or smile broadly as if consciously acting for the cameraman from Sheffield. The people on the street represent all social groups and all sections of the community. Well-dressed gentlemen and ladies whose suits, dresses and fine hats would not have been out of place in any other European capital walk alongside other people dressed as if just arrived from a village: men are in homespun clothes with loose-fitting shirts and baggy trousers called *čakšire*; women wear heavily embroidered skirts and head-scarves; both sexes have *opanci* on their feet, long pointed shoes curling up at the tip. These scenes offer images of the city on the cusp between tradition and modernity.

The first Belgrade film producers were also the owners of the first cinema houses, supplying themselves with material for screening to their paying customers. Their work consisted of not much more than taking a camera into the street and shooting events as they happened. In 1911 one of these producer-owners made the first feature film. Teaming up with Louis de Berry, a French cameraman, Svetozar Botorić financed and screened a movie based on the life and exploits of the leader of the First Serbian Uprising, Karađorđe. The veteran actor, Čiča Ilija Stanojević from the National Theatre, directed the enterprise and took the starring role. Other members of the cast were also drawn from the National's company. The story as told in the film is taken from a number of sources: a play by Miloš Cvetić, historical and biographical works about the Serbian leader and the folk poem "The Start of the Revolt against the Dahijas".

The film includes all the narrative motifs associated with the leader's life and death. Karađorđe kills his first Turk while still a boy and shoots his father for refusing to cross the river into Habsburg territory when an earlier rebellion failed. He eventually returns to Serbia and initially refuses the leadership of the 1804 Uprising. The Dahijas draw a bowl of water from the Danube which they take to the Nebojša Tower and foresee their own grisly fate in it. The rebels are successful, but they are finally defeated and there is only one possible end; Karađorđe is murdered by agents of his rival, Miloš Obrenović. The actors and directors were heavily influenced in their craft by their experience in theatre performance, although there are interesting moments when dramatic tension is heightened through the use of editing and cutting techniques to show dream sequences or simultaneous actions.

The film had its premiere in Belgrade on 23 October 1911 and its last recorded screening was to Serbian emigrants in the United States in 1928 after which it disappeared without trace. It was rediscovered in the Austrian film archives, Vienna, in July 2003 by Aleksandar Erdeljanović and Radoslav Zelenović on behalf of the Yugoslav Cinema Archive (Jugoslovenska kinoteka). The film was re-mastered and broadcast on Belgrade television, giving an opportunity after many decades to see one of the milestones in the development of cinema in the Balkans.

Other producers of early Serbian cinema were the Savić brothers, responsible for the next feature film to come from the nascent Belgrade studios in 1912, *The Woeful Mother* (Jadna majka). The home community expanded its scope in the production process and moved on from providing finance and actors to the technical side when Slavko Jovanović became the first Serb cameraman and worked on projects with Botorić and the Savić brothers. The First World War and occupation of the city brought a halt to Belgrade's film industry. The Serbian army, however, in its camp on Corfu developed its own film section, which was later used for propaganda purposes after launching its offensive from Thessalonica and advancing north into Serbia.

After the First World War Belgrade was the centre of film production in the Kingdom of Serbs, Croats and Slovenes, although filmmakers faced fierce competition from abroad. Imports from France, Germany and in particular from the rapidly expanding Hollywood studios were of superior quality and cheaper. To combat the problem, a new law was enacted in 1931 to oblige cinemas to show a proportion of home products, stimulating domestic studios with the release of, for example, Mihajlo Al. Popović's 1932 feature *With Faith in God* (Sa verom u Boga). Nevertheless, foreign imports began to creep back in their former numbers. The issue of *Politika* published on the day of the German bombing of Belgrade in 1941 contains numerous advertisements from Belgrade's cinemas showing Hungarian, Russian, French and Hollywood films—with not a single Serbian film available. Influence from abroad went much deeper, and many of the city's picture palaces have westernized names like Luksor, Koloseum, Siti (City), Rex, alongside the more Slavonic-sounding places like Slavija, Avala, Balkan and Drina.

LITERARY CRITICS AND BELGRADE STYLE

The ascension of King Peter to the Serbian throne coincided with, or perhaps in some way stimulated, a sudden growth in cultural activity and a rush towards modernity. The nineteenth-century village stories of Laza Lazarević and the Realists became a thing of the past. Greater literary contacts opened up between Belgrade and the wider world, especially Paris.

Most writers at the beginning of the twentieth century regarded a stay in the French capital as a necessary part of their literary education. Furthermore, Belgrade was beginning to attract people whose professional lives were tightly bound to the cultural life of the city. Some were book-binders and printers, with commercial interests in the production and sale of journals and books. Others were editors and critics interested in the promotion of culture, aesthetic values and literary tastes. The founding of the University of Belgrade was an important development, giving added impetus to the education of future generations who would continue to support and contribute to the arts.

Two of the foremost names in this field were themselves professors of literature at the new university: Bogdan Popović (1864-1944) and Jovan Skerlić (1877-1914). Both men were born in Belgrade, and their work signalled the city's leadership of Serbian cultural aspirations, rather than the Vojvodina community of Serbs. Popović studied literature in the Great School and in Paris. Returning home in 1893, he took up the position of Professor of Literature in his alma mater, and then transferred to the new university when it opened in 1905 and stayed until his retirement in 1934. He was a man of great learning and analytical consistency. His approach was to examine the internal working of the text, what makes art a special category of human experience and of creative expression. He had a deep and sincere belief in the influence of literature on the soul and mind as a source of inspiration. For him, this was the realm where language was able to reveal not empirical truths but symbolic truths that might point to greater understanding of the human condition. In his teaching and writing he tried to develop these qualities in his students and the reading public, to raise their aesthetic awareness. In the twentieth century Popović's legacy has reasserted itself on occasions as a contrast to the Yugoslav communists' utilitarian approaches towards culture and the purpose of art in society.

Popović published his *Anthology of Modern Serbian Lyric* (Antologija novije srpske lirike) in 1911, the first attempt to create a literary canon of the most significant poems down the ages. He chose examples that reveal a consistent and highly developed poetic expression as the hallmark of Serbian literary achievement. He distanced poetry from the folk heritage, proposing an alternative view of sophisticated forms with a broad poetic range and insight into the kind of understanding art offers. He founded the *Serbian Literary Herald* (Srpski književni glasnik) in 1901, the most noted journal for literature and art of its day. It ceased publication for the duration of the First World War, but continued after the liberation of Belgrade until the beginning of the Second World War. All important writers published their work in its pages, while the magazine also included reviews, criticism and general articles on film, foreign literature, feminism and women's writing. Popović believed in a broad church and provided a forum for all tastes and movements in literature and art, committing his life and work to nurturing this area of human activity.

Jovan Skerlić was much younger and died suddenly on the eve of the First World War. He was one of Popović's pupils in the Great School until leaving for Lausanne from where he returned with a doctorate in French literature. He first taught French at the institution where he had been educated, before becoming Professor of Serbian Literature when the university was established. He collaborated with his mentor on the editorial board of the *Serbian Literary Herald*, becoming chief editor for a time.

Skerlić's opinions differed in some ways from those of Popović. While also appreciating the finer points of art and aesthetics, he placed greater emphasis on the moral and social influence of literature as one of the vital weapons in the armoury of the nation. Skerlić was more of a political animal, taking an active role as a member of the National Assembly and helping to shape the society of which he was a part. He published scholarly articles and books, including the most thorough history of Serbian literature at that time, *History of Modern Serbian Literature* (Istorija nove srpske književnosti, 1914).

In this historical study Skerlić dates the beginnings of modern Serbian literature from the cultural achievements of the Serbs in Vojvodina during the eighteenth century, and in particular the role of Dositej Obradović. He closes his vast work with an analysis of contemporary culture and the strong affinities between Serbs and Croats. For him, the study of the history of literature was an important part of history in general, touching on matters of cultural and national identity. He considered that there was a future for the South Slavs in a political union, although there would have to be compromises on all sides if this state was to come into existence. He recognized the historic, linguistic and other affinities between Serbs and Croats, and also their differences. Yet it was the common identity that was crucial, underpinned by both communities as members of the same European family of nations, and thus capable of living together in cultural and political union. He was an idealist in his vision and a pragmatist in debate whose ideas were both realized and undone during the twentieth century. Belgrade entered the modern age very much under the cultural and literary direction of these two men. They produced an image of Serbia as an urban, sophisticated and cosmopolitan land, confident in the new architectural contours of the city and its busy streets. Its literature, for so long dragging behind the western models that most writers aspired to follow, was put on an equal footing with more established centres in France, Russia, Germany and Britain.

The contribution of Popović and Skerlić was essential not only in the sphere of literary output and attention to critical detail but also for the development of the modern language. The Serbian language was codified according to the norms proposed by Vuk Karadžić in the middle of the nineteenth century. Yet the drive towards a sense of European modernity reinvigorated the whole idiom of the contemporary Serbian language. Its vocabulary was extended, expression was clarified, sentence structures became simpler, and the focus fell on the need to produce a logically developed syntactic flow. Word order was liberated from the stifling tendency to place verbs at the end of their clause or sentence. This older tendency produced a somewhat staccato effect in the rhythm of the standard written form that was not at all natural to the language, being imported from the written and spoken norms of German. In short, the Serbian language became capable of more flexible expression, more urban and more urbane, an instrument fit for a complex social organization. This reformed way of writing and speaking was termed the Belgrade style (beogradski stil) and is regarded as one of the signs marking the passage of Serbian culture and society into the twentieth century.

LITERATURE BEFORE THE FIRST WORLD WAR

Belgrade literature developed at a rapid pace at the turn of the twentieth century. Its first poets in the new age were influenced by French trends and styles, but very quickly found their own idiom. Two distinct camps appeared with, on the one hand, Jovan Dučić (1874-1943) and Milan Rakić (1876-1939); on the other, Sima Pandurović (1883-1960) and Vladislav Petković-Dis (1880-1917). The first two were employed in the diplomatic service and wrote harmonious poems with great attention to the intricacies of metre and rhythm. They were known for their chiselled verses and finely tuned lines. For them, poetry was a challenge to create a sense of melody and elegance in language.

The second pair, from a slightly younger generation, were the *enfants terribles* of their literary world. Vladislav Petković chose his appellation "Dis" as a repetition of the middle syllable of his first name, but also as the name of the Roman god of the underworld. He was a frequent evening visitor to the city's kafanas in Skadarlija and elsewhere where he would drink and compose new verses at the same time. Both Pandurović and Dis were great poets, concerned to capture and project the poetic image even at the expense of the harmony sought by Dučić and Rakić. Their work was also decidedly pessimistic, open to the darker sides of humanity. In one of his more censorious moments Skerlić judged their poetry to be harmful to the health of the national community for whom it was more important to face the future with optimism. Popović was less inclined to dismiss the work of the young poets and included in his 1911 *Anthology* two of Pandurović's poems, one of which has the title "Svetkovina" meaning a holiday, particularly a religious festival. The lines evoke a scene in a lunatic asylum, beginning with the sonorously disturbing: "We went out of our minds one fine day" (Sišli smo s uma u sjajan dan). The poem was published in a collection called *Funereal Honours* (Posmrtne počasti) from 1908. Dis's 1911 collection *Drowned Souls* (Utopljene duše) has an odd sense of foreboding as the poet himself died when a boat on which he was travelling in the Adriatic Sea in 1917 was torpedoed by an Italian warship.

Besides poetry, new prose writers in Belgrade helped expand urbanized literary tastes with themes more in tune with their day, for example Radoje Domanović (1873-1908). Writing humorous and satirical stories, he is particularly remembered for his "Prince Marko for the Second Time among the Serbs" (Kraljević Marko po drugi put među Srbima). Re-inventing the folk hero Prince Marko, Domanović places him in the modern world. Hearing the wails and laments of his fellow Serbs, Marko asks permission from God to return to earth that he might help them. His wish is granted, and the brave and strong Marko finds himself in Belgrade. Unfortunately, his way of dealing with situations—by striking his enemies with his heavy mace—is not appreciated either by the authorities or by ordinary men and women in the street.

Writers were beginning to produce an independent expression of their own urban experience in these new works, and it was not long before the term "Belgrade prose" (beogradska proza) was adopted to refer to this trend in which the city played an important function, not just as the setting for action but almost as an actor itself. Large numbers of people were attracted to the capital city in the decade before the First World War taking advantage of the new institutions of higher learning, looking for employment, and chasing dreams. The writer Milutin Uskoković (1884-1915) was one such in-comer, working as a journalist on *Politika* and publishing stories and novels. His novel *The Newcomers* (Došljaci) appeared in 1910 and was the first serious attempt to give literary form to these events and to utilize the contemporary city as a setting. Jovan Skerlić in his history of Serbian literature welcomed this development and commented on Uskoković's achievement in glowing terms: "In *The Newcomers* he has given the hitherto best Belgrade novel, with faithful reproductions of various Belgrade scenes, troubled life in a young capital, the feverish struggle in a society not yet properly ordered, beautiful and vibrant descriptions of the Belgrade landscape."

The city is a magnet attracting unsuspecting men and women from the provinces with its vague promise of a better life, only then to destroy their hopes by making them live in a way for which they are hardly prepared. Uskoković focuses on this new life waiting for them, the development of Belgrade as a metropolitan centre with none of the comforting securities of a smaller community. Belgrade itself is a key symbol in the clash between urban and patriarchal civilizations in the new Serbia. One of the characters from a small Serbian provincial town says,

> We all, more or less, came here with honest intentions. But we were all also, more or less, without means. The temptation was still greater, because we did not know the world around us. We thought that no-one knows us and so it was easier for us to do things of which we would have been ashamed in our town, in our own home.

Miloš is the main character in *The Newcomers*, arriving from Užice to take a job as a reporter on a Belgrade newspaper. One day he is sent to cover the story of a young woman who has committed suicide but while visiting the house where she lived and researching her story, he meets another young woman, Zorka, and they begin a secret affair. This is the first time that sexual attraction is a motivating factor in the action of a Serbian novel. They meet in parks and public places, confident that a large city promises them anonymity and that they are unlikely to be recognized by a casual passer-by. The sheer mass of the population allows them their clandestine liaisons, in contrast to predominantly village locations in earlier literature.

Miloš has literary ambitions and writes a play that is hugely successful, but in which Zorka recognizes his resistance to the idea of their marriage. As an act of extreme self-sacrifice she commits suicide by throwing herself into the Danube. Miloš decides that Belgrade is an environment too hostile to newcomers, encouraging depravity, dishonesty and the break-up of family values. He feels defeated by the city and wants to return home, to his provincial small town and slower pace of life. At the end of the novel he walks with a friend to the railway station and observes the crowds filling the streets, simply commenting, "The large shop windows of the fashionable Belgrade stores were luxuriously illuminated." This is a world in which life spills out into the streets, parks and public squares in all the corners of the city. He once regarded this carnival atmosphere as an attractive opportunity, but now sees it as a lonely and alienating experience, a faceless existence. Belgrade takes an active role in determining the limits of human agency. Characters are forced to confront its challenges, adapt to its values, and struggle to understand its multi-accented landscape.

LITERATURE AFTER THE FIRST WORLD WAR

By the end of 1918 Belgrade was the newly liberated capital of the much larger Kingdom of Serbs, Croats and Slovenes. Lena A. Jovičić in her book *Pages from Here and There in Serbia* gives many little portraits of Belgrade from this time. Writing after the First World War, she relates the damage caused by siege, years of enemy occupation and the fierce fighting that occurred when the city was retaken by Serbian forces. Moreover, she describes the rebuilding programme which transformed the city:

> The extraordinary building epidemic which held sway for several years after the war, resulted in the town being completely transformed. It not only meant reconstruction, but, one may say, a new city was raised in place of the old one. With unparalleled speed, houses appeared like mushrooms after rain, and although this was but the first step in the

great evolution destined to emerge from a heap of ruins, the subsequent stages of progress still continue in a striking manner.

Miloš Crnjanski was also in Belgrade during the early post-war years and left behind his impressions in his 1929 article "Post-war Literature: Literary Memoirs" (Posleratna književnost: literarna sećanja). Arriving in 1919, he recalls the legacy of war: "Belgrade, full of holes and ruins and weeds, sensational political events, the return of writers from all corners of the world, uncertainty..." He later adds: "It was not yet possible to speak of any kind of literary atmosphere, public, and the like in Belgrade. It was still without water, lighting, it was wrecked and ugly..."

Although the city was largely preoccupied with the consequences of the war, Crnjanski found a small but enthusiastic collection of writers, painters and musicians, anxious to provide the city with a new beginning in art and culture who called themselves simply the Group of Artists (Grupa umetnika). They met in the kafana of the Hotel Moskva because, according to Crnjanski, it was the only place with light. They represented the cream of the avant-garde, uniting both the pre-war and post-war generations. It was here that Crnjanski met Sima Pandurović, whom he greatly admired and from whom he learned about Jovan Skerlić and Vladislav Petković-Dis. He got to know Bogdan Popović and published some of his first poems in the new series of the *Serbian Literary Herald*. He mentions the names of almost all the artists associated with Belgrade Modernism whose careers began around those tables in the Hotel Moskva such as Rastko Petrović, Ivo Andrić, Stanislav Vinaver, the essayist Branko Lazarević, and others. Belgrade was in ruins but this small group reinvigorated the art scene during its short span of activity with poetry readings, literary evenings, exhibitions, concerts, debates and polemics.

Members of the Group of Artists were behind the publication of little magazines that were a feature of literary life in those years across Europe and North America. These journals were founded with the intention of promoting one set of ideas about poetry or art, in support of one of the numerous "-isms" in fashion in those heady days. They provided an outlet for a small group to publish their poetry or articles which were then read by a slightly larger group of people who shared more or less the same views, until the group would split up in order to form new constellations in support of slightly different ideas.

The atmosphere was charged with a dynamic interest in the power of modern art. The artists wanted to shock the comfortable middle classes out of conventional approaches to culture with their antics and to see how far they could take their avant-garde experiments and eccentricities. Rastko Petrović in one of his travel articles after a trip to Africa describes a totem, symbol of a heathen religion, and compares it to the image of Christ on the cross. The piece appeared in one of those magazines, *Paths* (Putevi), of which Crnjanski was an editor during the early 1920s. The Serbian Orthodox Church was suitably horrified and threatened to excommunicate Petrović until he printed a retraction and apology.

The journals may seem from this distance to be minor by-products of the day, but they performed an invaluable function in promoting interest in the cultural life of the city and connecting it to the outside world. Some of them survived longer than others and became highly respected such as *Zenith* (Zenit) edited by Ljubomir Micić (1895-1971) from 1921 to 1926 and renowned for its excellent coverage of modern trends abroad.

The interwar period was remarkable for the way in which Serbian art and literature captured the same radical spirit found elsewhere in Europe and North America. There was also a group of poets who dedicated themselves to promoting Surrealism in Belgrade. Theorizing the experiments by the French poet André Breton and others, the *Surrealist Manifesto* appeared in Belgrade just a few months after its publication in Paris. The main local exponents were Dušan Matić (1898-1980), Marko Ristić (1902-84) and Milan Dedinac (1902-66), later joined by Oskar Davičo (1909-89). They were extremely active in all areas of literary and cultural life. Ristić and Dedinac, in addition to their poetry, were also known as publicists, writing about Surrealism rather than just practising it for themselves.

As in France, the Belgrade Surrealists were politically on the left and fellow-travellers of the Communist Party. Literary life, in particular, became fraught during the 1930s with polemical attacks from both sides of the political spectrum. Crnjanski and others expressed more right-wing views, which were to return to haunt them after the Second World War when the communists came to power and they found themselves condemned as enemies of the new regime.

The pre-war trend of the Belgrade novel also continued in the 1920s and 1930s in works by, among others, Rastko Petrović, Branimir Ćosić and Stevan Jakovljević. These reflect the consequences of rapid urban and commercial development leaving people caught between two cultures, two worlds of tradition and modernity. Much of the action in them is determined by the clash of patriarchal values and the new demands of the urban environment. Characteristic themes continued to highlight the breakdown of family life and the damage caused by excessive greed and materialist values.

The story of Branimir Ćosić's *The Two Empires* (Dva carstva, 1928) is quite typical. The main character is the son of a secondary-school teacher whose ambition is to make a name for himself and enter Belgrade's high society. His actions are conditioned by the way in which he lives in the city and what it expects of him. Beginning a love affair with a married woman, he hopes to further his aims through her social connections. At the same time, he befriends his lover's husband and is then caught between desire for her and a sense of moral obligation arising from his friendship with her spouse. The solution is found only when the three of them are staying away from Belgrade's corrosive influence in a monastery. The hero is helped by one of the monks to confront his conscience and he returns cleansed of the corruption of the city.

These kinds of stories gradually became predictable as a literary form, increasingly relying on sentimental and stereotypical characters and situations. By the advent of Second World War they were often wooden constructs, lacking the ability to shock their readership and capture the essence of a new social and cultural experience.

Literary and cultural life in Belgrade from 1900 to 1940 was a lively affair reflecting the city's growth in the modern world. Belgrade was witness to new forms of expression for the new urban experience in theatre, music, film and literature, with trends and styles reflecting contemporary tastes abroad. Citizens of Belgrade could travel around Europe or North America and feel equally as if in their own home. The city's institutional infrastructure and the ability of its artists to experiment with form and to develop their own poetic and prose traditions identified Belgrade as one of the new cultural centres on the old continent. Belgrade was learning to tell its own story, a narrative about a city and its citizens facing the challenges of the modern world after a somewhat shaky beginning. It was a society growing in self-confidence, adopting ideas from others and supporting its own indigenous artistic flair.

Chapter Five

KING ALEXANDER BOULEVARD
AND TAŠMAJDAN:
THE RISING STAR OF COMMUNISM

THE SECOND WORLD WAR AND LIBERATION OF BELGRADE

Prince Paul tried to keep Yugoslavia out of the Second World War for as long as possible. He never expected to become regent and felt it proper that such momentous decisions as war or peace should be taken by Alexander's legitimate heir, Peter, who would become of age late in 1941. But he could not keep the threat at bay for ever. Italy had significant interests in Yugoslavia and south-eastern Europe generally. It had been awarded territory after the First World War in Dalmatia and the Istrian Peninsula, home to large numbers of Croats. Albania became an Italian client state.

With an eye to expanding his influence in the region, Mussolini invaded Greece in 1941. The campaign did not go as well as hoped and he turned to Hitler for help. The quickest route for German troops to support the Italians in Greece was to cross Yugoslavia and immediate overtures were sent to Paul to allow the army's passage. Prevarication was no longer an option, but the prince faced a difficult choice. He had strong Anglophile leanings, but could not expect help from Britain at the time. There was little popular support for an alliance with Germany. Serbia in particular maintained its traditional support for France, which was now a defeated country in the war. On a personal level, his wife was herself from the Greek royal family. Yet if he refused to cooperate with Hitler, he would place Yugoslavia in danger. In the end, he was forced to sign a pact with the Axis Powers in Vienna on 25 March 1941.

Reaction in Belgrade was swift and Paul was ousted in a coup led by General Dušan Simović supported by the army during the night of 26/27 March. Large numbers of demonstrators took to the streets chanting *Bolje rat nego pakt* (better war than the pact) and *Bolje grob nego rob* (better the grave than a slave).

In his play *Prince Paul* (Knez Pavle, 1991), Slobodan Selenić focuses on the dilemma faced by the regent, particularly his personal predicament, and even goes so far to suggest that Britain may have had a hand in persuading the army to act. There is, however, no historical evidence to support the claim. Winston Churchill welcomed the events in Belgrade, announcing,

> Early this morning the Yugoslav nation found its soul. A revolution has taken place in Belgrade, and the Ministers who but yesterday signed away the honour and freedom of the country are reported to be under arrest. This patriotic movement arises from the wrath of a valiant and warlike race at the betrayal of their country by the weakness of their rulers and the foul intrigues of the Axis powers.

Alexander's son, Peter, was declared to be of age, six months short of his eighteenth birthday, and Prince Paul went into exile in Kenya. Hitler was enraged and vowed to bring ruin to Yugoslavia. The German air force bombed Belgrade on 6 April, a land invasion followed, and final victory came quickly when Yugoslavia surrendered on 17 April. The bombing campaign was as vicious as it was unexpected. Miodrag Pavlović's poem "Belgrade 1941" (Beograd 1941, 1977) expresses the outrage, horror and fear instilled by the brutality of the attack on the city:

> With a torch between its legs
> a foul insect flies around
> setting fire to houses
> > skins
> > cemeteries
> books turn to bubbles
> birds ask themselves
> if people are cold
> to light all those fires
> the town quickly gathers
> its own ruins
> trees clutch at their heads
> who's this who dares
> take the apocalypse
> into his own hands?

Peter and his ministers fled the country and eventually formed a government-in-exile in London. The country was immediately dismembered with Germany, Italy and their allies, Hungary and Bulgaria, each taking a share of its territory. Croatia became an independent state under the Ustaše led by Ante Pavelić, who conducted a brutal campaign of terror and liquidation against Serbs, Jews and gypsies. Serbia was reduced to its borders from before the Balkan Wars, with a quisling government under General Milan Nedić although real authority was with the occupying German forces. Belgrade became a frontier town once more, looking out at Zemun, now in the independent state of Croatia, and Vojvodina as part of Hungary.

The Belgrade-born film director, Dušan Makavejev, known in the West for, among others, his film *W. R.: Mysteries of the Organism* (W.R.-Misterije organizma, 1971), was a boy when the war began. He recalls the bombing and later occupation of the city:

> Then the incendiary bombs began to fall, the National Library was burned down, as was a third of the city, all the bridges destroyed, the young King in flight. The German Wehrmacht arrived in town. Buildings were cut in half. Once they were opened up, you could see dining tables, chandeliers, pictures untouched on the wall, here a dentist's surgery, there a bathroom with its tub. In the first days of the occupation there was neither water nor electricity. Various smells wafted through town. A temporary public toilet was hastily opened in the interests of order and hygiene, made by joining together bomb craters in the very centre of town behind a large fence with separate entrances for men and women.

This makeshift convenience was in Terazije. Makavejev remembers other events:

> A couple of months later when they had cleaned Terazije up, five Communists were hanged from lamp-posts. A little to the left of them was an advert for the horse races, and under that, people from the town and refugees would drink beer.

Wartime Belgrade bore no relationship to the civilized pre-war city.

Elsewhere in Serbia remnants of the army continued to resist under the command of Colonel Dragoljub "Draža" Mihailović (1893-1946). The government-in-exile made him chief of staff of what loyal forces were left, but it was difficult to impose overall strategic planning. His fighters were called Četniks, after the name given to the guerrillas who used to harass the Turks. They were a disparate army split into small units and their communications in occupied Serbia were sporadic. Leader of a Serbian rather than Yugoslav resistance group and loyal to the king, Mihailović was convinced of a future Allied victory. His policy was to wait, holding his soldiers in reserve to support the inevitable defeat of Italy and Germany in Europe. In some areas the Četniks disbanded altogether, in others they formed temporary alliances with the occupying forces in order to take revenge for Ustaše atrocities against Serbs, or to fight against their ideological opponents in the alternative resistance movement, the Partisans, led by the Communist Party of Yugoslavia and Josip Broz Tito.

The Partisans were eventual victors in the complex Yugoslav conflict—a mixture of resistance to outside invaders and internecine civil war—and have been awarded credit for most of the armed activity against Axis troops. Mihailović's policy proved to be a mistake as he was unable to control those who ostensibly accepted his authority—for which he paid the price. Captured by the security service of the new communist state, he was executed in 1946 as a collaborator.

Tito (1892-1980), real name Josip Broz, was born in the border country between Croatia and Slovenia in 1892. He fought in the First World War for the Austrians on the Eastern Front where he was captured by the enemy and taken to a prison camp in Russia. The camp was liberated by the Red Army during the 1917 revolution, and the prisoners were given freedom in return for joining the Bolsheviks. Josip Broz accepted the offer and after the revolution was sent back to Yugoslavia as a trade union organizer. He served a term in prison from 1929 to 1934 for being a member of the Communist Party, an illegal organization, and returned to the Soviet Union. As an agent of the Moscow-run Comintern, he was appointed general secretary of the Yugoslav party in 1937. Tito was one of the code names which he adopted in order to hide his true identity from the authorities.

The Yugoslav communists arranged to meet in Belgrade on 4 July 1941 to discuss resistance to the occupation. Their destination was a

modest house at 5 Botić Street in the exclusive residential area of Dedinje, belonging to Vladislav S. Ribnikar (1900-55), owner of the *Politika* newspaper and—in those desperate times—willing to help Broz against the invaders. His wife, Jara (1912-2007), a prominent writer after the war, recalled Tito's visits to their house and in particular the meeting of 4 July, when seven men arrived at the house to plan the uprising. She describes in detail the bizarre ordinariness of the occasion:

> First, they gathered in the garden, divided into small groups, sat on the grass and chatted. It was a beautiful, sunny day. The garden was empty as we had sent the children to friends for lunch, and they were to return only in the evening. We took a walk down the garden and explained the disposition of the house to those comrades who were not yet acquainted with it. It was agreed that in the event of danger they would leave via the

neighbouring estate, make their way to Dedinje Boulevard and try to save themselves. We kept guard, but nothing happened. It was exceptionally quiet. There were no unexpected callers or neighbours popping round that day. Our guests withdrew from the garden into the dining room where they continued to work. Whiffs of cigarette smoke would float out the window from time to time. They asked for a snack for lunch, and drank a great deal of black coffee. They worked without a break, very intensively, until six o'clock in the evening. Then they began to come out, cross the terrace and into the garden. They breathed in the air, satisfied, in good spirits. Comrade Tito was the first to leave. The others walked a while more in the garden, joking and behaving as if they were having a picnic.

Although they took the decision to organize the resistance in Belgrade, the heart of the Partisan movement was in the countryside. The city was occupied and not a place to wage a guerrilla war. The communists also felt uneasy in the old capital. It was not their natural habitat and it exuded the atmosphere and values of the pre-war regime and society, which they were committed to transforming. Consequently, once in power, they said little about the Belgrade experience of the war. The city was not part of their narrative, and it was not theirs to commemorate. Refugees flooded into the city from Croatia and Bosnia with stories of atrocities against Serbs. Corpses would float down the rivers, some coming to shore, victims of the Ustaše on the other bank. From the point of view of the Allies, Belgrade was a resource used by the enemy, and as such a legitimate target. In April 1944 British and American planes systematically bombed the city in a series of attacks with much greater destructive effect than the Germans in 1941. The new government after 1945 did not record the full extent of all the damage inflicted on Belgrade nor all the names of those who perished.

Belgrade was liberated by the Partisans, with the help of the Soviet Red Army, in October 1944. Fitzroy Maclean, head of the British military mission to Tito's headquarters, recorded his memories of the event in his book *Eastern Approaches*. The German army was in retreat and shelling Belgrade from Zemun as its troops tried to withdraw across the River Sava. Maclean noted the chaos in the streets, which were "crowded with civilians, some enthusiastic, some just standing and gaping. From time to time a shell would land full amongst them, killing several." He was in the company of a senior Partisan officer who was taking his guest on a tour of the city centre with no regard for the obvious dangers. Maclean attributes his guide's behaviour to his Partisan experience: "Accustomed to the hand-to-hand fighting of guerrilla warfare, long-range shelling meant little to him." They reached Kalemegdan from where he could see the enemy withdrawing across the bridge over the Sava and racing on to Zemun. For a brief moment the bridge was empty, and then immediately filled with soldiers of the Red Army in full pursuit. Maclean recounts how German attempts to destroy the bridge failed due to the efforts of one old man who spied German sappers laying explosives under it on the night of 19 October 1944 and, realizing their intentions, disconnected the charges.

The arrival of the Partisans in Belgrade was not good news for many in the capital. Besides those who had collaborated during the occupation, others who had simply continued in their work or who did not wholeheartedly welcome the new ideology of their liberators discovered that they could easily be denounced as traitors. On Monday 27 November *Politika's* front page contained the names of 105 citizens who had been shot the previous day. The charges against them were accompanied by an article justifying the executions in the name of the people; it was signed by the Surrealist poet, now politician, Marko Ristić. Many of the victims were leading members of the pre-war elite, figures who might act as focal points for opposition to the communists, and their elimination was part of the new regime's drive for mastery over the city.

The communists took to government in order to build socialism based on the Soviet model. Land, industry, transport and banks were nationalized. Elections were conducted on the basis of one list of approved candidates, giving the communists a legal mandate for their aspirations. Yet they were also genuinely popular, promising stability and some degree of normality after the years of bloodshed.

The new constitution was rooted in the 1936 constitution of the USSR. Yugoslavia was divided into six republics based on the national structure of the country: Serbia, Croatia, Bosnia, Montenegro, Macedonia and Slovenia. Serbia itself was further divided with two autonomous provinces in the north and south, Vojvodina and Kosovo. Each constituent part had its own government and capital city, but real power was tightly centralized in the hands of the Communist Party. Belgrade was the capital city of both the Republic of Serbia and of the federal government with responsibility for the whole country. Officials, military officers and bureaucrats came to live in the city from all parts of the country, making a significant impact on its demographic composition. The old Belgrade rapidly disappeared as the new elite brought with them a new ideology. The city stopped looking westward and there was no further discussion of cultural and artistic contact with London and Paris. Instead, the new regime sponsored links with the people's democracies of Eastern Europe and in particular with the first land of socialism, the USSR.

Yugoslavia was regarded in the West as one of Stalin's most loyal acolytes. But a rift soon opened between the leadership of the two countries over differences in defining their relationship. The Yugoslav communists liberated their country with little help from the Soviet Red Army and were quick to establish control over government. They were self-confident and naïve in equal measure, seeing their relationship with the Soviet Union as one of equals, as comrades in arms furthering the cause of international socialism. The Soviet Union, on the other hand, viewed its East European satellites as a buffer zone separating it from a hostile West and as markets to be exploited.

Stevan Pavlowitch in his book *The Improbable Survivor* has characterized the reason for the break as follows:

> The difference between Yugoslavia and other East European states in these post-war years lay in the extent of Tito's hold over his regime, and in his country's position bordering on the Mediterranean and on non-Communist Europe. This combination would be the cause of difficulties both with neighbours and with the Soviet Union. Because of increasing tension in Europe, Stalin wanted to prevent the development of a situation likely to cause trouble in the Communist camp that he was setting up. His need to be able to control Yugoslavia more directly because of her geopolitical position led to the break.

The main areas of frictions revolved around economic, military and foreign policies. The Soviet Union wanted to dominate Yugoslav markets by selling finished goods from its factories in return for raw materials. The two sides established joint stock companies for air and river traffic in which decisions tended to be made to the benefit of the Soviet side. From the end of the war the Soviet Union had installed military advisers in the Yugoslav armed forces. Complaints began to arrive from Belgrade that these advisers behaved in an arrogant and domineering manner. In matters of foreign policy Yugoslavia supported Soviet demands against those of the western allies, but rarely received Soviet support in return for its claims over, for example, Trieste. It rapidly became apparent that Stalin was not going to treat Yugoslavia as an equal partner, and that Yugoslavia under Tito was reluctant to accept subordination to the state interests of the Soviet Union. Stalin considered it necessary to get rid of the upstarts in Yugoslavia before other leaders in Eastern Europe began emulating them.

Matters came to a head in 1948 with Soviet criticism of the leaders of the Yugoslav Communist Party. They responded by publishing all their correspondence with the Soviet leadership, calling on the nation to defend itself against outside interference. People suspected of supporting the Soviet line were dealt with severely. Some high-ranking party members were shot while ostensibly trying to leave the country. Many others were imprisoned on the notorious island of Goli Otok, which was nothing more than an outcrop of bare rocks in the Adriatic Sea. The prison regime was extremely harsh, intended to break the spirit of anyone with pro-Soviet sympathies, forcing them to admit their guilt and to recant. Many of the inmates came from Belgrade, returning home only after several years of incarceration and inhuman and degrading treatment. Stalin's attempt to squash the Yugoslav leadership failed. The result of his action was to force the country to look westward for financial support and for reasons of state security.

TITO'S YUGOSLAVIA

The break with the Soviet Union was the defining moment in Yugoslavia's post-war development. The leadership of the Communist Party of Yugoslavia was committed to introducing a Soviet-style of government, genuinely believing in its advantages over the pre-war system. For most communists the break represented a crisis of direction in which they had to re-examine their Marxist principles. In the process many found themselves increasingly attracted to the idea of workers' co-operatives with less involvement from central administration in the day-to-day running of industry.

The first law on workers' councils was introduced in 1950. Designed to hand more responsibility for financial decisions to the factories themselves, it was a tentative move away from Soviet-style central planning in which government ministries gave out directives on matters of production, pay and investment. Some have seen this as an attempt to establish a true workers' democracy in which the state would wither away as superfluous. Fred Singleton sees a more pragmatic Tito behind the decision: "Tito did not accept the idea simply because it was a fulfilment of a Marxist dream. He did so because he saw that it suited Yugoslav conditions in 1950, by presenting to the workers a credible alternative to the Stalinism which had failed them in 1948." If the first councils were largely symbolic since real power at all levels in the country was still in the hands of the Communist Party, the system of self-management as it was termed developed through the ensuing decades and became a distinct feature of Yugoslav political identity.

Over the next 25 years self-management went through numerous changes, each stage contributing to the drive for greater decentralization and encouraging mass participation in all spheres of public life. In his book, *Self-Management on Trial*, Milojko Drulović summarizes the aims of the system "to allow the greatest possible participation of the individual in management and direct democracy". Workers elected delegates to represent their interests in the workplace. Factory councils would then elect delegates to the next tier consisting of a group of enterprises, or factories, operating locally. From there another delegation would be sent to the next tier through to the republic and federal levels, each delegate team representing the level immediately below.

A similar system operated in the political sphere beginning with the lowest tier of political representation, the communes, through to the city, republic and federal authorities. At each stage there were opportunities for delegates in the economic and political structures to meet and discuss issues of common concern. In May 1974 it was reported that some 700,000 people were serving as delegates.

In the latter stages of self-management attempts were made to include all institutions, including education and health. The Faculty of Philology at the University of Belgrade was organized like other universities around the world: academic staff elected a dean; heads of department were responsible to the dean, policy and budgets were decided at Faculty Boards, with student representation where appropriate. Another tier of delegated committees was bolted onto this fairly standard set of practices to involve others with an interest in the running of the Faculty. Ancillary staff were represented, since salaries and wages were determined by councils in a manner similar to those in factories. Delegates came from local political structures and local enterprises—as their taxes helped finance the facility—as well as from textbook publishers and other institutions in the educational sector. Agreements had to be reached by consensus, so decisions often stood for months waiting for all parties to agree a common policy. The Faculty, in the terminology of the time, was known as a Self-Managing Community of Interests. Self-management was regarded by some as a utopian aspiration of maximum democracy and by others as bureaucratic and too cumbersome to operate efficiently.

The renewed socialist Yugoslavia also turned more to the West, introducing selected aspects of free market economics, decentralizing the processes of decision-making, and handing more powers to the individual republic governments. The Communist Party changed its name to the League of Communists of Yugoslavia as a symbol of its new role—to act by persuasion and example rather than insisting on its place in the vanguard of the revolution. The country opened its borders, its citizens being amongst the very few in the world who did not require visas for travel abroad to either Western or Eastern Europe. About one million Yugoslavs had jobs as temporary guest workers in Germany, France and Switzerland, regularly sending remittances home. Yugoslavia, meanwhile, was admired for its liberal government policies and apparent lack of dissent, and its Adriatic coast was a favourite destination for western holidaymakers. The country represented the most successful example of socialist doctrine anywhere, acting as a bridge between the two most powerful blocs in the world.

In many ways, all this was a dream. Economic success was built on easy loans from abroad, not an increase in productivity or capacity. Political harmony relied on two factors. Firstly, the federal government bought the support of the republics by a careful distribution of the largesse available to it from foreign money. Secondly, the same government was quick to pounce on any real threat to central authority. There emerged a paradox whereby the League of Communists appeared receptive to greater freedoms, especially in the economic sphere, but at the same time never intended to relinquish its monopoly on political power. In the 1950s

Milovan Đilas, a leading figure from the Partisan movement and the post-war government, was imprisoned for publishing abroad his views on the need for internal reform and to allow political pluralism. In the 1960s a group of philosophers at the Universities of Zagreb and Belgrade gathered around the journal *Praxis*, which represented a humanist view of Marxist ideology, opened a debate with more orthodox Marxists and were critical of some official lines. The Belgrade *Praxis* group showed some sympathy for the students who protested in the city in 1968, the only student protest in Eastern Europe. The episode came to an end after Tito made a personal appearance on television promising to meet the students' demands. Afterwards, however, the tolerant approach to the Praxis group was replaced by a campaign to oust them from their posts.

In 1971 the leadership of the Croatian League of Communists was purged in response to its calls for even greater decentralization and its increasingly nationalist sentiments. The League of Communists decided that it was time to re-assert its central authority and action was taken to remove other rogue elements in other republics. The head of the Serbian League of Communists, Marko Nikezić, lost his position for being too much of a liberal. Self-management operated by alternating sticks and carrots, and it worked very well for a time.

The Tito years also resulted in a distinctive non-aligned foreign policy. Many countries in Asia, Africa and Latin America were emerging from their colonial past and mistrusted the actions of the world's two most powerful alliances. The idea for an organization of nations not committed to either NATO or the Warsaw Pact came from talks between Tito, President Nasser of Egypt and President Nehru of India in 1956 held on the Yugoslav president's island of Brioni. The first conference of the Non-aligned Movement was held in Belgrade in 1961 with representatives from 25 countries.

Tito successfully found an international role and strengthened Yugoslavia's position, as Fred Singleton comments:

> The Belgrade summit conference of non-aligned nations in 1961 was a triumph for Tito's policy of steering a careful route between the two power blocs. Neither side dared offend him too much, lest they drive him into their opponents' arms. His popularity amongst the Third World countries, which his vigorous denunciations of the neo-colo-

nialists greatly enhanced, also strengthened his position in dealing with the big powers. Neither could afford to alienate the champion of the Afro-Asian nations, over whose destinies both sides were struggling to gain control. Therefore, both offered non-aligned Yugoslavia economic aid and diplomatic support.

Attitudes in Belgrade, meanwhile, did not differ from those anywhere else in Yugoslavia. Most people got on with the daily routine of their lives, a few made careers out of being seen and heard in various committees, a small minority would question the taboo areas of public life. Direct criticism of President-for-life Tito was not permitted, nor were attacks on the basic principles of the system, self-management and non-alignment. The police, the army, and the decision to open Goli Otok in 1948 were also no-go areas for open discussion. Those who went too far would be discouraged by being denied better apartments or losing their jobs. The system avoided highly visible and controversial action against individuals whose case might attract international attention, preferring to hand out pensions rather than prison sentences. Yet the fact remains that the system was mostly benign; the vast majority of Yugoslavs were loyal, enjoying a higher standard of living than elsewhere in Eastern Europe and an open-door policy toward the West.

Nikola Pašić Square

Nikola Pašić Square is located at the beginning of King Alexander Boulevard as the road curves round from Terazije. From the end of the sixteenth century a large mosque, the Batal-džamija, stood near or on today's square. By the middle of the nineteenth century, after Knez Miloš began plans for development on Terazije, the old mosque was clearly situated in the growing Serbian district. Miloš faced a very difficult decision, for the Ottoman authorities wanted to include it within their jurisdiction. He resisted their attempts as a matter of principle, but unwilling to antagonize them over the issue, he made no effort to demolish it. The building was simply neglected and the site became better known as a market for trading livestock, which was otherwise forbidden in the town's Big Market. Consequently, the space in front of the Batal-džamija was known as the Cattle Market (Marvena pijaca), from the Serbian *marva*, cattle or livestock, and *pijaca*, market. The area around was planted with corn and a winding track connected it to the Town Gate district below. Miloš's son, Knez Mihailo, toyed with the idea of converting the mosque into the state archive after the Turks left the city in 1867, but his untimely death led to a change in plans and the old building was pulled down in 1869.

After the First World War the Cattle Market was renamed after one of Serbia's famous generals of the time, Vojvoda Mišić, only for the communists to rechristen it after their own heroes as Marx and Engels Square (Trg Marksa i Engelsa) in 1954. The name Nikola Pašić Square was adopted in 1992, adding yet another historical figure to the list of those who have been inscribed on this particular landmark.

Nikola Pašić (1845-1926) was one of the leading Serbian politicians of his age. As a young student in Zurich, sponsored by the Serbian government, he was influenced by radical political ideas and there he met the Russian anarchist Bakunin. On his return to Serbia he moved in those circles closest to the young socialists of the 1870s. In 1878 he was elected to the Serbian National Assembly and founded the People's Radical Party, with a political programme based on universal suffrage, popular sovereignty, parliamentary government and decentralization of the state. These aims were threatened by the Austrians who wished to subordinate the interests of Serbia to their own plans, and by King Milan who did not care for the nuances of parliamentary rule. The Radicals encouraged an armed uprising, the Timok Rebellion of 1883, which was successfully put down. Pašić fled to Bulgaria and was sentenced to death in his absence. He later returned and took up the reins of the People's Radical Party once again and, with the support of a parliamentary majority, introduced the 1888 constitution. By the beginning of the twentieth century, older and more experienced, he also became more conservative in his politics. Favouring the rule of King Alexander Obrenović, he worked alongside less liberal factions in order to secure continuity and stability in government.

His actions alienated some of the younger members of his own party. With the change of dynasty in 1904, Pašić became the single most influential figure in Serbian politics until his death just over twenty years later. He supported the aims of the Balkan peoples to establish their own nation states during the Balkan Wars in 1912 and 1913. He was the Serbian government's chief representative during the next war and at the Paris peace conference in 1919. As one of the architects of the 1921 constitution of the Kingdom of Serbs, Croats and Slovenes, he earned the animosity of many Croats who favoured a greater degree of autonomy from Belgrade. Even so, his ability to negotiate and compromise eventually led to a political alliance with the leader of the Croat Peasant Party, Stjepan Radić, in 1925. Pašić's death the following year removed one of the few politicians who might have made a difference to the Serb-Croat quarrels facing Yugoslavia.

The square was not properly constructed until the twentieth century as part of the general plan for regulating the flow of traffic more efficiently around the city centre. Furthermore, it occupied a prestigious site close to the Old Palace and other government buildings. It was decided to build a new National Assembly (Narodna skupština) above the square in 1907. It was finally completed in 1936 and was followed two years later by the main post office across the road. The architectural evolution and context of the square then took on ever larger and more grandiose turns.

At the end of the Second World War the communist government expanded on this theme with an addition of their own, demolishing the low buildings separating the back of the square from Terazije in order to construct the huge semi-circular shape of the House of Trade Unions (Dom sindikata) as the base for the Central Committee of Trade Unions. This organization did not really represent the interests of workers, but was responsible for ensuring access to health treatment, running holiday hotels, and in particular acting as a conduit through which government and party organizations could communicate with ordinary citizens. The House of Trade Unions was completed in a typically socialist-monumental style, with its clean lines and huge proportions announcing it as a spectacle in itself. The principles governing such architectural planning removed excesses of ornamentation and eradicated any indication of a private or intimate space. Its minimalist intentions reduced outward appearances to the display of ideological purity and strength.

Built in 1955 as an artificial amphitheatre, it provided a backcloth for public performances organized by the party. The square offered a bare stage, with no trees or fountains as now, but with a clear view of the structure's massive curved lines on which huge pictures of President Tito and other dignitaries were hung for the May Day parade. This celebration of workers would pass down the boulevard, in front of the National Assembly where leaders of the party and government waited, continue round Marx and Engels Square and then enter Terazije. Today the square is broken up by the natural outlines of trees, water cascading from fountains and the buzz of the constant human traffic crossing from one side to the other.

KING ALEXANDER BOULEVARD

This impressively broad and long thoroughfare provides one of the main exits from the centre toward the periphery of Belgrade, leading eventually to Smederevo. It also used to be the beginning of the main route connecting Kalemegdan with the sultan's court at Istanbul. Its various names down the ages reveal layers of the city's history. It has been called Smederevo Highway (Smederevski drum), Constantinople Highway (Carigradski drum), and in 1895 it was renamed King Alexander Obrenović Boulevard (Bulevar kralja Aleksandra Obrenovića). In 1946 the communists christened it Red Army Boulevard (Bulevar Crvene armije) in recognition of Soviet help in liberating Belgrade.

The Yugoslav Partisans joined forces with the Red Army in 1944 for the final push against the Germans in the capital city. The main force entered Belgrade down this street, fighting along its whole length, from house to house, against very fierce resistance from an adversary with little left to lose. The Partisans, more used to operating in open country than in the confines of a major city, lost many soldiers in this action.

One of the consequences of the change in ideological direction after 1948 was to change the names of some streets in the city that honoured Yugoslavia's previous co-operation with the USSR. From 1952 the road was called Revolution Boulevard (Bulevar revolucije), eclipsing the debt owed to the former ally. This name survived to 1997 when the advent of a different ideological climate prompted a new change to King Alexander Boulevard.

The authorities responsible for the Serbian quarter around the Town Gate in the early days were terrified by the danger of fire. A small spark could easily spread through the tightly packed houses and cause great damage. Smoking on the streets was already banned by public edict, and it was decided to follow this precaution with another. Merchants who traded in gunpowder and firearms were required to leave the old town and relocate their shops in 1845 to the Constantinople Highway above the Batal-džamija. The area became known as Fišekdžijska čaršija, from the Turkish word *fišekdžija* used in Serbian for someone who trades in gunpowder and cartridges. Although this was the main route out of Belgrade for Istanbul, the road that wound its way up from the Town Gate district resembled a wide cart track. In 1859 the stretch of road from the mosque to the end of the Fišekdžijska čaršija was cobbled, but afterward the track narrowed back to its former dimensions and made its way through thick undergrowth and reeds growing on the marshy ground. The gunpowder merchants were joined by the rag-and-bone men whose trade was considered too unhygienic for the markets in town, and by the end of the nineteenth century only about forty per cent of the shops here traded in weapons. The area became a flea market with a poor reputation among the more respected members of the community. By 1892 three tram lines converged into the street and ran as far as the tramway stables, as they were locally called. The term was apt as the early trams were drawn by horses that required stabling. There is still a depot for electric trams on the same spot.

Belgrade developed along this route from the Batal-džamija, past Tašmajdan, to the tram depot. By the beginning of the twentieth century this represented the city limits in this direction. The first track for horse racing, the Trkalište, was established here on the open spaces at the edge of the city until it was moved in 1906 to its present position at Senjak. The intensive building of more accommodation along this street dictated the founding of another market for residents and in the 1920s the Đeram Market was opened a little further down the road from the tram depot. The King Alexander Obrenović Boulevard had a splendid appearance, far removed from its origins, now with wide pavements, a properly surfaced road and shops and kafanas along its length from Terazije to the market and beyond.

The major period of architectural development took place in the period between the two world wars with the construction of the National Assembly, post office, and across the road the Czechoslovak Embassy, the building in which the capitulation of the country was signed in 1941. The University of Belgrade expanded along the boulevard during these same decades with the university library (1921-26), a hall of residence commissioned by King Alexander for 500 students (1928), a Technical Faculty (1926-31) and a Law Faculty (1935-38). The statue of Vuk Karadžić was placed at the corner of the park where the student hall stands in 1937, a reminder of the cultural contribution made by one of Serbia's foremost language reformers. Not far from the university complex is a museum dedicated to the famous scientist Nikola Tesla at 51 Crown Street. Tesla (1856-1943) moved to New York and made many important discoveries in the fields of electrical engineering and radio technology. This was the golden age of Belgrade's emergence as an urban centre. Outward modernization was symbolized by the completion of large residential and commercial premises, the introduction of a proper transport system and the supply of electricity, water, sanitation, and all the other attributes of contemporary city life. The handsome proportions of the boulevard contributed toward the self-affirmation of Belgrade society and its place in the modern world.

TAŠMAJDAN AND ITS NEIGHBOURHOOD

Stone was quarried from the district around today's neat park of Tašmajdan, providing after many years a system of underground caves and corridors. Units of Karađorđe's cavalry hid in these caves, waiting for passing Turks during the First Serbian Uprising. They were used as a shelter and makeshift hospital during the city's bombardment in the First World War. Later, they housed the German army's communications centre in the Second World War, with plans for the network of tunnels to be strengthened and transformed into the military command post for the whole of south-eastern Europe. The raised plateau where the St. Mark's Church now stands was an ideal position for artillery batteries besieging Belgrade, as proven in the successful Austrian attack of 1717 and again by the Serbian rebels in 1806.

The most significant political event associated with Tašmajdan took place in 1830 with the reading of the *hatti-sherif* granting the Serbs greater autonomy and rights on this spot. The decree was read out to Knez Miloš and then handed over in a formal ceremony for which a large tent was erected; the tent had two entrances, one for the Ottoman officials and a separate one for the Serbian officials to allow them to meet in the middle.

The ground is now more associated with the large church dedicated to St. Mark, which towers above the park. In 1826 the Orthodox Church wanted to move the main Christian cemetery from the Town Gate as the district was planned for expansion as a residential area. Tašmajdan was an obvious choice as it already possessed a small graveyard used by the people down the hill in Palilula. Many more people now made their way along the old road to Istanbul from Belgrade but for an entirely different purpose.

Funeral processions coming slowly up the hill and passing in front of the arms-dealers on their way to the Tašmajdan cemetery became a common sight. A small church dedicated to St. Mark was opened in 1835. However, by the 1870s the Church hierarchy was beginning to reconsider the best use of its property on the bluff overlooking the town and expressed a desire to move the cemetery once more for two reasons: it was no longer adequate for the needs of the community and could not be made bigger as it was hemmed in by the old quarry workings on one side and by the road on the other. It was also felt that more profitable gain could be made by increasing the space available to rent to the growing number of new businesses opening here. The decision to forbid further burials was taken in 1883, but it was not until the 1920s that the graveyard was dug up and moved. The small shops and the original Fišekdžijska čaršija have long since been demolished in later developments.

Further changes and additions were made in the twentieth century, firstly with the foundation of the Seismological Institute in 1909, and then with the erection of the small Russian Orthodox Church dedicated to the Holy Trinity in 1924. The largest architectural project was the con-

struction of the new St. Mark's Church, between 1932 and 1939, to
replace the smaller one from the previous century. The church is modelled
on that from the old monastery at Gračanica, near Priština in Kosovo. It
is much larger than the original and built in a more grandiose, if not to
say theatrical, style. It caused a controversy at the time as many people felt
that it was not appropriate to update and modernize a historical monument with such strong associations for Serbian national feelings. Others
felt that the solution was an excellent marriage of traditional architecture
with the possibilities of twentieth-century construction techniques. The
interior decoration of the church was interrupted by the Second World
War and never completed, although the body of Tsar Dušan was transferred here.

Tašmajdan Park was designed in 1952, and some 800 people had to
be resettled in new apartments elsewhere in the city to make room for it,
although they left behind nothing more than shacks without basic facilities. The area below the park, away from the main road, was given over to
sports with skating in winter and tennis, basketball and volleyball in the
summer months. In the 1960s these facilities were upgraded with a proper
sports complex, including an Olympic outdoor swimming pool. At the
beginning of the twenty-first century a project to install external lighting
at St. Mark's was approved, which in the evenings shows off the architectural details of the building to best effect.

Near Tašmajdan and across the road from the National Assembly is
another park, Pionirski Park, named after the youth movement of socialist Yugoslavia, the Pioneers. All children over the age of seven were
members and wore bright red scarves. It was a national organization for
promoting patriotic pride but was also, for most of the time, a place to
have fun, to go on excursions and mix with friends. The park has a number
of statues and sculptures, and contains examples of a variety of trees. On
the corner by the traffic lights where Knez Miloš Street begins is a striking
monument, the Lookout Post of the High Command of the Serbian Army
(Osmatračnica Vrhovne komande srpske vojske). Alexander Karađorđević, as head of the Serbian army, alongside Vojvoda Živojin Mišić and
other members of the HQ, observed his forces break through enemy lines
on September 15 1918 at the end of the First World War. It was moved
here in 1928 to commemorate the jubilee celebrations in memory of the
Thessalonica Front.

Takovo Street begins from the post office on the corner with the boulevard. The offices and studio of Belgrade Television are at 10 Takovo Street, although the complex of buildings brings it quite close to the back of St. Mark's. The first experimental broadcast was made in the city in 1939, but regular transmission did not begin until 1958. The television company was closely associated with the Milošević regime during the whole of the 1990s and was therefore a target for NATO in 1999, and also for anti-government demonstrators in the protests against his government and their policies in 1996-97 and again in 2000 when he was toppled from power.

The first street on the left is Kosovo Street and at no. 47 is the building of the old telephone exchange, the first in Belgrade, the façade of which bears a strong resemblance to the Vuk Karadžić Foundation on King Milan Street. Its architect, Branko Tanazević, was responsible for the highly decorative interpretation of this neo-Byzantine style in both cases. The exchange was built in 1908 when Belgrade had a population of some 80,000, of whom 6,000 were subscribers to the new telephone system. The building was constructed quite deliberately to house the latest technology in an architectural wrapping that provided an eloquent statement of national tradition.

Kosovo Street leads down towards the city centre and eventually arrives at the House of Youth (Dom omladine) at 22 Macedonia Street. Built in the early 1960s, it contains versatile spaces for theatre groups, film projections, exhibitions, concerts, literary evenings and discussion groups, and also hosts the Belgrade Jazz Festival. Further along the same street at no. 29 is the building of the *Politika* newspaper, while on the corner at Hilandar Street is Radio Belgrade. The close proximity of these two institutions has been a source of constant custom for the kafanas here. Journalists and other media people mounted a campaign to protect their favourite watering holes from globalized over-modernization. A particular effort was made to save the Under the Linden Tree (Pod lipom) kafana across from the *Politika* building, although the garish sign of Pizza Hut above the entrance attests to its failure. The home of the Atelje 212 theatre is not far away, at 21 Sveta Gora Street. It has been here since 1963 with its emphasis on promoting modern productions. The original theatre was in a building on Nikola Pašić Square, which contained exactly 212 seats.

ARTS AND POLITICS AFTER 1945

In 1945 the Communist Party of Yugoslavia intended to run the country according to the models and lessons of the Soviet Union. It appointed a commissar to oversee artistic production and to ensure that it conformed to the norms of a socialist society: in short, literature, painting, cinema and music existed in order to promote Marxist ideology and the creation of communism.

The first holder of the post was Radovan Zogović (1907-86), although from the beginning there were differences between standard Soviet interpretations on how these goals might be best achieved and the Yugoslav practice. The events of 1948 set the Yugoslav communists on a different path, allowing greater diversity—so long as the taboos were respected. Artists were too important to be left to their own devices. One of the consistent features of dictatorships and one-party states is their awareness of the power of art as a producer of meanings. Art does not just reflect what exists in reality, but is also a medium for the articulation of that reality. In this very important sense, it actually constructs an idea of the current possibilities of the imagination. Art is an important feature in the processes of how a society sees itself, what it wants to say about itself and the kinds of images which it mirrors back to itself. The control of the range of meanings available for consumption and exchange, in other words culture, remained within the unspoken remit of government until the end of communism.

In the early days poets and others known to be opponents of communism were publicly criticized and vilified; their works were not studied in schools and universities and went unpublished, and their names and voices were simply not heard. Miloš Crnjanski was a writer whose pre-war rightwing views were no secret. He spent the war years in London and preferred to remain in exile rather than risk returning to Belgrade in 1945. He was attacked by his former friend Marko Ristić as a "dead poet", a metaphor which may easily have been made literal had he dared to appear in Belgrade.

As the years went by, however, the party's policies on cultural matters changed. Crnjanski became a visitor to the Yugoslav Embassy in London, overtures were made for him to return, his books were published again, his influence on Serbian literature was discussed and his works were included in school curricula. He eventually returned to Belgrade in 1966. His arrival was an instant event, significant both to the older generation of intellectuals who recalled his presence from before the war and to the students at Belgrade University who saw in him the embodiment of a change in official policy. He lived the rest of his days as a celebrated writer of Serbian Modernism and a classic of twentieth-century literature. The reformed communists in Belgrade found that their relaxed attitude to cultural questions did them more good in the world than it caused problems at home. They were able to point to figures like Crnjanski as evidence of their change of heart and an example of how the Yugoslav system was socialism with a human face.

Most culture did not, in fact, require policing. People were wealthier than their parents had been and the standard of living was increasing during the 1960s and 1970s, so unsurprisingly there was a growing sense of self-confidence in the stability of Yugoslav society. Critical attitudes and images were tolerated within the limits set down by the League of Communists. It was only important for art to be made safe, neutralized, to be a cathartic space for letting off steam. The state helped the process by providing artists with what they usually lacked, some kind of security of employment. Very few writers could earn a living from the sale of their books, so many were given jobs in publishing houses or on editorial boards, providing a regular income. This kind of security was equally important for actors, musicians and painters, if not even more so. State involvement in their activities, guaranteeing the provision of facilities, maintaining permanent employment in large orchestras and theatre companies, was essential in a society and economic system which frowned on income gained from self-employment.

Artists were divided into associations through which they could work, be recognized as a writer or translator, and in particular be registered within the welfare system. Membership also conferred other benefits since the associations were responsible for awarding prizes for contributions in their particular field. The distribution of housing was also channelled through these organizations. The industrial and commercials sectors would invest some of their profits into residential building projects from which employees would be eligible to receive accommodation. But housing built by public funds was made available to the non-commercial sectors through the offices of social or government bodies. Participation in the official associations was hence driven by personal interest as much as by the knowledge of taking part in worthwhile guild activity.

The Association of Writers of Serbia (Udruženje književnika Srbije), for example, is at 7 France Street near Republic Square. The association had an elected president and assorted secretaries responsible for different aspects of the organization. The premises were used for meetings and book promotions. The association distributed money in the form of prizes, funded delegations on official trips to meet writers overseas and held a large international conference every October. The managing board of the association also had access to social housing, and one of its functions concerned the distribution of apartments to writers who met the official criteria. These benefits were a strong incentive to membership. It still exists although there are now other bodies and the arts are more open to market mechanisms as in the West.

Despite patronage, the Association of Writers became a platform for the intellectual opposition to many aspects of the system by the 1980s. Protest meetings were organized and a committee established to protect the rights of its members to free speech; it also often defended writers who were being hounded by the authorities in other republics. The infrastructure established by the regime as a method of quiet control became in communism's last decade a source of opposition.

CHALLENGING IDEOLOGY

When the communists came to power, all areas of public life were subject to scrutiny by the party: not only political and security structures, but also all places where people might meet and exchange ideas. The circulation of anything of aesthetic significance came within this remit, and the wider the possible audience, the greater the care that had to be taken over its dissemination. The communists adopted the tenets of Socialist Realism from the Soviet Union, requiring that the arts play a part in the construction of socialist Yugoslavia and form its citizens into standard bearers for the future. The message of literature, painting and film was to be positive, showing that the ultimate success of the class struggle will wipe away the remnants of the past, that the socialist model of economic and political organization is superior to all others, and that in the Yugoslav context the victory of the Partisans in the Second World War was the first inevitable step in this direction. The emphasis in art was on reproducing this message, not in encouraging stylistic experiments and departures that would only confound what was to be a simple matter of communication. Yet the break with the Soviet Union in 1948 profoundly influenced this approach to cultural politics in Yugoslavia. Socialist Realism, along with other Soviet models, became discredited.

There was no official announcement that the Communist Party's cultural policy was about to change, but a series of events in the early 1950s heralded a new direction. The painter Petar Lubarda (1907-74) opened his first major exhibition in Belgrade in 1951, an occurrence accepted by many as a crossroads in the development of modern Serbian art. He introduced a bold way of using colour and abstract techniques, emphasizing the autonomous dynamism of painting to express multiple meanings directly or metaphorically. He was joined by others such as Bata Mihailović and Mića Popović who were interested in pushing at the boundaries of aesthetic interpretation and the possibilities of what painting can express.

It was well known that President Tito himself did not care for abstract painting, but these artists broke through onto the international scene and took Serbian art beyond the borders of the country to exhibitions abroad. Their stance also forced the art establishment to revive the work of painters from before the Second World War whom the communists had regarded as decadent. The Museum of Modern Art in New Belgrade has a large collection of these modern masters. This change was happening not just in painting but in all branches of art, and especially in Belgrade. The communist hierarchy made the city the home of its most powerful institutions; it also became home to the newest artistic credos.

One of the factors influencing the new directions in Yugoslav art was the re-opening of contact with cultural trends in Western Europe and North America. After 1951 Belgrade theatre blossomed in the more tolerant and artistically creative atmosphere ushered in when foreign plays were performed. Under the old cultural policy any kind of display of capitalist art was looked on with great suspicion by the authorities. But between 1951 and 1958 the Belgrade Drama Theatre (Beogradsko dramsko pozorište) staged plays by Arthur Miller (*Death of a Salesman*), Tennessee Williams (*Cat on a Hot Tin Roof*), John Osborne (*Look Back in Anger*) and other western playwrights. Styles of acting became more adventurous and opened up more expressive possibilities for the stage. The Yugoslav Drama Theatre, under its highly innovative artistic director Bojan Stupica (1910-70), toured abroad with great success, with a review in the

Parisian *Le Figaro* praising the ensemble for its "spirit of unity, which acts with a high level of consciousness and emanates dignity".

The new direction was not all plain sailing and the authorities could react high-handedly if minded. The Belgrade Drama Theatre attempted to put on Samuel Beckett's *Waiting for Godot* in 1955, but the production was banned. Yet once having tasted a more liberal approach in cultural policy, the artists themselves were not willing to succumb to each official backlash. The play was performed the following year in the newly established theatre, Atelje 212, its first performance in Eastern Europe. Atelje 212 went on to produce plays by Jean-Paul Sartre (*Huis Clos*), Eugene Ionescu (*The Chairs*), Harold Pinter (*The Caretaker*) and other examples of controversial modern drama. The manager of the theatre, Mira Trailović (1924-89), and its literary consultant, Jovan Ćirilov, founded the Belgrade International Theatre Festival (BITEF) in 1967, which has operated every year since then in September. BITEF brings the best of international stage companies to the city, and provides a conduit for Belgrade groups to perform abroad. Many aesthetic barriers were overcome, which was not the case elsewhere in Eastern Europe, and the authorities were forced to reconcile themselves to a certain degree of artistic freedom, provided that political boundaries were not overstepped.

From Red Reels to Black Wave

Film, like other art forms, fell under the demands of Socialist Realism and the Soviet model. The Second World War had effectively destroyed what little existed in the way of studio facilities, technical equipment and personnel in Belgrade. Despite these obstacles, after the liberation of Belgrade the communists established a film section, which was to produce documentary films about the war and the first efforts to re-build the country. In 1945 a state film enterprise was founded, taking over control of the funding, production and distribution of film. Although facilities were sparse the Central Committee took the role of film very seriously, with the first studio Avala Film in operation on 15 July 1946. New facilities were concentrated in Belgrade as the federal capital and the urban centre with the greatest infrastructure. The party established a Film City (Filmski grad) on the outskirts of Belgrade at Košutnjak; the first professional school for acting and directing was also opened here, along with another institution for the training of technical staff, and a journal *Film*.

The first movie from Avala Film was called *Slavica*, released in 1947. The action is set in Dalmatia, telling the story of a small resistance group struggling against the occupying forces and against traitors and collaborators. The nucleus of the plot revolving around a small band of heroic Partisans fighting a lonely local battle against much greater odds became staple cinematic fare in the first years of communist rule. Characters in these films were stereotypical depictions of brave guerrilla fighters with impeccable ideological credentials, in complete contrast to the rather vain and stupid Italians, brutal Germans with their military airs, and the domestic traitors, the Četniks and Ustaše, who were deceitful and cowardly by nature. Such films were important in creating a deliberate mythology of the Second World War, presenting a romantic and simplistic version of events as historical truth. They were epic narratives recounting a struggle between contesting forces and the difficult birth of a new country.

The film industry in Belgrade during the 1950s continued to glorify the heroes of the war and post-war reconstruction but also introduced a note of greater depth. Heroes had some flaws, mistakes were made, but the same message ultimately stressed that what was done was necessary at the time. Greater diversity was introduced into the repertoire with light comedies and some careful attempts at portraying contemporary themes.

The split with the Soviet Union ushered in many changes, including consequences for the organization of the film industry in Yugoslavia. One of the main thrusts of the reforms was to hand over a more meaningful role to republic governments. Each republic was duly handed its own studio system, technical facilities and personnel with institutional facilities at the federal level to allow collaboration. Central funding was removed in 1957 and replaced by a tax on tickets as a way of raising revenue to finance the film industry. Nevertheless, government subsidies were available for large, prestigious projects. Foreign films also began to find their way into Belgrade and Yugoslav cinemas as part of the policy to open the door to the West. The influence of Italian Neorealism particularly made itself felt in cinema. The presence of other aesthetic sensibilities and competition from abroad were a force for good in stimulating the cinematic infrastructure at home.

Belgrade filmmakers began to take a more independent stance in the 1960s, which evolved into a trend known as the Black Wave (Crni talas). This radical group of directors had at its centre Aleksandar Petrović,

Živojin Pavlović and Dušan Makavejev. They risked government displeasure by offering individual perspectives on social themes, the meaning of suffering in the war of national liberation and personal visions of uncertainty about the future. Their work is often pessimistic, filled with the realities of urban squalor, exposing the gulf between official aspirations and the lack of direction and drive of a new generation. Their world was one of ambiguity, filled with primitive and unknown appetites that can swallow beauty, innocence and intelligence.

One of the first films in this wave was Pavlović's *When I'm Pale and Dead* (Kad budem bled i mrtav, 1960). The story is set in the post-war period concerning a young man who is a drifter with no purpose in life. He tries his hand at singing, and finds that his poor voice is acceptable in small kafanas or army camps where the audience is not too discriminating. He goes to Belgrade to try his luck but faces two problems: his lack of real talent is recognized, and his choice of material—old-fashioned ballads—is at odds with the city's demand for western pop music. He returns to the provinces and the corruption of communist officials who use their influence to satisfy their desires for money and women. Confronting one of these men, the disillusioned popular singer is shot and killed. He dies in a most undignified position, in an outdoor lavatory with his trousers round his ankles.

In the end, the authorities decided that these directors' work overstepped the political boundaries on which the party insisted. In their hands, contemporary life was a struggle for survival set against the backdrop of the new slums created by massive post-war movements of population. They focused attention on themes of social dislocation and individual alienation, which was seen as too critical of contemporary Yugoslav reality. So the Black Wave came to an end.

LITERARY IMAGES OF BELGRADE

The turning point for literary production after 1948 came in 1951 with the publication of Dobrica Ćosić's novel *Far Away Is the Sun* (Daleko je sunce). The story follows a fairly standard Partisan narrative but with the additional themes of doubt and possible ideological miscalculation, which were not typical at the time. More generally, there are few examples from this period of the kind of Belgrade literature that had flourished before the Second World War. The authorities did not forbid such expression, but neither was it part of their agenda for cultural policy. The city was not a centre of Partisan activity during the war; it was occupied and then liberated only in the latter stages of the war. It was also a place with many physical reminders of the previous regime. The communist authorities were anxious to promote their arrival as year zero, and to suppress memory of what existed before them.

Literary life in the 1950s was dominated by the polemics between the Modernists grouped around the journal *Delo* and the Realists around *Savremenik*. The differences between the two groups were founded in their attitudes to the role of the literary work. The Modernists emphasized the autonomy of the text and its potential meanings from direct social and political engagement. The Realists regarded literature as an expression of social forces that could not and should not be separated from that world as its raw material. In some senses, the latter were closer to official views on the responsibility of the artist to practise his or her art with an eye to the possible influence the text might have on the public imagination. Yet it would be too simplistic to see their differences just along these lines. By the end of the decade their polemical relationship was over, as literature followed the same kind of cosmopolitan and varied styles to be found in other creative spheres.

The city became a literary topic during this period in the work of two authors who came from very different poetic backgrounds, Dragoslav Mihailović and Borislav Pekić. After the debates between the Modernists and Realists most writers wanted to take literature out of the public sphere and tended to produce work with little connection to contemporary life, especially with its more squalid aspects. Literary prose became more contemplative. Then, at the end of the 1960s, a new wave of authors, most probably under the influence of the Black Wave in film, saw literature and particularly the novel as a source for depicting the new urban reality. Mihailović was one of their number. He published his novel *When Pumpkins Blossomed* (Kad su cvetale tikve) in 1968. The narrator is a Yugoslav worker living in Sweden and recalling the events that forced him to leave Belgrade some twenty years earlier. He reveals how he lived in one of Belgrade's poorer districts, and in the aimless poverty of the immediate post-war years took up boxing. While undergoing his compulsory army service he hears that his sister has died. She was raped and, as a result, committed suicide. Learning that the rapist was a member of a rival gang from another district, he resolves to take his revenge. Eventually catching up with his quarry, he beats him to death and, when he feels that he may be arrested for murder, flees the country.

The novel was one of the first to make use of post-war Belgrade not just as a setting for action, but also as part of the structure of the novel and its fictional world. The places where events happen are real, and the grinding difficulties of the urban environment in this period are relevant to understanding motivation. Characters speak the authentic language of the Belgrade streets, and their mental and emotional horizons are bounded by that same geography. The action of the novel even includes an obvious allusion to the arrest and transportation of people from Belgrade to Goli Otok in the purges following 1948.

Borislav Pekić published his novel *The Houses of Belgrade* (Hodačašće Arsenije Njegovana, 1970) two years later. The narrator and hero of the story is Arsenije Njegovan, who has not left his apartment since 1941. He was a landlord in Belgrade before the Second World War, the owner of numerous houses which he rented to tenants. The novel is set in 1968 when Arsenije decides to leave his flat for the first time in over 25 years. He resolves on a pilgrimage round his former properties, thinking that he is still their owner, unaware that the war and the subsequent arrival of a communist government have changed his city.

Pekić's urban landscape takes on a much greater symbolic presence than is the case in Mihailović's novel. As he goes around recalling his Belgrade of 1941, Arsenije remembers the event that frightened him into his seclusion. Caught up in the demonstrations at the end of March against the pact that Prince Paul signed with Hitler, he was badly injured and has been unable to face the world since. Now, once more, he witnesses another demonstration on the streets of Belgrade, this time the student protests of 1968. He sees these events as symptoms of the collapse of order, the actions of the crowd contrasting with his houses, which represent examples of symmetry and beauty.

Arsenije is obsessed by the houses which he once owned, giving them names and personalities. In his vision of the world, all problems are eventually seen as issues of architectural or urban design. When watching the demonstrating students in early June 1968 he gets into conversation with some fellow-bystanders. They discuss the events unfolding in front of them, the behaviour of the mob and its destruction of property. They are aghast at the display of lawlessness, while Arsenije feels more for the hurt caused to dwellings than to people. The bystanders comment on the police response, while one of them calls the situation "a political error". Arsenije offers an alternative explanation:

> "That's a political error," said the man behind us.
> "It's an urbanist error, gentlemen!" I shouted. "*C'est une faute urbanistique!* The workers' suburbs have been located in an encircling belt which grips the commercial heart of the city like a vise. This has concentrated the proletariat in breeding grounds of revolt and destruction. Why, gentlemen, didn't they place those people in closed-off Soleri cones?"
> "What's all that crap about?" said the colonel.
> "I'm speaking of Paolo Soleri, who designed a town like a beehive, or rather a conical anthill with internal passageways. All its exits can be easily controlled, and production carried on without any fear of revolutionary ideas or attitudes. In a word, a real town for workers."

It is difficult to imagine such sentiments finding their way into a published novel elsewhere in Eastern Europe at the time.

SYMBOLIC ENDINGS

At the end of Tito's final decade in Belgrade the city was again represented in fictional works, but this time with a potentially broader meaning in a short story by Danilo Kiš and a film by Slobodan Šijan. The film, *Who's That Singing over There* (Ko to tamo peva), made in 1980, has been voted the most popular piece of cinema made in Serbia. It tells the story of a ramshackle bus with its strange conductor and driver, taking a group of passengers from a village somewhere in the Serbian countryside to Belgrade. The journey takes place in 1941, on the very eve of Germany's attack on the city. The passengers represent people from all walks of life and all ages, as if a microcosm of the country itself. They include two gypsies, itinerant musicians, who introduce the film with a song. The journey extends into the night when the passengers come across the army making preparations for something, although the danger is not named. The atmosphere is generally light-hearted but as the bus approaches its destination the mood begins to change. One of the passengers is sure that

From *Who's That Singing over There*

his wallet has been stolen, and all eyes turn inevitably to the gypsies. Daylight is breaking, the bus is entering the outskirts of the city, and unwarranted violence is about to be inflicted on two innocent men. Then, without warning, the bus is hit by a bomb dropped by the Luftwaffe. It explodes and the bus is blown over, the sudden silence indicating that everyone is dead. But the two gypsies emerge as the only survivors, and the film closes as it opened with their song. It is a symbolic journey of a country heading toward a catastrophe of which it is completely unaware. Looking back on the film from a vantage point after the year 2000, it seems to suggest a much wider resonance than that of Belgrade facing the Second World War. It was made in the same year that Tito died, when another unseen hand began work at the long process of unravelling Yugoslavia.

The short story by Danilo Kiš, "Encyclopaedia of the Dead" (Enciklopedija mrtvih), was published in 1981 and contains another kind of symbolic reference. The narrator is visiting Sweden when one night she is taken to a strange library comprising a dimly lit series of rooms, each chamber full of volumes chained to the shelves. Each room contains books beginning with the same letter in alphabetical order. She quickly realizes that the library is the Encyclopaedia of the Dead, with a reference to each departed soul. She races to the volumes beginning with M to look for the entry on her father who died just two months earlier. She finds the entry, which is both a document of his life and at the same time an account of his country in the twentieth century as it affected him. A Serb, born in Croatia, he moves to Belgrade where he studies surveying and eventually is one of the men given the task of making maps of the Kingdom of Yugoslavia. Staying in Belgrade during the Second World War, he witnesses events under the occupation, then the liberation of the city by the Partisans amidst scenes of violence. After the war he returns to his profession in order to produce maps for the new order:

> The post my father held after the war in the land office, which undertook to re-measure and re-record the land, as is usual after major historic upheavals, is accorded the detailed treatment it demands: quality of terrain, title deeds, new names for former German villages and new names for freshly colonized settlements.

At the end, however, after all this careful elaboration it turns out that the whole episode has been a dream, and the narrator did not read the Encyclopaedia of the Dead. There is here a similarity with Pekić's *The Houses of Belgrade* in that the city provides a solid framework around which the story is embellished. The presence of Belgrade is stronger than the fragility of fiction and stronger than the changes and transformations that have shaped its development during the twentieth century.

Chapter Six

KNEZ MILOŠ STREET, DEDINJE
AND TOPČIDER:
FROM TITO'S DEATH TO CIVIL WAR

TITO'S LAST DECADE

When Tito died in 1980 and his funeral cortège made its solemn way down Knez Miloš Street, Yugoslavia appeared to be the most successful state in Eastern Europe. The country had defied Stalin in 1948, forged good relations with the West, patched up its differences with the Soviet Union and established itself as one of the leading countries in the Non-Aligned Movement—an international grouping committed neither to the Warsaw Pact nor NATO. Yugoslav passports were welcomed in more countries than most others without the need for visas. Large numbers of tourists sunned themselves on the coast, arriving by car from Germany and Austria or by cheap charter flights from Britain. Yugoslavia was held in high esteem for its liberal domestic policies by western governments and by dissidents in Eastern Europe. It offered a third way, not based on the market demands of capitalism nor run according to a centrally planned state system. Neither in the West nor the East, it had an identity of its own. Its citizens had enough disposable income to take holidays or go shopping abroad, while the old quarrels between the different nationalities were forgotten by a generation of younger people. Yet a decade later the country was in a state of civil war, and Belgrade was ostracized by its former friends.

There was real fear in international circles that Yugoslavia might become a trouble spot after Tito's death if the Soviet Union tried to assert its influence in the region. This, in fact, did not happen. Rather, the country became embroiled in its own problems of an economic and political nature. The Yugoslav economy began to falter in the early 1980s, with some everyday items in short supply and restrictions on energy consumption. Inflation and unemployment both began to rise, while those

Knez Miloš's *Konak*

entering the job market after 1980 found a dormant economy with few new opportunities. At the same time, foreign banks and governments began to call in the debts that Yugoslavia under Tito had borrowed. The republics began to pull in different directions, each trying to maximize its share of reduced resources. This situation was not unexpected as each unit had its own strengths and weaknesses, the federation having been held together in a spirit of compromise and by a willingness to negotiate between the more and less advanced regions. Tito was effective in bringing the country together by a combination of charisma, personal prestige and the power he represented at the federal level in the government, the League of Communists and the armed forces. After his death no single person held all the important positions he had enjoyed. Instead, the federal system operated according to the principle of consensus and all parties had to agree before policies could be enacted.

The republics increasingly asserted their independence from the central organs, however. Competition in the deepening economic crisis became worse, and the republics' leaders blamed their neighbours for lack of progress. So began a cycle of recriminations, which eventually turned into more overt nationalist rhetoric, causing further anger and frustration in each constituent part of the country. Communities looked inward to themselves for salvation and anyone who was different became a potential enemy.

The federal institutions, the symbols of a united Yugoslavia, were disintegrating by the end of the decade. The League of Communists met in January 1990 to try to resolve some of the issues but broke up without agreement when the Slovene delegation walked out of the meeting. The federal government was powerless to prevent the referenda held in Slovenia, Croatia, Bosnia and Macedonia to secede from Yugoslavia. This move frightened national minorities in those areas, influenced by the recent waves of negative nationalist rhetoric. This fear was particularly evident among the Serbian communities in Croatia and Bosnia, which led to the beginning of conflicts in the former in 1991, and the latter in 1992. The Yugoslav army no longer existed, and the civil wars that broke out were unmistakable evidence that Tito's Yugoslavia had come to an end.

BELGRADE UNDER SANCTIONS

The Serbian government was dominated by the Socialist Party—in fact the renamed League of Communists of Serbia—led by Slobodan Milošević. He and his policies were by no means universally popular at home, and especially not in Belgrade. A huge opposition rally of some 40,000 demonstrators met on Republic Square on 9 March 1991. Milošević sent in riot police with tear gas and water cannon, then called on the military for support. The army entered the centre of Belgrade during the night, with tanks gouging deep holes in the asphalt between Slavija Square and Terazije. They departed the following day, but not before a bond of trust between the city and the institution entrusted with its defence was broken.

Milošević gave in to some demands, enough to defuse the situation, but he also bussed in his own supporters from the provinces to provide a counter-demonstration. With the secession of the other republics, the remaining government deputies in Belgrade declared the formation of a new country, the Federal Republic of Yugoslavia, made up of the republics of Serbia and Montenegro, on 27 April 1992. The city was the capital of a country with a new name for the seventh time in the twentieth century; but with a clearly uneasy relationship between the citizens and the state government.

The Serbian communities in Croatia and Bosnia called on support from Milošević, which he supplied but then withdrew to leave paramilitary organizations in Serbia to continue the fight over the borders. The United Nations expected greater efforts from the Serbian president to control these forces and to exert his influence to stop the fighting in former Yugoslavia. Consequently, the UN Security Council voted for Resolution 757 on 30 May 1992 to impose sanctions against Serbia and Montenegro. The measures included a very strict ban on all trade, financial, sporting, cultural and educational links and prohibited air and sea traffic. The country was cut off from the rest of the world and the Milošević regime left to rule behind its hermetically sealed borders with no interference from outside.

This situation sparked a series of events in the country over the coming years which for all those who lived through or witnessed what was to come brought some of the most bizarre experiences possible. Some people amassed huge personal fortunes but most suffered the opposite effect: poverty, unemployment and the disappearance of normal life.

The monthly inflation rate for retail prices in June 1992 exceeded 100 per cent and the German deutschmark became the unofficial currency in a city that no longer trusted the domestic dinar. By September almost half of factories were closed and thousands of workers were put on what was known as "forced holiday". Salaries, for those who still received them, were not enough to cover basic costs of living and it was necessary to do something to find extra cash. The routine and discipline of regular work disappeared and many took to the streets in a chaotic and disorganized way, either selling goods or changing currency. Some of these activities were supported by organized syndicates breaking sanctions by importing cigarettes, clothes, petrol or virtually anything since nothing was being produced in Serbia itself. The need to survive was slowly pulling a majority of the population into nebulous criminal or semi-criminal forms of activity.

The Milošević government ended up forming an alliance with those groups who could break the sanctions regime and prosper in an atmosphere of corruption and intimidation. These were essentially criminal gangs, formerly part of an underground mafia, now pushed to the surface and cruising the streets openly, flaunting their new respectability and their celebrity status. They were rich and successful, while everyone else could only stand by and watch their rise to a position of power.

One way offered to ordinary people to make ends meet was via the huge interest rates for deposits in private banks. One of these was run by Dafina Milanović, a larger-than-life character who would appear in public adorned in furs and jewellery when not overseeing the money mounting up in her vaults. By December 1992 she was offering an interest rate of 15 to 17 per cent per month on deutschmark savings. In other words, an investment of 500 deutschmarks would provide a monthly income of about 75 marks—not a huge amount but enough to provide a welcome addition to a family budget. Investors would pick up their monthly payout, and immediately take it onto the streets to convert into dinars on the black market. Dinar banknotes were going straight from the state mint onto the streets through the connivance of the government operating hand-in-glove with crime bosses. The system was perfect. Citizens put their money into a bank run with the approval of the government and then gave their deutschmarks earned in interest to the dealers on the street. Meanwhile, corrupt politicians received payback from both the bank and the dealers. The momentum of this scheme could only be kept up for as long as new money was being deposited to finance the monthly interest, and it eventually collapsed—with investors losing all the savings they had committed.

The figures for inflation in this period provide some barely believable statistics. At the end of September 1993 one deutschmark was being traded for 1,000,000,000 dinars. In October the government resorted to removing six noughts from the currency, making the value of one mark 1,000 dinars. Yet the daily rate of inflation was such that by the middle of November the deutschmark was again worth 1,000,000 dinars and the average monthly salary dropped to about ten marks (approximately five euros). By the end of the year the deutschmark reached a value of 1,000,000,000,000 dinars (really 10,000,000,000,000,000,000 if compared with its value earlier in the year before the noughts were removed). The price of a loaf of bread had risen from 12,500 dinars on 2 November 1993 to 4,000,000,000 dinars on 22 December. The retail price index recorded a monthly inflation rate of 313,563,558 per cent, or a daily inflation rate of 62 per cent and an hourly rate of almost 3 per cent. Goods no longer had price tickets in shops as values changed so much during the course of one day. Cash registers could no longer be used to add prices together because of an excess of noughts. Sales staff sometimes quoted prices according to the pictures on the banknotes, so that an item might cost "two sunflowers and a little boy". Stores were largely empty of goods and a supermarket might display widely spaced boxes of cornflakes or chocolate but little else. The streets were eerily empty of traffic in the summer of 1993 since petrol was expensive and only available on the black market from gangs who smuggled it illegally. Of course, the new elite making money from this chaos was subject to no restrictions.

These figures only tell a small part of everyday life in Belgrade. Daily existence was dependent on maximizing all available resources. Those who could left the country. Community services collapsed and society fragmented under the strain. Streams of desperate refugees arrived from across the borders. People were living a doubly isolated life: first, behind the wall of sanctions separating them from the world at large; second, behind a psychological barrier that prevented integration into the abnormal world which was now the norm at home. The history of the collapse of social and economic order in Belgrade during the period of sanctions is also the story of the simultaneous collapse of moral authority, value systems and all the small decencies that are the hallmark of civilized society.

By the end of 1993 the dinar was no longer used as currency and there was little profit left to be made from manipulating the black market, so the period of hyperinflation had outlived its usefulness. The government appointed a new governor to the National Bank of Yugoslavia, Dragoslav Avramović, and on 24 January 1994 hyperinflation came to an end. A new dinar was introduced and exchanged for the old one at a rate of 12,000,000:1, with no more wild and indiscriminate printing of money. The solution could have come much sooner.

GANGLAND CULTURE

A gangland culture emerged and took over the city during the 1990s. Tim Judeh, a journalist who lived in Belgrade from 1991 to 1995, describes the beginning of this process in his book *The Serbs*:

> The end of Yugoslavia turned Serbia and the Serb-held lands in Croatia and Bosnia into a patchwork of mafia fiefs. The unprecedented breakdown of law and order and the fantastic business opportunities provided by sanctions-busting meant that many Yugoslav gangsters who had hitherto operated in the richer pastures of Germany and Switzerland returned to reap the profits of war. Some became involved with Serbian paramilitaries, which under the cover of patriotism became rapacious looting machines. After they had stolen all the cars and other goods from the frontline towns, they turned their attention to the home front.

Two such patriots were Branislav "Beli" Matić and Đorđe "Giška" Božović who helped establish the Serbian Guard, a paramilitary formation under the auspices of the Serbian Renewal Movement and its leader Vuk Drašković. When Drašković's political career began in earnest he distanced himself from the Serbian Guard. The lives of criminals were short; Matić was shot outside his home in August 1991, Božović a month later in one of the Serbian enclaves in Croatia. It was rumoured that he was shot in the back by his own side. In October 1992 another gangster, Aleksandar "Knele" Knežević, described by Judeh as "the icon of a younger generation of the Belgrade underworld", was killed in a room in the exclusive Hyatt Hotel. He was just twenty-one years old.

During the following years gangland murders, turf wars and assassinations were common on Belgrade's streets. In addition to the more usual drug, prostitution and protection rackets, the criminals were in charge of imports, smuggling goods through the wall of UN sanctions into Serbia.

The particular circumstances of the time dictated the kinds of criminal activity that would be most lucrative. The shortage of petrol in Belgrade stimulated a lively illegal trade with plastic bottles of fuel sold in back streets. Weapons were also in high demand across the whole of former Yugoslavia. The lack of proper border controls across the region facilitated the international trafficking of stolen cars shipped from Germany through Serbia and then, if not intended for the home market, sent further east to Russia or Asia. This route quickly developed into a conduit for drug smuggling and people trafficking from east to west. It is said that the opportunities for profit in those days of mayhem united the criminal elements on all sides, bringing together Serbs, Croats, Bosnians and Albanians.

Željko Ražnatović, better known as Arkan, was one of the first criminals to return to Belgrade. In the 1970s he operated in Western Europe, where he was wanted for armed robbery and murder. It is also said that he worked for the Yugoslav Secret Service as an assassin of political dissidents abroad. He returned in the 1980s and set up business as the owner of a pastry shop. With the outbreak of civil war in Croatia he went there at the head of his own paramilitary unit, the Tigers, with the support of senior government figures, including a deputy Serbian minister called Radovan Stojičić, nicknamed Badža (meaning Bluto from the Popeye cartoons).

Arkan had a varied career in the 1990s: he led his own paramilitaries, was elected as a deputy representing Kosovo in the National Assembly and owned a Belgrade football club. In 1995 he married the country's most popular "turbofolk" singer, Svetlana Veličković, otherwise known by her stage name Ceca. Their wedding was a huge media event broadcast on television. He was dressed in the uniform of an officer in the Serbian army from the First World War and the occasion was treated like a day of national celebration. Videos of the wedding were later put on sale. In the eyes of the media and the public they were the new celebrities; an Arkan calendar was even issued with a different picture of him for each month. Later indicted by the international court in The Hague for war crimes, he was shot and killed in the lobby of the Intercontinental Hotel in January 2000.

The fact that the gangsters did not live long did not diminish their status, and probably even enhanced it with false notions of a romantic demise. The independent radio and television station, B-92, made a documentary film about Belgrade's criminals and their social influence called *See You in the Obituary* (Vidimo se u čitulji, 1995). In the programme the older criminals bemoan the disappearance of a code of honour among the city's thieves, regarding the new arrivals as too eager to make quick money and forgetful of their place in the pecking order. Dina Iordanova in her book *Cinema of Flames* describes the appearance of the younger set: "Other elements of their B-movie-inspired styles include multiple gold chains and bracelets, sleeveless T-shirts, muscular bodies, expensive jogging suits, silk shirts, state-of-the-art pistols, well-shaven faces and trimmed hair, dark glasses, leather jackets and underage girlfriends." By the time the documentary was complete, three of them had been killed, and by the end of the decade they were nearly all dead.

An official position offered no immunity from gangland warfare. In the early hours of 11 April 1997 Radovan Stojičić was murdered in a Belgrade restaurant. He was buried in the Avenue of Honour in the New Cemetery, normally reserved for citizens whose life and work have made a positive contribution to culture and society. On 24 October 1997 Zoran Todorović was shot and killed as he arrived for work. He was director of the company Beopetrol and general-secretary of the pro-government coalition JUL (Yugoslav United Left) led by Mira Marković, the wife of President Slobodan Milošević.

A peculiar trace of the kitsch culture spawned in these years is to be seen in the tombstones dotted around Belgrade's cemeteries marking the graves of the fallen gangsters. Božović is immortalized in a bronze statue dressed in his military uniform. His effigy stands in front of a construction resembling a doorway decorated with two large crosses and an inscription to his "heroism" in life. Mileta Prodanović has written on these monuments in his ironically titled book *An Older and More Beautiful Belgrade* (Stariji i lepši Beograd). He describes Božović's hieratic pose placed symbolically before the door on "the border of the world of the living and world of the dead". Arkan's tombstone features him in his favourite First World War uniform and sporting a medal, the Karađorđe Star, which he may have thought that he deserved but was never awarded. Another criminal, Zoran Šijan, is depicted by a life-size bronze statue and is dressed in a sharp suit. By his side stands a small table on which there is a bottle of Coca-Cola, a packet of cigarettes and an ash-tray, all fashioned from stone and marble. Prodanović considers that these elements of pop-art iconography added to his sepulchral monument, since they:

> embody the value system which—in the shadow of wars and the total
> pauperization of the population—was established in the everyday life
> of the most important subculture of Belgrade in the 1990s. Its essence
> is best articulated in the lyrics of a popular song:

> Coca-Cola, Marlboro, Suzuki,
> discotheques, guitars, bouzouki,
> that's life, that's not an ad,
> no one is more than us glad.

Many of these realities of life in Belgrade are found reflected in the films
and novels of the decade.

OPPOSITION TO MILOŠEVIĆ

Sanctions were lifted at the end of 1995 when the conflict in Bosnia ended.
Yet economic problems persisted, travel abroad was still difficult because
of visa conditions imposed by foreign embassies, and criminals continued
to live and operate openly. On 17 November 1996 local elections were
held throughout Serbia in which the government's candidates were faced
by a coalition of opposition parties jointly known under the name *Zajedno*
(Together). The opposition estimated that they easily won in all the major
towns including Belgrade. However, Milošević and his allies refused to
recognize these results. In reply, the opposition called on the populace to
protest at such blatant gerrymandering.

The most spectacular events unfolded in Belgrade where the demonstrators were joined by students from the university in daily marches
through town that continued for three months. The streets rang to the
strains of a carnival atmosphere with ever more imaginative slogans, such
as "I think, therefore I walk" (Mislim, dakle šetam). One day, instead of
walking, people were invited to drive into the centre of town where, mys-
teriously, every single car broke down at the same time and the whole city
centre was blocked for the rest of the day. Every evening at 7.30 the city
was filled with the noise of whistles and people banging on saucepans or
whatever else came to hand for a solid half hour in order to drown out the
lies broadcast on the main television news programme. The student body

was particularly adept at putting its feelings across with a sense of humour bordering somewhere between farce and irony. Students took to standing by traffic lights, stepping out only when the red light appeared to warn pedestrians not to cross, and in so doing disrupted the flow of traffic. The point of their actions was to show that nothing meant what it was supposed to mean any more in Belgrade.

The demonstrators were supported by many national institutions such as the Serbian Academy of Sciences and Arts and the Orthodox Church, and by a strong chorus of voices from outside the country. In February 1997 the government finally conceded that it could not continue to defy the daily demonstrations. But rather than admit defeat, the National Assembly passed a special law to recognize the opposition's electoral successes—as if it had not really won but that the government was giving in to outside pressure.

This was not the end of the stand-off between Milošević and the liberal opposition in Belgrade. The ruling coalition tightened its control on the media to ensure that television stations and the main newspapers reported in their favour. Then the government decided that appointments to the directorships of public enterprises, social service institutions, all spheres of education and health, and commercial enterprises where possible, should become part of the political process. This move brought the Socialist Party two advantages: first, the opportunity to reward its supporters in other political parties; second, to reinforce control over large parts of the country's institutional infrastructure. Milošević was particularly anxious to bring the University of Belgrade to heel and passed a law to make the deans of faculties government appointees. The measure met with fierce opposition from staff and students but the Socialist Party and their allies were determined to divide the spoils among themselves. The opposition group Together did not survive much longer, dividing into a number of factions with recriminations on all sides.

The world that emerged from the period of hyperinflation looked a very different place from what had existed before. A country had disappeared, but one had barely been constructed to take its place. Ordinary citizens were still reeling from the effects of sanctions, the civil wars in former Yugoslavia and the corruption of the very people who were supposed to be guardians of public order. Little actual help was coming from outside and by 1999 Belgrade was drained, disillusioned and confused.

Knez Miloš Street

Knez Miloš Street runs from King Alexander Boulevard to the large road intersection called the Mostarska petlja (*petlja* corresponding in meaning to a "spaghetti junction"), or more often simply Mostar, the name of a kafana that was built hereabouts. The route was known as the Topčider Highway, or Topčiderski drum, until 1872 when it took its name from the man who became knez of Serbia twice. Between 1922 and 1946 it had the grander title of Miloš the Great Street (Ulica Miloša velikog), but the reference to the nineteenth-century knez as "the Great" was dropped after 1945—which is a pity since the origin of this wide and impressive thoroughfare was his idea. The Topčider Highway had some advantages, from his perspective, as a district to develop. It lay at a safe distance from the immediate reach of Ottoman Belgrade's guns. The way to reach it from the city was through the newly conceived way stations on Terazije, the growth of which he was also trying to stimulate. Unaware that the street would be honoured with his name, Knez Miloš built for himself a palace here and surrounded it with barracks and other military facilities. Very little is left of these projects from the 1830s except for the 1837 Turkish bathhouse (or *amam*) that belonged to the palace and can still be seen in the courtyard at 12 Admiral Guépratte Street topped by a tiled roof and distinctive cupola. As he had done elsewhere, Miloš gave out free parcels of land for building. One story tells how he gave such a plot to one family, only to take it back without warning when he saw that not even so much as a fence was put up around the property. Rulers of Serbia after Miloš continued the trend of developing this particular street in both functional and aesthetic terms.

Miloš provided his soldiers with a makeshift church, but this was replaced in 1863 with a new church at the top of Admiral Guépratte Street, the Church of the Ascension (Vaznesenska crkva), to serve also the religious needs of those living in this expanding suburb some distance from the Cathedral. A new building for the National Assembly was opened on the corner of Knez Miloš and Queen Natalija Streets in 1882. It was, alas, a squat and ugly building, rather small for the purpose of running the country, and replaced before too long. The Ministry of Defence was constructed at the crossroads with Nemanja Street, completed in 1895 but burnt down in 1941, and on the opposite corner from 1908 stood the Ministry of Finance.

Individuals were allowed to build villas and private dwellings on the street, provided that they were of an appropriate grandeur and with the regulation line facing the street. Elsewhere in the city private villas tended to be planned with a garden in front separating family life from the street. Here, however, the city authorities deemed it important that a continuous architectural line was required behind the trees planted the length of the pavement. The street became a chic area at the end of the nineteenth and beginning of the twentieth centuries. Everything was neatly planned and regulated, offering a safe environment for the country's elite. Men of importance would go from one ministry building to another, attending the meetings where they ran the country's affairs. Industrialists, politicians, actors and public figures lived in their opulent homes, secure in their private world on one of the main roads at the edge of town. It was almost as if someone had designed the street for chaperoned walks by fashionable young men and women among the parks where small concerts were given.

Construction of new government and army buildings in a monumental style of architecture continued in the 1920s and 1930s along Miloš the Great Street. The communists, in power after the Second World War, carried on the trend and built a new federal Ministry of Defence and General Headquarters of the Army of Yugoslavia at the crossroads with Nemanja Street. It was a centre of state activity, graced with government ministries and numerous foreign embassies. In the decades after the split with the Soviet Union, when Yugoslavia was establishing its own identity and place in the world, this long and straight stretch of imposing roadway provided a fine opportunity for prestigious processions. Foreign dignitaries could be driven down the street in a cavalcade of open-topped limousines. The broad pavement provided ample space for flag-waving crowds cheering from the side. Schoolchildren were drafted in to ensure impressive numbers by taking a morning or afternoon from the classroom.

The last great event, however, was of an altogether different nature, marking the funeral procession of President Tito who died after an illness at the age of 87 in May 1980. His body was brought back to Belgrade for burial by rail from the hospital where he was being treated in Slovenia. His coffin was carried down Knez Miloš Street on a plain gun-carriage, watched by huge crowds mostly in tears lining the pavements, then taken up the hill to Dedinje and his final resting place behind the Museum of 25 May and next to his own villa where he had lived since the end of the war. The occasion was attended by presidents, kings and statesman from around the world in a show of respect for the man who over a remarkable career kept his country united and improved its standing in global politics.

Knez Miloš Street was intended to be a symbol of the new country from the time of its first ruler, housing the highest offices of government and the army. It has served as the showpiece in the capital of the principality of Serbia when it still owed allegiance to the Porte; later in the Kingdom of Serbia; then in the Kingdom of Serbs, Croats and Slovenes; the Socialist Federal Republic of Yugoslavia; and most recently the Republic of Serbia.

It has also been the scene of other, more violent, events. One of the targets for intensive German bombing in April 1941, it was where one of the war's catastrophes occurred. A bomb shelter in the grounds of the Church of the Ascension where some 180 people were taking refuge was struck by high explosives. A small memorial in the church grounds today marks where the shelter stood. Nearly sixty years later, some of the government and military buildings on the street were deemed to be legitimate targets by NATO strategists, giving rise to huge damage in 1999. Some buildings have been restored and some are still waiting for sites to be cleared and reconstruction to begin. In 2003 the President of Serbia, Zoran Đinđić, was assassinated in the grounds of the building of the Government of Serbia on the corner with Nemanja as he was leaving to get into his official car at the back of the building. The history of Belgrade seems to demand that its landmarks bear witness equally to all the triumphs and disasters that befall the city.

The end of the street in the nineteenth century was marked with a flourish by a handsome, cobbled square, home to the kafana Mostar. Today it is a junction sitting at the crossroads of a number of important and fast roads. It was built in 1970 to bring the motorway over the River Sava from New Belgrade via the bridge called the Gazelle (Gazela), so-called because its elegant sweep is said to represent an antelope leaping over the water. At this intersection, following from the end of Knez Miloš Street, one road goes down to join Vojvoda Mišić Boulevard, and another crosses straight over into Vojvoda Putnik Boulevard. The lower road leads to the Belgrade Fair (Sajam), which regularly hosts industrial and commercial exhibitions, an annual car show and in October the book fair attended by publishers from home and abroad. Vojvoda Mišić Boulevard then proceeds to the entrance to Ada Ciganlija, the island on the River Sava used by people in Belgrade as a welcome retreat during hot summer weather, and into the Topčider valley via the Belgrade racecourse. Vojvoda Putnik Boulevard goes straight up the hill toward the city's most prestigious residential district of Dedinje.

These two boulevards are named after famous generals of the Serbian army who held long and distinguished military careers. Radomir Putnik (1847-1917) initially turned back the Austrian invasion of Serbia, then in 1915 was faced with certain defeat by a combined offensive of German, Austrian and Bulgarian armies. He withdrew the whole army across Montenegro and through the mountains of Albania to reach safety on the island of Corfu rather than surrender. Živojin Mišić (1855-1921) served in all the major wars from 1876 to 1918. Leading the Serbian offensive in northern Greece during 1918, he broke through the enemy lines and after just a month and a half brought his men to Belgrade on 1 November.

DEDINJE

By the side of the Mostar intersection where Knez Miloš Street joins Vojvoda Putnik Boulevard to go up the hill towards Dedinje stands the brewery originally founded by the Weifert family. After the Second World War it was nationalized and given the more anonymous name of the Belgrade Beer Industry (Beogradska industrija piva), although it has since reverted to its previous name and it is once more possible to buy Weifert beer. Further up the hill, Knez Alexander Karađorđević Boulevard is the lower marker of the elite district of Dedinje. The term is sometimes used to refer to this whole area incorporating Topčider, Košutnjak and Senjak. Strictly speaking, however, it should be confined to the area bounded by the Vojvoda Putnik Boulevard and the ridge at the top of the hill.

The area was formerly known as Dedija or Dedina taken from the Serbian word *deda*, which usually means grandfather but was also applied historically to community elders and particularly heads of religious houses. It is thought that the name has its origin in the fact that, according to an Ottoman census of 1560, a Moslem order of Dervišes from Belgrade owned some land here. At the beginning of the twentieth century the area was known for its orchards, small summer-houses and vineyards kept by some of the rich families in town, who would use their property as a handy retreat from the city.

It owes its transformation into the desirable address that it has represented for nearly a century to King Alexander Karađorđević when he decided to build a new family residence for himself on the ridge of the hill. He chose a spot from where there were long views on all sides, particularly to the south over the wooded Topčider valley. He began to buy up land and between 1924 and 1929 built the Royal Palace (Kraljevski dvor) for himself in the kind of national Byzantine style found in some of the architecture in the centre of Belgrade. The building has a quiet elegance suited to its function as a family home, not an institution of state. Later, as part of the same complex, a new palace was completed in 1936, the White Palace (Beli dvor) in a neoclassical style. Tito used the White Palace as a place for holding state functions and receptions after the Second World War, and since the end of Milošević's regime the complex has been returned to the Karađorđević family for their use.

King Alexander set a trend with his palace development, which was immediately followed by Belgrade's wealthier families who built luxury villas for themselves in Dedinje, pushing the city's boundaries up the hill from Knez Miloš Street. The parkland to the side was planned in the 1930s with pathways for walking and riding and given the name Hyde Park (Hajd park).

Dedinje rapidly became more than just a district of Belgrade. It became a social goal, as a villa in this part of town was taken as a sign of arrival in Belgrade's high society and represented success, money, sophistication and elegant living. It attracted the attention of foreign representatives who saw the value of having their embassy, or more often an ambassador's residence, in Dedinje with the more functional embassy building in town.

When the communists arrived in 1944 they took it upon themselves to take over control of Belgrade in all ways, including the symbolic significance of the Dedinje villas. Their goal was not just to assume the outward appearance of having taken power, but to take over the prestige and position of the pre-war elite. To this end they requisitioned the houses in Dedinje, moving out the previous owners and installing themselves and their families. Property was handed out to loyal followers of the Communist Party like a medieval king would give castles and lands to his feudal barons.

The same mentality dominated among the new elite of the 1990s. They were not interested in emulating the political coup that the communists strove to achieve, but wanted to show the rest of their world that they had truly arrived. Old-style leaders of criminal gangs became new-style businessmen, hiding their origins behind a Dedinje villa. Yet their taste for kitsch styles in dress, music and finally architecture led them to treat their prestige addresses in a different way. They would enlarge the property, or even pull down the original house and replace it with some hugely vulgar monstrosity, ruining the unassuming elegance for which the district was famous. Their trademark has acquired the term "turbo" architecture, coined from the more widely known turbofolk, a fast and furious version of popular music from the 1990s produced by adding disco rhythms to the slower oriental melodies of traditional folk songs.

The basic orientation of "turbo" forms, according to Slobodan Bogunović in his encyclopaedia of Belgrade architecture, is founded on a "reinterpretation and politicization of folklore, a nationalist mania for mythmaking based on incorrect readings of national history". He characterizes the stylistic content of its architectural design as follows:

> The absence of any feeling of measure, an intoxication with physical size, a visible tendency towards a sense of the theatrical overburdened by motifs and details; a somewhat mellow, indulgent and shallow under-

standing of architectural tradition, alongside a shameless flirting with dreams of a fairytale, ideal home, bring these objects close to the nature of kitsch production and kitsch perception.

These "turbo" blunders mix a layman's vision of a hi-tech future with a confused sense of the purpose of architecture. They appear to some as a Postmodernist expression in building materials. Yet such a view overlooks the social, economic and political chaos that shaped Belgrade in the 1990s, and the desperate situation of most of its inhabitants as a result of the collapse of Yugoslavia. The appearance of these weird buildings is a sign of those times of crisis, just as the Baroque and classical monumentalism of many of the buildings in the centre is a sign of the city's early growth and sense of self-confidence.

House of Flowers

A little way along Knez Alexander Karađorđević Boulevard, set back from the main road behind a broad swathe of park, stands what used to be the Museum of 25 May. The date is taken from Yugoslavia's Day of Youth (Dan mladosti), which was also Tito's birthday. It used to exhibit the official presents that the president received on his state visits to other countries, and items sent to him from various organizations and individuals from within Yugoslavia. It was a shrine to the popularity of Tito, which with the fall of communism became out of place, and the museum no longer exists. The space is used for temporary exhibitions, and the area in front for small musical or theatre performances. Just inside the front door, however, two of Tito's official cars remain on display. One of them, a Rolls Royce, was slightly damaged during the 1999 bombing campaign. It was kept in a garage at the late president's villa which became a target when it was rumoured that Milošević was living there.

Another museum used to be close by but is now considered irrelevant in the new times. The Museum of 4 July was dedicated to the Partisan uprising in 1941, as it was in this house, formerly belonging to Vladislav S. Ribnikar, that the leadership of the Yugoslav Communist Party met to organize resistance to the German occupation.

Behind the ex-Museum of 25 May is a small mausoleum, the House of Flowers (Kuća cveća), where Tito's coffin was laid to rest in 1980. His tomb is made of plain white marble with his name and years of his birth and death in gold letters. The whole building is a modest homage to the man who led the country from the end of the Second World War to 1980. By the side of the House of Flowers is a small museum of artefacts from his life, mainly gifts given on state occasions. Behind the wall lies his former residence, a villa constructed as the family home of Aleksandar Acović in 1934. When Tito arrived in Belgrade at the end of 1944 he lived briefly in the White Palace before moving to 15 Užice Street. The site is now closed to visitors, but the damage caused in 1999 is obvious from the street.

TOPČIDER AND SURROUNDINGS
Vojvoda Putnik Boulevard continues to climb the hill beside Hyde Park to meet the Topčider Star, or Topčiderska zvezda, a roundabout where seven roads converge. From here the boulevard drops down the other side of the hill with a pleasantly wooded area on the left through which paths cut down to the bottom avoiding the main road. On the other side of the road the slope forms a residential area known as Senjak; its name comes from the Serbian word *seno*, meaning hay. Kalemegdan used to provide storage space for hay until there was a serious fire in 1857 that caused a great deal of damage and presented a serious danger to the fortress and the buildings inside. It was decided, thereafter, for reasons of prudence, that such easily combustible material should not be kept so close to the centre of Belgrade. The collection and storage point for hay was then moved out of town to here, hence Senjak.

This innovation was followed toward the close of the nineteenth century by the building of new industries near the square marking the end of Knez Miloš Street. People looking for work began to migrate to this district and, since it was outside the city boundary and not subject to any planning regulations, built rough dwellings on the slope of Senjak. Not much attention was given to these hastily constructed shacks, thrown up with no regard for any kind of urban plan, until the development of Dedinje as a residential quarter was under way in the 1920s and 1930s. Although it was less prestigious than Dedinje, Senjak was very close and it rose in popularity among Belgrade's middle classes who replaced the slums with family villas. The old racecourse, the Belgrade Hippodrome, was relocated to the bottom of the Senjak slope from its original site near the Đeram Market on King Alexander Boulevard at the beginning of the twentieth century and, later, the state mint was built close by.

The area known as Košutnjak begins just to the south of Senjak. It is thickly wooded parkland with mixed deciduous and evergreen trees spreading up the hill away from the valley floor of Topčider. In the nineteenth century it was known as a hunting ground, košuta being the Serbian word for a hind or a doe. It covers a substantial area and has retained a rather wild appearance. People come here to have a picnic or go walking. Residential areas have since sprung up around Košutnjak, too, so it is no longer on the very periphery of Belgrade, yet building within the park area is controlled to keep it a green oasis. The air is much clearer than closer in to the city where there is a concentration of exhaust fumes and noise. Knez Mihailo Obrenović was assassinated in Košutnjak on 29 May 1868. The spot is commemorated with a simple monument, which is inappropriately small and hidden away, really deserving a more prominent and visible place. A railway line marks the boundary between Košutnjak and the Topčider valley.

Topčider valley nestles in the middle of the area bordered by Dedinje, Senjak and Košutnjak, down the hill from the Topčider Star. The area is known for its very pleasant microclimate, enjoyed by the rulers of Belgrade, whether Ottoman or Austrian, who escaped business in town and came here for picnics, hunting or country parties. In times of war it was a strategic point for armies attacking the city where they could put up camp in relative safety, separated by the hill from the defenders' guns. The valley also gave control of major approaches to Belgrade from the south. The Turks made use of the area when taking the city in 1521, and later Karađorđe during the First Serbian Uprising.

Miloš Obrenović decided to build a small palace complex in the bottom of the valley for himself after receiving the *hatti-sherif* of 1830. The konak, or residence, intended for use by the church next door, was the first building to go up in 1830-32, constructed in a traditional Balkan style. The church, dedicated to the apostles Peter and Paul, was built over the next two years and designed according to more western taste with a tall bell tower like the Cathedral church in Belgrade, but on a much smaller scale. The prince's own residence, Konak kneza Miloša, was sited close by and was also constructed between 1832 and 1834 in a typical Balkan style of architecture. These buildings still stand today, except that Miloš's konak now houses a museum with exhibitions about the Serbian uprisings against the Turks.

After his exile abroad, Miloš took up residence here again in 1859, and after his death the Obrenović rulers continued to use it as a summer house. Other workshops, a military store and a garrison were built, but most of the area was developed as a park. Miloš did not want a defensive fortification on this spot and he modelled his residence on the kind of environment that the ruling families in Western Europe were then making for themselves. One French visitor, quoted by Bogunović, remarked that the residence at Topčider was "the Versailles of the Serbian Princes".

REINTERPRETING THE PAST

Literature in the 1980s became obsessed with looking at the past in new ways. The taboos of Tito's time gradually gave way to a much bolder approach to recent history. Even so, the League of Communists of Yugoslavia was not prepared to allow creative artists simply to express any views or images without a struggle. The Serbian poet Gojko Đogo found himself in court for his collection titled *Woolly Times* (Vunena vremena, 1982) in which he provided very unflattering sketches of the late president himself. He spent a period in prison before an early release on conditional discharge after public protests at his treatment.

The Croatian League of Communists published a report in 1984, *The White Book* (Bijela knjiga), criticizing contemporary artists who allowed themselves too much liberty. The 237-page document detailed instances in which it was felt that novels, plays, films, aphorisms and literary criticism were spreading messages hostile to the regime. By far the greatest amount of offending material was taken from Serbia with considerably less from Slovenia and Croatia. The report stated that some criticism in recent times had gone beyond the bounds of acceptability and had attacked "the very direction of Yugoslav social development and the basis of the economic and political syste". The themes to which the party hierarchy objected in particular were stories about the prison island Goli Otok, narratives rewriting the story of the Partisan struggle and stories whose bleak pictures of the contemporary world indicated that not all was well with socialism in Yugoslavia. Authors were publishing work that questioned assumptions about the past and the present—"open attempts to devalue the revolution and its achievements in the name of demystification".

The *White Book* was correct in its basic assumption that writers in 1980s Serbia were re-assessing the story of communism in Yugoslavia. This is not to say that all were dissidents or intent on pulling the regime down; for many it was an attempt to open a debate on the nature and direction of contemporary society. This kind of Serbian writing, with its concentration of talent in Belgrade, was epitomized by one member of the Serbian Academy of Sciences and Arts, Predrag Palavestra, as "critical literature". Writers were interested in the process that brought the communists to power, the consequences of their policies and the gap between official versions of history and what was preserved in folk memory from those times.

The novelist Slobodan Selenić took this topic as the theme for his address to a conference held in Belgrade in June 1990. Participants at the conference from the Serbian and Swedish Academies were examining the responsibility of science and the role of intellectuals in contemporary society. Selenić spoke about mainstream tendencies in the modern Serbian novel and compared them to the fate of historiography as an academic discipline. He described how history under the communists in Yugoslavia ossified, how it "ceased being the branch of knowledge that records and explains past events". Instead, it became a series of convenient slogans and assumptions about what happened. History, the academic subject entrusted with the responsibility of investigating what has made us what we are today, was emasculated. For decades after the end of the Second World War the primary task of the historian had been to reinforce the place and prestige of the communist movement in Yugoslavia. Hence, Selenić insisted that only the imaginative scope of literature was free to take a fresh look at Serbian history. Novelists had the task to exhume and disturb the ghosts of the past, to offer alternative visions of what happened, to take on the responsibility of confronting accepted wisdoms. For some Belgrade novelists, the story of their city during the war and its subsequent liberation was one of those topics that had not received the treatment it deserved.

The Partisan novel was typically set in the mountains and among the small villages of provincial Yugoslavia while German and Italian forces were in possession of most major towns and communication routes. Consequently, there were very few stories about the war set in Belgrade. One exception was the novel *The Poem* (Pesma, 1952) by Oskar Davičo (1909-89)—except that the plot offers a standard view of Belgrade as a corrosive and corrupting environment. Then Aleksandar Đorđević (1924-2005) directed the 1974 film *The Written-off* (Otpisani) about a group of young communists in Belgrade fighting the Germans and bringing the guerrilla war into town, followed by a sequel two years later, *Return of the Written-off.* Both films were transferred to the small screen and became very popular television series.

The story of war-time Belgrade, however, received a much more vigorous re-interpretation in two novels, translated into English: Slobodan Selenić's *Fathers and Forefathers* (Očevi i oci, 1985) and Svetlana Velmar-Janković's *Dungeon* (Lagum, 1990).

The story of *Fathers and Forefathers* is told by two characters, the married couple Stevan and Elizabeth Medaković. Stevan meets the English girl Elizabeth in Bristol when he goes to study at the university there, taking her back to Belgrade as his wife in 1925. The novel covers their life together from when they meet to some forty years later when they are both alone in their rooms on the second floor of 52 Knez Miloš Street.

The novel dramatizes a series of clashes of different cultures as Serbs and English, parents and children, communists and non-communists, traditional and modern worlds, rub up against one another, repelling and attracting. Elizabeth is particularly struck by the contrasts she experiences in Belgrade. One side is characterized by poverty, backwardness and cruelty. On arriving at the Sava quay by boat at the end of their long journey from England in 1925, she is frightened by the sudden appearance of men in rags racing through the mud to fight over their bags and earn a tip. She rails against the way in which the draymen whip their horses on steep streets and slippery cobbles. This is the barbaric side of Belgrade, which she sums up as "the Orient". The other side of her life is epitomized by Stevan, who lectures at the Faculty of Law, and his friends, all of whom are highly educated and cultured people. They are knowledgeable about world affairs and some are amateur chamber musicians who meet regularly to play for their own enjoyment. This is the civilized, European Belgrade.

Selenić's novel allows ample opportunity for reflection on Belgrade society and Serbian culture. At the time of its publication, however, readers were more alert to its picture of life in the city when the communists arrive in 1944. For Stevan and Elizabeth, the Partisans are hardly liberators, and Stevan recalls—in contradiction to the regime's propaganda—how the citizens of Belgrade knew very little about the resistance movement during the occupation since its distant operations were of little relevance to the daily grind of surviving the war in the city.

Mihajlo, Elizabeth's and Stevan's son, is intensely drawn to the young comrades from the hills and villages of Bosnia and Serbia with whom he comes into contact. He invites them into the family home which they use to paint banners and posters to take on demonstrations in support of Tito. As they prepare their materials they spill paint and carelessly put their muddy boots on furniture. Stevan describes how "I clenched my teeth, kept my silence and watched how the Huns and Visigoths devastated my home from one day to the next." They have, he says, the "spontaneity of jungle creatures" unconscious of what they are doing "because they knew no order". Selenić also draws into his fictional world the names of the party hierarchy whom Stevan meets and who force him to work for them because they want to make use of his legal expertise. He calls that period "those ugly and perilous times".

The worst, however, is yet to come. Mihajlo in his euphoric support for the Partisans is sent, along with many other young people from Belgrade, to fight on the Sremski Front, the final battle to push the enemy out of the country. The battle is a disaster, where many of the recruits, poorly trained and badly armed, are killed. Mihajlo dies and Stevan brings his body home for burial. His death holds a symbolic significance, for something in Stevan and Elizabeth dies with him, destroying any chance of future happiness together.

Svetlana Velmar-Janković's novel *Dungeon* was published in 1990, five years after *Fathers and Forefathers*. The work is presented as if the diary of Milica Pavlović, wife of Dušan Pavlović, a respected professor at Belgrade University. In her recollections she depicts the liberation of Belgrade and its effects as a complete break with the city's past. The arrival of the Partisans sets off a train of events based on betrayal, execution and requisition. As the city is liberated, the Partisans arrest Dušan for being a collaborator. During the war he accepted a post in the quisling government, which gave him responsibility for refugees, and he was able to save the lives of many Serbs who would otherwise have been killed by the occupying forces or by the Ustaše. In his opinion his actions were honest and honourable, but his view is not shared by the new authorities and he is led away. Milica later discovers that he has been executed along with others accused in the mass trials held at the end of November 1944. She is devastated by the news, but this is not the end of her story.

Dušan is arrested in the presence of people both he and Milica know.

One of them is the caretaker of their building in the district of Dorćol, a man who would always help the wealthy families who live there, until the revolution comes and he joins the fight out of weakness. Another is the son of the Armenian grocer whose shop was on the corner of the street. He reappears in the city as a Partisan officer determined to establish the new ideological order. Their sumptuous flat is immediately divided. Milica and her two children are allowed to live in the smaller portion, while the larger area is given to their maid, now known as Comrade Zora. She is one of the lucky few from a small village near Šid whom Dušan managed to save during the war and whom he brought home to live with them. She now turns on her former benefactors and directs the soldiers to the most valuable paintings in the flat, which are confiscated. Milica has difficulty in obtaining food and fuel, and cannot work as she is regarded as an enemy of the people. Eventually, she is able to get a job as a translator, although she is not allowed to sign her work with her own name. She is a person without a past or a present and barely exists in this brave new world.

Her children, however, are brought up in this environment and do not see it or experience in the same way as their mother. They learn the new language, where words change to suit the circumstances. (The grocer's shop is now called a general store because the latter "does not presuppose an owner".) The communists retain only those elements of the pre-war city that are useful to them. Milica eventually asks herself who has betrayed whom: "Who then is the one who is saved and who the saviour, who is sacrificed and who is the victim?"

She ultimately finds that there are no clear lines of demarcation in Belgrade to divide traitors from patriots, honest people from dishonest, lambs from wolves. Terms such as innocence and guilt become irrelevant in times of crisis, when history is out of control and events follow no clear logic. Belgrade's position at the turbulent meeting of the Sava and the Danube becomes a metaphor for life in *Dungeon*, suggesting that the city has been formed from sudden and irreversible clashes of history and culture.

Belgrade in Literature and Film
Film and literature from the 1990s obsessively examine the consequences of the disappearance of Yugoslavia. The images of Belgrade incorporated

into these narratives are based on the perception of a world turned completely upside down in which nothing is as it seems. The city of this period has been summarized in a book about organized crime in the country, *Criminal Activity which Changed Serbia* (Kriminal koji je izmenio Srbiju, 1995): "Belgrade epitomized Chicago in the twenties, the economic crisis of Berlin in the thirties, the cloak-and-dagger plots of Casablanca in the forties and the cataclysmic hedonism of Vietnam in the sixties." The story of Belgrade in the 1990s is an amalgamation of crime, instant poverty, conspiracy theories and a destructive delight born from the lack of restraint which the war brought in its wake—all concentrated in one city. The problem of artists in all branches was to convey the palpable breakdown of order on a collective level and of moral value on an individual level.

The contemporary films and novels set in Belgrade emphasize the atmosphere of constant crisis. By focusing on a particular aspect or group of people, they isolate the reactions and effects of war, sanctions and a criminalized society. Some films look at the lives of a particular social group, such as the elderly in *Diary of Iniquities* (Dnevnik uvreda, dir. Zdravko Šotra, 1993) or a generation coming to maturity in *Neither in Heaven nor on Earth* (Ni na nebu ni na zemlji, dir. Miloš Radivojević, 1994). Šotra's film records the experiences of an older couple whose lives seem settled and comfortable. They have friends who visit them in their home to play music, they go to literary evenings, and they are in contact with the city and society around them. Slowly, as the effects of sanctions begin to bite, their lives too become isolated and fragmented. Friends stop visiting and social contact is reduced to a club for the elderly, serving only as a reminder of the distance they have travelled from the lives they formerly led. Food becomes scarce, shopping becomes a humiliating experience and life regresses to a more primitive form, represented in one scene by the wild dancing of a village *kolo* or folk dance in a Belgrade supermarket. Their son has been forced to leave the country to avoid the military draft, which causes a major rift between the wife, who is only concerned for her child's safety, and her husband who considers him a traitor for running away. Such daily pressures force them apart, and they eventually make separate homes in different rooms of the family apartment. In desperation, the wife begins to make toys and hats for sale on the Belgrade streets where one winter night she dies of the extreme cold.

Radivojević in his film of the following year focuses on a group of young friends who are just starting out in their careers. Their story records the destruction of their opportunities and dreams for the future while all the time the criminal presence around them presses threateningly closer until one of them is killed and others leave the country. One stays behind, and he is finally depicted alone, unkempt, in an empty room, dressed in a blue jumpsuit as if an inmate in a prison or a patient in an asylum.

Stories of crime and conspiracy were common. One of the first films set in these new circumstances was a gangster movie that adapted some of the generic elements of the early films about Chicago, Vladimir Blaževski's *Revolution Boulevard* (Bulevar revolucije, 1992). A young criminal befriends and protects a young girl, a refugee from Bosnia, and in the end they attempt to leave the country together. The plan is foiled by the girl's father but she dies in the cross-fire between him and her boyfriend. A partnership re-worked on the model of Bonnie and Clyde ends in a tragedy on the streets of Belgrade.

At the end of this period the director Srđan Dragojević made the film *Wounds* (Rane) in 1998. This is a much more violent story of two young men born at the time of Tito's death, brought up in a vastly different world from that of their parents. The blossoming of crime as Yugoslavia disintegrates is an exciting time and offers opportunities for them to act without the usual framework of social and legal restraints. They live in a paradise for those who do not care to reflect on the difference between what they want and the necessary means to achieve those aims.

Two novels, both published in 1996, also relate stories of crime, but wrapped up in more conspiratorial plots. Mileta Prodanović in his *Dance Monster to My Tender Music* (Pleši čudovište na moju nežnu muziku) tells the story of a contract killer employed by the communist security services to eliminate state enemies abroad who is called home when conflict breaks out in Bosnia. He meets his old controllers who are now part of a new nationalist *Nomenclatura* and serving new masters in changed circumstances. The communists have gone and his task is now to lead paramilitary units over the border.

Nenad Petrović in his novel *The Man Who Should Have Been Killed* (Čovek koga je trebalo ubiti) imagines a plot to assassinate the man considered most responsible by the British Secret Service for the current crisis in south-eastern Europe, Slobodan Milošević. The CIA learns of the plan and puts into operation a counter-strategy to prevent the killing on the grounds that it is in American global interest to save Milošević in order to maintain chaos in Europe.

Some of the novels and films set in 1990s Belgrade found their way abroad and have been translated or subtitled for foreign audiences, for example: the two novels *Premeditated Murder* (Ubistvo s predumišljajem, 1993) by Slobodan Selenić and *In the Hold* (U potpalublju, 1994) by Vladimir Arsenijević; the two films *Underground* (Podzemlje, dir. Emir Kusturica, 1995) and *Cabaret Balkan* (Bure baruta, dir. Goran Paskaljević, 1998). Each story is peopled with characters whose attempts to give purpose to what they are doing are met with failure and an overbearing sense that everything is an illusion.

Two of these works have a historical dimension, taking a longer view of the contemporary tragedy. The main character in Selenić's novel, Jelena, is alone in the city. Her parents are divorced; her father is caught in a hopeless second marriage and her mother has left with her new husband for New Zealand. Jelena discovers a bag of mementos, letters and diaries belonging to her late grandmother. The find encourages her to piece together the life of her grandmother, significantly also called Jelena, at the end of the Second World War when she had an affair with a Partisan officer, Krsman Jakšić. Her grandmother is the daughter of a wealthy industrialist accused by the communists of collaboration, the family home on Senjak is requisitioned, and her brother Jovan does not hide his disgust at the barbaric ways of the new rulers. In truth, they are not real brother and sister, only becoming siblings when their widowed parents marry and they are brought up together.

Jovan is sent over the edge in these times of unbearable crisis and, in a fit of rage, he rapes his sister. Finally, he ends up shooting Krsman before turning the gun on himself. For Jelena, this revelation gives rise to a vital question: does she issue from Jovan or Krsman, from a civilized but nervous and drained personality, or from the mountain peasant bent on destroying the city's heritage? Jelena and Belgrade of the 1990s have elements of both in their veins.

Kusturica's film also links the Second World War with events of the 1990s. The story opens as Belgrade is about to be bombed in 1941. The narrative follows the exploits of two petty criminals, Marko and Blacky, who use their talents to support the communist resistance and line their own pockets. Fearing that they may be captured by the Germans, Marko hides his family and friends, including Blacky, in a cellar. But, he does not tell them when the war has ended. Instead, they keep producing weapons from their hideaway which Marko, now a successful politician in the post-war regime, exports. The allegoric status of a government keeping its own people in the dark is not lost on the audience, but Kusterica's exuberant cinema style does not labour the symbolism of his plot. Instead, life below the city develops a logic and rationale for its existence, while Marko above ground continues to peddle lies about the past and his own exaggerated role in the war until the two worlds collide.

Blacky and his son, born in the cellar, escape and find themselves on the streets at night. They stumble across a film set where a motion picture is being made based on Marko's false version of events in the war. The actors playing German soldiers look real enough to the people from the cellar. The scene is Blacky's heroic execution which Marko has invented in order to hide his betrayal of his friend. The simple allegory now leaps to a far more complex series of potential references in which the people, the city and the whole country are complicit in keeping alive the lies of the past in order to support the illusion that all is well in the present.

Both Selenić and Kusterica present history as a repository of myths and build up complex narrative plots that intertwine those legendary motifs with images of Belgrade as a city of doubled and re-doubled identities, sometimes even in conflict with itself.

The other two stories focus on the impossibility of making sense of the current crisis. Arsenijević's novel is narrated by a young man from Belgrade trying to cope with the catastrophe of the situation in which he finds himself. Though not in the city, the war's effects are all around. His teenage brother-in-law is called up for military service and his body later returned for burial. The narrator, his wife, and their friends survive by taking drugs and trying not to notice what is happening. Belgrade seems like a nightmare, a city crowded with refugees who speak with the same accent as the supposed enemy—a reference to the fact that most refugees were Serbs who came from Bosnia or Croatia. The narrator repeats how everything appears unreal, as if in a film, where even grief is not real but "an ugly parody of grief". He and his generation suffer from two contradictory feelings of innocence and guilt. Paradoxically, between these two extremes they also feel the lack of all constraints. Death is just around the corner and their lives are already destroyed. No-one goes to work anymore, all routine of life is gone, and anything is permitted. The narrator recounts a nightmarish vision that encapsulates the death of the city:

> I felt sorry for all of us. In the glare of a sudden and all-pervasive vision that split the ordinary street scene before my eyes, I caught sight of all of us, running, while the ground beneath our feet was breaking up and opening with a terrible cracking sound, and out of those depths came the unbearable stench of the centuries which, in our inertia, we had omitted to use in a dignified way, a great, slimy pulsating monster was mocking us from in there, unconcerned about the horror which we were conjuring up with our irresolute movements, and our desire not to be. In the course of this carnal bacchanalia, which lasted for one second, the chosen victims had vanished randomly in the depths of that well of flesh. There were many of them. All those who had not managed to find a shelter, all those who had been caught unawares, they were all whisked away, like kites snatched from our hands by the November gales.

The title of the film *Cabaret Balkan* neatly summarizes an inter-textual reference to Berlin in the 1930s, the setting for the earlier film *Cabaret* and the dizzy Sally Bowles character played by Lisa Minnelli. In the earlier film the glamour and spectacle of the cabaret functions as a contrast to the repellent images of Nazism in the background. In Paskaljević's setting the cabaret act opens and is part of the story itself, not a piece of compensatory colour. The cabaret is introduced by a ghoulish compere, a painted face that extols self-pity while mocking the audience. The war is over and sanctions have been lifted, but Belgrade continues to reel from their effects.

All the events of the film take place one night in Belgrade towards the end of the 1990s. It is a narrative of unconnected episodes that begin with a minor road accident after which tempers flare. There follows a series of almost separate vignettes strung together through the night. Characters who move from one event to another serve as the only link between them. Two friends are showering after boxing together at the gym when their conversation leads them to the discovery that they have both slept with the other's wife and the child of one of them may not be after all his. These remarks culminate in anger and a brutal murder. The film is heavily laden with an accumulation of fear and desperation, characterized by sudden and random violence. Belgrade is in chaos, its citizens experiencing life as if with no past and no future, just a series of present moments.

The imaginative depiction of 1990s Belgrade is one of reckless fury trying to come to terms with the end of Yugoslavia, civil wars, the pariah status conferred by sanctions, feelings of guilt and powerlessness. Working through allegory and metaphor, novels and films try to give form and meaning to what has little sense or shape. They succeed not only in conveying the atmosphere of those times, but also in representing a society and culture at odds with itself. Internally fragmented and internationally isolated, the city is vulnerable and alone. Novels and films offer an insight into the crisis characteristic of those years, expressing in powerful individual terms the impact and drama of lived history. More than simply a place, Belgrade appears as a metaphor for what can happen when civilization itself comes under attack.

Chapter Seven

SLAVIJA, ENGLEZOVAC AND THE VRAČAR PLATEAU: BELGRADE UNDER A FOREIGN GAZE

SLAVIJA

Slavija Square lies at the end of King Milan Street. When the pasha finally quit the city in 1867, this point marked the edge of Belgrade in this direction. Beyond here, going up the hill and toward where Kalenić Market (Kalenićeva pijaca) stands today, the land was marshy and well known as a good spot for hunting wild fowl. But Belgrade developed rapidly after this event, spreading up the hill toward the Vračar plateau and further. A large hotel was constructed at Slavija between 1883 and 1888 by the Czech engineer and architect František Nekvasil, who was also its first owner. There have been many changes since then, but a hotel has remained more or less in the same place as a landmark of the square.

Nekvasil came to Belgrade in the early 1880s when the railway arrived and the station was built because of the work that urban expansion promised. He was one of many who came to the city anxious to make use of their professional skills and qualifications. They numbered lawyers, doctors, architects and engineers, mainly from other Slavonic lands in Central and Eastern Europe under the rule of the Austrian Habsburg dynasty.

There was another impetus for their coming to Belgrade. These Czechs, Slovaks, Croats and Slovenes nurtured a pan-Slavonic feeling, a belief that there exists a basic unity amongst the Slavs underpinned by similarities in language and culture. At the same time, and linked to pan-Slavism, their desire for national independence grew. The organizations they joined were, of course, treated as hostile by the authorities in their home states. Belgrade was a beacon for such people hoping for freedom from foreign domination, since it was the capital city of a country of Slavs and of a sovereign state.

It is difficult to find final confirmation, but it would appear that Nekvasil, intentionally or not, actually gave the square its name. He put a statue of a female figure in a niche on the first floor of the façade of his hotel in honour of Slavija. There is no such word in Serbian, but in his native Czech Slavia was the title of a popular student organization with very strong pan-Slavonic views, to which Serbian orthography would demand the addition of "j" for the word to be adopted. Given the circumstances, it is not unreasonable to suggest that his aim was to commemorate the feelings that drove him and other East European immigrants to Belgrade. The hotel and then the square as a whole acquired the same moniker.

From its beginning Slavija Square had regular evening visitors to its famous kafanas, some of which even predated the hotel. One of these was the Three Peasants (Tri seljaka), which is mentioned in a list of similar establishments from 1860. The composer and art historian D. Gostuški recalls it from his childhood in the early twentieth century as a place that may have been in need of some repair but which was popular among the city's intellectuals. Next to it, the Rudničanin kafana was another evening venue known for its jovial atmosphere and music. The same D. Gostuški also remembers this establishment chiefly for its regular pianist who would play for the guests and who was an Englishman "with absolutely white, shoulder-length hair".

The merchant Vlada Mitić bought the Rudničanin in 1935, giving him a fairly large plot on the corner of King Milan and Belgrade Streets on the edge of the square. He demolished the building and cleared the site intending to redevelop it as the city's first department store. A very ambitious businessman, he planned to build a retail outlet of fourteen storeys, 200 feet tall, which would have made it the tallest building in Belgrade before the Second World War. The aim, as reported in the press at the time, was to present the ordinary person with the opportunity to buy just about all that he could need in one shop. Architects drew up plans and Mitić deposited twenty million dinars in the National Bank toward building costs. The plan was interrupted, however, by the Second World War and never came to fruition. After the war the communist authorities accused Mitić of selling goods to the enemy—tantamount to a charge of collaboration—and he was imprisoned. Mitić's Hole, as the site was popularly called in the city, remained empty and an eyesore for decades after.

It was eventually taken over by gypsies until the decision was taken to clear the site once more, landscape it, and turn it into a small park. On the opposite corner to Belgrade Street from the Rudničanin, the Scottish philanthropist Francis Mackenzie (1833-95) built his Hall of Peace (Sala mira) in 1889. He wanted it to serve as a community centre for the district, which it did for a while. But in 1910 it became the head-quarters of the Social Democratic Party of Serbia; thus began a link between Slavija Square and leftist circles that was to continue for some decades. The Socialist Workers Party was formed from a number of separate groups which met at a congress held in the Hotel Slavija in 1919. After the Second World War the communist government renamed the square after one of the country's early socialists, Dimitrije Tucović (1881-1914). His remains were transferred here and re-interred under a small statue in the middle of the square. Despite this official act, the square continued to be called Slavija by everyone who lived in Belgrade. The Social Democratic Party left Mackenzie's Hall of Peace, which changed yet again, becoming a kafana for a period, then after the Second World War housing the Slavija cinema.

During the 1980s it was decided that the square should be given a more harmonious appearance and function. All around it stood a jumble of small shops, a cinema, cheap places to grab a snack, bus stops, kiosks and a constant stream of cars, buses, taxis, trams and people. The first Macdonald's restaurant, not only in Yugoslavia but in the whole of the Balkan Peninsula, was established here, adding to the colourful mix to which Slavija Square played host. It may have been hoping for too much, but the aim of the new plan was to transform the square into the centre of Belgrade's modern financial district, with a concentration of banks and other institutions. The hotel added an annex on the opposite corner with more up-market rooms and apartments attractive to foreign businessmen and investors. Work began on the project with enthusiasm; the old Slavija cinema was demolished, as were some other of the older buildings on the north side including a pharmacy. Some people objected to the changes on the grounds that these buildings were of some architectural merit or historic interest.

Then came the crash of the 1990s. Yugoslavia collapsed and a combination of war and sanctions destroyed the Serbian economy, while the government under President Milošević was considered abroad to be entirely untrustworthy. Investment in the project dried up and at the beginning of the twenty-first century the only bank to survive from this project is housed in the ultra-modern building at the end of Nemanja Street. The old picture palace has become a car park, and the square as a whole has kept its disordered appearance, a place where all is in transit and nothing is permanent.

The main problem posed by Slavija is its function as a vital point in the city's road network. Its significance in this respect was recognized early on, with the first horse-drawn tram service running from here to Kalemegdan, and the second service when inaugurated from Slavija Square to the railway station and the quay on the River Sava. It is a large intersection where seven roads meet bringing traffic from out of town to the city centre. It is also a vital spot in the public transport system with trams, trolleybuses and buses passing through. The national airline, JAT, has its terminus for buses running to and from the airport at the hotel. The main railway station and bus station are situated down Nemanja Street, below the intersection with Knez Miloš Street. One of the roads leading into the square, Belgrade Street, connects with King Alexander Boulevard and the residential areas of Zvezdara and the west of the city. Liberation Boulevard, opposite Belgrade Street, goes up to the Vračar plateau, the site of the National Library of Serbia (Narodna biblioteka Srbije) and the massive new church dedicated to St. Sava (Hram svetog Save), continuing out to the southern suburbs.

This is always a busy part of town and the city authorities have been trying to grapple with its congestion from the beginning of the twentieth century. Various ideas have been put forward, including reducing the number of roads entering and leaving the space, but cars and public transport would need to turn at another point in order to approach the centre of town—which would cause bottlenecks elsewhere. Plans have been drawn up for overhead walkways and a complex of pedestrian underpasses with entrances to shops in order to separate people from vehicular traffic, a difficult aim given the large numbers who change public transport here. Slavija Square requires two or three policemen directing traffic at what has become Belgrade's biggest roundabout.

ENGLEZOVAC

Francis Mackenzie, the founder of the Hall of Peace, was an important figure in Belgrade's urban development. He was born into a well-to-do background; his father's family owned a large estate in the north-west Highlands of Scotland around Gairloch, while his stepmother's family was also wealthy. He came to Serbia in 1876 with the intention of helping the refugees fleeing the troubles in Bosnia and Herzegovina. He was already acquainted with one or two influential Serbian families in Belgrade, probably through contact with the anglophile statesman Čedomilj Mijatović, and decided to buy a plot on the edge of Belgrade in 1877. He purchased land owned by Đorđe Simić, the son of Stojan Simić from whom Knez Alexander Karađorđević had bought the Old Residence on Terazije in the 1840s. Mackenzie became the owner of a piece of land roughly in the shape of a fan stretching on one side of Slavija up toward the site of the National Library, and on the other side a little way up what is now Belgrade Street, with the area in between crossing today's Mackenzie Street, named after the Scotsman himself. He has been described in an article by Michael Palairet as "one of those quintessentially Victorian apostles of the virtues of his age", meaning that he was a financially independent philanthropist with a strong religious streak.

Determined to do good, Mackenzie divided his sizeable estate into small parcels of land that he intended for the construction of individual homes. He sold the plots with very favourable repayment terms to poorer families but with certain conditions attached. Householders had to ensure that their houses followed the line of the street frontage; they had to promise that they would use solid building materials, provide proper drainage and a clean water supply, pave the section of the street in front of their property, and limit the number of persons in the dwelling to prevent overcrowding. In short, he adapted "various British urban improvement and low-income housing schemes of the time" that had brought some good to the working class.

His religious zeal was of a somewhat puritanical nature, however, and it prompted him to add an extra condition forbidding the sale of alcohol within the area of his estate. This last provision proved impossible to enforce and was overturned when a group of householders took the matter to the Serbian courts. Mackenzie was determined to improve life for others, firmly believing that the path to happiness was based not just on a housing programme but also on education, religion, moderation and sobriety. His Hall of Peace on Slavija Square was a centre for the whole community used for prayer meetings, literary classes for adults in the evenings, sewing classes for young women, gymnastics and fencing, while religious instruction was conducted for a while under the auspices of an Orthodox priest. Mackenzie's stamp was set on this district when it was eventually incorporated officially into the city to the extent that it was known, out of a misguided sense of his nationality, as *Englezovac*, which might be translated something like the Englishman's place.

The Orthodox Church was not enamoured of all Mackenzie's efforts. He was an avid supporter of religious tolerance and defended various Christian sects against attacks on the rights of their members to worship freely. He defended in particular the Nazarenes, giving the Orthodox Church to assume—wrongly—that he was himself a member. Yet he was able to dampen the suspicions of this powerful institution and redeem something of his reputation. Part of his estate touched on the Vračar plateau where, in 1595, the Ottoman authorities under Sinan-Pasha burned the exhumed remains of St. Sava. The pasha was moved by a series of rebellions in Serbia to give a demonstration of his power and attack the self-confidence of the rebels. The cult of the Serbian patron saint was growing in influence, so Sinan-Pasha had his bones taken from the Monastery of Mileševa in the south, brought to Belgrade, and thrown on a pyre intending to subdue and humiliate the insurgents.

The Church had long wanted to build an edifice dedicated to the most exalted figure in its history on the very spot where the offending spectacle had taken place. Its desire was sharpened by the approach of the tercentenary in 1895 and Mackenzie, who owned the land hereabouts, gave a plot for this purpose. A small chapel was erected in time for the commemoration but was then superseded by a more ambitious project for a much larger church. Mackenzie apparently obliged with a plot of about two acres but he died in London before any papers could be signed. There was no written evidence of the agreement, and the Church duly approached the man who inherited Englezovac, Henry Gratten Guinness. He honoured the commitment allowing the Church to acquire the required piece of land for their new plans.

Not much remains of the original housing planned by Mackenzie in the last quarter of the nineteenth century. The name Englezovac has also been lost. Nonetheless, in 1896 it was decided in memory of the Scotsman to give the name Mackenzie Street to the road that runs up the hill from Slavija Square. In 1930 the name was changed to Tsar Nicholas II Street

(Ulica cara Nikole II), after the last Romanov Emperor of Russia. It was subsequently rechristened Marshal Tolbukhin Street (Ulica Maršala Tolbuhina) after the Second World War in honour of one of the Soviet commanders who helped liberate Belgrade. The original name was restored in 1997, although, truth to say, there are not many citizens today who know who Mackenzie was or why he should be remembered.

Vračar Plateau

Slavija Square and Englezovac form part of the western end of Belgrade's borough of Vračar. The name is first recorded in the fifteenth century and then again in Ottoman sources from the sixteenth century. It comes from the old Slavonic word *vrač* meaning a sorcerer or a soothsayer. It is thought that a man called Stephen the Lame (Stevan Hrom) who was known for such occult gifts lived in the area. The term has been applied over the centuries with a certain geographic vagueness to its precise limits, but certainly to include the level patch of ground at the top of the rise above Slavija Square from where the massive dome of the new church dedicated to St. Sava looks across the whole central district of Belgrade and indeed is visible from much of the rest of the city.

The broad Liberation Boulevard that climbs the hill was originally known as the Kragujevac Highway (Kragujevački drum) and after the Second World War as the Boulevard of the Yugoslav People's Army

(Bulevar JNA). The first sight as the road tops the brow of the hill is of Karađorđe's Park (Karađorđev park) with its lawns and flower beds, fronted by a statue of the leader of the First Serbian Uprising. This is the plateau of Vračar where the Serbian rebel forces pitched camp when laying siege to Belgrade in 1806.

Immediately beyond here, as the road begins its descent, is another smaller park that follows the curve of the boulevard. A number of other monuments can be found at this spot. The first, erected here in 1975, is a simple block at the entrance into the grassed area marking the site of an air-raid shelter hit by a German bomb in 1941 with many lives lost. The next one is an imposing statue of a soldier from the First World War dedicated to the memory of those who gave their lives to defend their country in 1914-15. Then there is a monument to the members of the International Brigades who went to fight in Spain against Franco and the fascists in 1936-39.

Close to this spot stands the only memorial here that does not refer to a war: a bust of the French writer Alphonse de Lamartine (1790-1869) who visited Belgrade in 1833 when returning from a long trip to the Near East. He made extensive notes about his stay which give an interesting picture of the city at the time and which he published as part of his memoirs. On arriving at Belgrade, he wrote in his journal dated 2 September 1833:

> We crossed the barren slopes around midday from where we at last came upon Belgrade spread at our feet. Belgrade, destroyed by shells so many times, sits on a raised bank of the Danube. The roofs of its mosques stand out; its ramparts have fallen in; those parts of the town outside its walls are deserted and covered in hovels and heaps of ruins. The town itself, like all Turkish towns, descends in narrow and crooked lanes toward the river. Zemun, the first town in Hungary, gleams from the other side of the Danube with all the magnificence of a European town; its church towers rise up facing the minarets. When we came to Belgrade, while resting in a small inn, the first we had come across in Turkey, Prince Miloš sent me a small company of his principal officers to invite me to spend a few days at the fortress where he resides a mile or two from Belgrade.

Having spent some time in and around Belgrade, listening to the stories about the Serb rebellion and fight for freedom from Ottoman rule, he writes on 25 September in a Byronic mood: "The history of this people should be sung, not written. It is a poem yet to be completed."

Toward the bottom of the park is a large square monument topped by a cross inscribed with the date 1806. This was the first public monument to be erected in Belgrade by Knez Alexander Karađorđević in 1848 and is dedicated to the memory of the rebels who captured Belgrade from Ottoman forces in the Serbian Uprising under Karađorđe.

It is surrounded by twelve gravestones of insurgents who died in the battle for the city.

The modern building on the Vračar plateau nearest the main road is the National Library of Serbia. As an institution the library was established in 1832 by Gligorije Vozarević in his bookshop near the Town Gate during the rule of Knez Miloš Obrenović. When the Second World War broke out it was situated on Kosančić Crescent and was completely destroyed during the German air-raid of 1941. After the war, the library was moved temporarily to the old hotel at the end of Knez Mihailo Street where the City Library is now to be found. The new premises were completed in 1970 and provide space not just for books and periodicals but also halls for lectures and exhibitions.

Its work as the leading state library was interrupted during the 1990s. The regime of sanctions applied to Serbia was intended to isolate the country as completely as possible, including in the fields of culture and education. Libraries abroad were forced to cut all exchange agreements and the National Library, even if it had the funds, was not allowed to purchase books. In the last few years its staff has made huge efforts to make up for this period of bibliographic deprivation.

Old St Sava's Church with new church in background

The first church dedicated to St. Sava on the plateau was built in 1895. Later, the decision was taken to build a much larger church on the same site. The old chapel was demolished and its stones used as material to construct what is now the smaller of the two existing churches here in 1935. Work on the bigger replacement church was, like much else, interrupted by the Second World War, and at the end of the war the communist authorities refused permission for construction to continue. The site was boarded up and deserted, leaving it unclear whether it was a building that had been bombed or an abandoned building site. Negotiations opened up again in the early 1980s and permission was granted for building to resume in 1984. The basic plan for the new church remained unchanged in terms of its size and internal space but it was updated to allow for the possibilities of modern technology.

The dimensions of the building are vast for an Orthodox church, which is usually to be found on a smaller scale. The floor area is 265 by 300 feet, the central cupola has a diameter of 100 feet and a height of 230 feet, the gold-plated cross on top stands a further forty feet high and weighs about four tons. The edifice on one of Belgrade's highest points dominates the city skyline. Opinion about the building varies from those who consider its construction an important landmark not just in a physical sense but also for its wider cultural significance as a symbol of Serbian national identity. Then there are others who regard it as too big, a sign of nationalist megalomania and an ill-fitting memorial for true religious feelings.

TRAVEL WRITING FROM BELGRADE

Mackenzie was unusual in his prolonged stay in Belgrade, although it has to be admitted that he tended to spend summers back in Scotland or London. Most foreigners visit the city for short periods and sometimes as part of a longer journey. British visitors in the twentieth century have left a record of their impressions and feelings about the city that are quite telling in their more graphic imagery.

Two such travellers arrived in Belgrade at the beginning of the twentieth century, and published their journals in London in 1907. The authors were the journalist Harry De Windt (1856-1933) whose book boasted the long title *Through Savage Europe: Being the Narrative of a Journey (Undertaken as Special Correspondent of the "Westminster Gazette") throughout the Balkan States and European Russia*, and the writer and traveller William

Le Queux (1864-1927), who chose to publish his book *An Observer* in the Near East anonymously. Both men undertook very similar routes through the Balkans, arriving by boat at Kotor and going to Montenegro first, then on to Dalmatia, Bosnia, Serbia, where they stayed in Belgrade, and finally to Bulgaria. Both had letters of introduction from London and were very well connected, giving them access to the most influential circles along their way, including Habsburg officials, senior politicians, and figures from the royal courts and palaces of Montenegro and Serbia. They discussed many and varied topics, met people both formally and informally, and moved around the cities and countryside gathering information. In short, they saw more or less the same sights and talked to the same people. Yet the two authors came to opposing conclusions about everything they witnessed, largely because they came with a set of their own predetermined ideas, which their visit was not intended to test but to confirm.

These were dangerous times in the Balkans; then as now foreign journalists tended to visit at times of international crises with negative consequences for the region. One Serbian king had recently been killed to be replaced by a rival dynasty, while the Habsburgs were attempting to extend their influence and territory in south-eastern Europe. De Windt was a supporter of Austrian influence in the Balkans, believing that Slavs generally could not be trusted to introduce civilized behaviour and modern ways. He felt that Montenegro was a little backwater overrun by quarrelsome and warring tribes. By contrast, he saw that Bosnia, with its Austrian administrators, was an example of a perfectly oiled machine. He justifies the pejorative title of his account by simply stating that "the term accurately describes the wild and lawless countries between the Adriatic and Black Seas". For him, the Austrian presence was needed in order to tame native barbarism.

Unlike De Windt, Le Queux was opposed to Austrian influence in the Balkans. He felt that the spread of Habsburg power was the result of rapacious political greed and that its mission to bring civilization was nothing but a sham. He wrote of the political situation in the region: "All through the Balkan peninsula the weak are to-day being crushed by the strong. The Austrian eagle has over-shadowed and grasped Bosnia, she has her talons in Servia, and is casting covetous glances upon gallant little Montenegro." He concluded that negative reports in the British press about the Serbs were the result of Habsburg propaganda, spreading "false news, being supposed to emanate from reliable sources in Belgrade". In fact, the two men looked for and found the evidence they needed to support their more general views on the politics of the Great Powers at a time of international tension. Their interpretations of what they experienced in the Balkans had little to do with what they saw and heard, rather reflecting the political baggage they had brought with them.

De Windt, not generally considered a friend of the Serbs, made a surprising discovery on his arrival in Belgrade. He had first come to the city some thirty years earlier when the country was at war with the Ottoman Empire, at about the same time that Mackenzie arrived, and he recalled the town as if some squalid village. Remembering his first visit, he writes:

> In 1876 a dilapidated Turkish fortress frowned down upon a maze of buildings little better than mud-huts and unpaved filthy streets. I had to splash my way from the river to the town through an ocean of mud carrying my own luggage, for no porters were procurable, and the half-dozen rough country-carts at the landing place were quickly pounced upon by local magnates.

His hotel was a festering hole that served black-bread and paprika stew, offering rooms that had to be shared with strangers. But years later, and De Windt's second taste of Belgrade is incomparable:

> To-day it seemed like a dream to be whirled away from the railway station in a neat fiacre, along spacious boulevards, with well-dressed crowds and electric cars, to a luxurious hotel. Here were gold-laced porters, lifts, and even a Winter Garden, where a delicious déjeûner (cooked by a Frenchman) awaited me.

It is striking that he feels duty bound to add in brackets that the meal that he enjoyed so much was not cooked by a Serb. Even so, Belgrade in 1906 was a modern and vibrant city even to a visitor evidently reluctant to be too impressed by his surroundings. He noted that hotels, private residences and shops illuminated by electric light were strung along Terazije and King Milan Street, which in the evening "becomes a fashionable promenade, and smart carriages, brilliant uniforms, and vienna toilettes add to the gaiety of the scene".

For De Windt, boorish behaviour is equated with provincial and rustic settings, while civilization and modernity are exemplified by an urban environment. In Belgrade he found the citizens were usually as he would want them to be, probably on account of the fact that the new elite sent their children to Paris for an education and they all spoke at least three foreign languages, adding to the cosmopolitan atmosphere of the place. In other words, he did not recognize the city as a part of Serbia. The real Serbia, however, was never far away. On a visit to a Belgrade music-hall he commented on the restrained public and their sobriety, which he explained by observing that the average Serb "is a temperate being, who dislikes alcohol in any shape or form—and generally prefers water to any other beverage. This, however, does not apply to the provinces, where drunkenness appeared to be almost as prevalent amongst the peasantry as it is in parts of the Russian Empire."

De Windt could not resist qualifying his own experience, assuming that there lurks somewhere the real Serbia to which Belgrade does not belong. He generally expressed an ambiguous relationship toward the city, which had only recently lost its oriental appearance and was still regarded, whether deservedly or not, as if on the crossroads between East and West, the Orient and the Occident. De Windt's image of Belgrade is of a place surviving on the very edge of civilization.

Other writers have relied on imagery similar to De Windt's. The American journalist John Reed (1887-1920) provides another example of this striking sense of ambiguity. Reed is more famous as a witness of the Russian Revolution, which he captured in his book *Ten Days That Shook the World* (1919), but prior to this he reported from Serbia during the First World War as one of a group of foreign newspapermen assigned to visit the Serbian army in 1915. They were put in the care of a representative from the military press bureau whom the western journalists called Johnson—this being a literal translation of his name, which was probably Jovanović. Johnson was a lecturer at the University of Belgrade in peace time, teaching comparative literature. Reed describes him in the following terms:

> Johnson was saturated with European culture, European smartness, cynicism, modernism; yet scratch the surface and you found the Serb; the strong, virile stock of a young race not far removed from the half-sav-

agery of a mountain peasantry, intensely patriotic and intensely independent.

His choice of expression is in itself telling. The representative from the press bureau is given a false Anglicized name, making him appear more like a citizen of the West, which on the surface he resembles. But underneath this urbane veneer, he hides a true self closer to his rustic origins. Whereas De Windt finds this true self repellent, Reed transforms the vices of the peasant into virtues, not least because he is fighting alongside the Allies during the war.

Some foreign visitors preferred the image of the village Serbs to that of citizens of Belgrade. Rebecca West (1892-1983) recorded her lengthy stay in Yugoslavia on the eve of the Second World War in her book *Black Lamb and Grey Falcon* (1941), probably the most famous travelogue from this part of the world. She is generally considered to have been very favourably impressed by the country, and particularly by her experiences in Serbia. Yet it is again in her attitude towards Belgrade that we find an element of ambiguity. Spying a group of businessmen at a hotel bar in the centre of town, she does not like the way in which they try to emulate their counterparts from the West in dress and manners. Nor does she care for the hotel itself, which she considers to be akin to any other Savoy or Plaza anywhere in the world. Both have lost their authenticity in her eyes. She continues:

> Belgrade, I thought, had made the same error. It had till recently been a Balkan village. That has its character of resistance, of determined survival, or martyred penury. This was a very sacred Balkan village; the promontory on which it stood had been sanctified by the blood of men who had died making the simple demand that, since their kind had been created, it might have leave to live. Modern Belgrade has striped that promontory with streets that had already been built elsewhere much better. I felt a sudden abatement of my infatuation for Yugoslavia.

West's romantic view is charged with a highly emotive account of a historical struggle for survival. She conjures up a world of heroes and deeds of great sacrifice in her mythic Belgrade, her sacred place. Her faith is restored when the scene in the bar is interrupted by the arrival of a stranger, a peasant, dressed in village clothes, and clutching a black lamb in his arms. She transforms him into a tableau portrait of her ideal: "He stood still as a Byzantine king in a fresco, while the black lamb twisted and writhed in the firm cradle of his arms, its eyes sometimes catching the light as it turned like small luminous plates."

This dual image of the city has been redrawn by visitors in more recent times. The destruction of Yugoslavia and the following Wars of Yugoslav Succession attracted many journalists to the country and more than a few wandered through Belgrade. Mark Thompson presents his impressions in his book *A Paper House: The Ending of Yugoslavia* (1992). Visiting all the main towns of the country, he arrives at Belgrade's railway station, which he describes thus: "Belgrade at last. The train station makes no distinction between goods and passenger trains. Some travellers have to make their way between pens of sheep on the platform; others are left where there's no platform at all."

The station, a stop on the old Orient Express, is a large and busy junction with both international and local trains. It was built in an imposing architectural design, appropriate to its function. Whatever was happening on the day when Thompson arrived, he chose to follow an interpretive framework used by writers and visitors to the city for the last one hundred years. He concludes his description of the city in similar vein: "Those sheep-pens at the station are no anomaly. Belgrade hasn't moved far from its origins: the garrison and the village. Its focus remains the Ottoman fortress of Kalemegdan." His Balkan village is not the stronghold of Rebecca West, defended by heroes straight out of the Serbian folk epics. Rather, he paints a picture of a muddy dung-heap, governed by a medieval militant order and commanded from the heights of a fortress. Official Belgrade was then stoking the nationalism and violence that accompanied the end of Yugoslavia, and Thompson finds the image that corresponds to expectations.

Such views are part of a tradition of ambiguity that leaves the reader waiting for the author to discover something positively romantic in the city. Thompson finds his antidote in the old frame of Milovan Đilas, the first Yugoslav political dissident who denounced the Communist Party for losing its revolutionary aims in the early 1950s. Thompson interviews him in his flat and is clearly impressed by his clarity and energy, so much so that, while listening to his words, he remarks, "I gazed back, fascinated by the transformation of man into Dinaric legend, re-enacted before my sceptical English eyes." Thompson, like Reed before him, finally finds his intensely independent hero, whom he places on a pedestal like West's Byzantine king in a fresco painting.

Belgrade Gap

This issue of ambiguity is not lost on Belgrade's own internal commentators. Many of the novels that have been introduced on earlier pages reveal an uncertainty about Belgrade and its history, although in recent times this has reflected a new freedom to articulate that past without the dogmatic constraints imposed by the League of Communists. This revised tension in relation to the past has often revolved around Belgrade's oriental heritage, as identified by Elizabeth Medaković in Slobodan Selenić's novel *Fathers and Forefathers*, and by the Hungarian wife of Knez Mihailo in Svetlana Velmar-Janković's *The Abyss*. Such expression is also elaborated in non-fiction works, particularly those written from the curious position of someone in-between, with a foot both in the Serbian and the foreign camp.

Lena Jovičić was one such figure, the daughter of a Serbian father and a Scottish mother. She divided her time between her two countries and was in a unique position to know them both. In 1928 she published her book *Yugoslavia* in a series aimed at younger readers called "Peeps at Many Lands". She writes about the life of children and how it differs from life in England, telling her readers, for example, "You may find it difficult to believe that, except in Belgrade, there are no real toy-shops in Serbia," and later, "You will never find people still asleep at half-past seven or eight o'clock in Serbia!"

Jovičić includes some observations that go much deeper, and one wonders if a child would fully see the point. The following paragraph is worth quoting in full:

> Extremes and contrasts are the most striking feature of Belgrade. You see opposing forces everywhere: in the streets, in the houses, in the lives of the people even. Side by side with the peasant in homespun clothes and sandalled feet, walk the smartly dressed people of the wealthier classes. The creaking ox-cart has the right of way alongside the luxurious limousine car, and tall modern structures tower above dilapidated

little houses in the strangest fashion. Thus East meets West in a curious jumble, and in view of such extremes and contrasts you cannot but feel that there is a gap somewhere. The connecting link between the one and the other is missing, and so you constantly find that you suddenly drop into the gap.

The passage has an incongruous tone, especially given that it was written at a time when class division was certainly not unknown to the British public for whom she was writing, and where motorized traffic had not entirely usurped the horse and cart. It is almost as if the Anglicized self of Lena Jovičić has picked up and absorbed the model that foreigners apply when looking at life in Belgrade. Stressing a division between East and West, her description goes beyond economic and social class and enters the realm of historical experience, drawn from a marked discontinuity in cultural expectations. The gap that she evokes is that ambiguous space that many writers see in Belgrade, a place from which one may be metaphorically exiled—and a hole into which it is possible to fall.

Chapter Eight

THE CITY ACROSS THE RIVER:
TWENTY-FIRST CENTURY BELGRADE

ZEMUN

From the platform at the base of the Victor in Kalemegdan, the tower on the top of the hill overlooking Zemun is visible down the Danube. It is not far away and Zemun now forms part of the administrative district of Belgrade, but it is a settlement with its own history, closely tied to the fortunes of the larger city but not entirely part of it. In Roman times it was called Taurunum, and to the Austrians it was known as Semlin. The first record of the Slavonic form, given as Zemljan, is to be found in the ninth century. A fortress in medieval times dominated the hill at Zemun, which was used at different periods by Byzantine, Hungarian and Serbian forces. The town fell, like Belgrade, to the Ottoman army in its offensive of 1521 as it made its push further into Europe. For two centuries Zemun was a small provincial town in the Ottoman Empire, subordinate to its larger and more important neighbour whose significance was geographical and political as the residence of the pasha. Yet historical circumstances were to have a huge influence on developments across the river from Kalemegdan. When the Austrians attacked and took Belgrade in 1717 they also captured a large swathe of Ottoman territory including Zemun. When they returned their conquests to Ottoman rule in 1739, they did not give back all they had taken, and the border between the two empires now followed the Danube and Sava. Kalemegdan remained as a Turkish watchtower, while the land on the other side of the rivers, to the north and west, was Habsburg territory. Zemun was transformed in status into the last Austrian outpost on the border with the enemy.

This change in Zemun's geopolitical position was crucial for the development of the district over the Sava from Belgrade. There was a Serbian community already established in Vojvodina to which Zemun now gravitated. Most of its population was comprised of Serbs, with some Greek, German, Jewish and a sprinkling of Turkish inhabitants, drawn here mainly by business. It rapidly became a wealthy staging post for land and water traffic between Austria and Turkey. It contained a small garrison and administrators representing Habsburg authority in order to regulate commercial and political relations on this crucial border crossing. Talks would often take place between representatives of the Belgrade and Zemun sides in order to resolve any local disputes. The town was given some autonomous functions, increasing its identity as a local municipality and its inhabitants' sense of belonging to a specific community. Zemun was a visible symbol to the Serbs in Belgrade of a successful westernized community of their co-nationals. This complicated relationship between the Serbs in the Ottoman Empire and those in the Habsburg Empire who left in earlier decades is one of the themes in Miloš Crnjanski's 1929 novel *Migrations* (Seobe).

The work is generally regarded as Crnjanski's greatest contribution to Serbian Modernist prose. It concerns two brothers, Vuk and Aranđel Isakovič, and Vuk's wife, the lady Dafina. The two brothers are brought up in the Serbian community of Vojvodina. Vuk serves as an officer in the Habsburg army, defending the frontier against the Turks, the traditional enemies of his people. He is even posted to Belgrade for a short period during the Austrian occupation between 1717 and 1739. Meanwhile, his brother becomes a rich merchant, trading up and down the Danube and dedicating his life to making money.

The novel revolves around these two contrasting characters. While Vuk dreams of overcoming the Turks and leading his people home, Aranđel has no such fanciful notions and wishes his brother would abandon his ambition, which only obstructs the wheels of commerce and his business ventures. He represents the pragmatic new generation, having come to the West determined to make the most of the new opportunities. When on one of his trading trips he almost drowns in the dangerous waters separating the two settlements, we are made to understand that the distance between them is metaphorical as much as geographical. Between the West and the Ottoman Empire lie uncharted waters, separated by the tension between modernity and tradition.

Belgrade and Zemun epitomize two different but linked paths in their architectural and urban designs. Zemun expanded in the nineteenth century, adopting from an early stage western styles of architecture that are easily discernible in its main streets and squares. But since the town had no ambition to become a capital city, there are far fewer signs of the more monumental styles found in the centre of Belgrade. It is more modest and unassuming, giving the impression of a greater self-confidence in its identity, evolving more slowly and steadily than its big brother. Zemun even gave responsibility to the city engineer for overseeing new building projects in the second half of the nineteenth century, thereby assuring greater coherence in the architectural appearance of the town. In time, the advent of steamships on the Danube and the weakening of the Ottoman grip across the river sent Zemun into a relative decline. But the arrival of the railway in 1883 with a bridge to Belgrade emphasized once more its geopolitical significance. Austria increasingly saw Serbia as a rival in southeastern Europe, and Zemun rediscovered a function as a customs point with border controls, the last staging post on the edge of the Balkans. This fresh impetus brought a new wave of German and Jewish settlers, merchants and artisans, eager to supply Belgrade with western goods and more.

Isidora Sekulić (1877-1958) was a writer who was born in Vojvodina, spent her childhood in Zemun and lived most of her adult life in Belgrade. Among her work she has left many accounts of her travels and memoirs of Belgrade and Zemun. At one point she turns her attention to this relationship between the two cities:

> Culture and civilization, magazines with the latest fashions, silver-plated cutlery, upright pianos, lace-up shoes for ladies, recipes with fine dough for bread and rolls (something like at the time of Gospodar Jevrem) and a little of the German language—all that came from Zemun on boats as private freight, or in parcels addressed in the name of Master so-and-so.

Zemun did not just supply goods to Belgrade, but was regarded as a cultural model, teaching western tastes to its co-nationals across the water.

Zemun could not, however, escape its status as a community in the Habsburg Empire. The Hungarians of the empire decided to celebrate 1,000 years of their settlement on the Pannonian plain by building five tall towers, one in Budapest and four others. The southern millennium tower was erected in Zemun in 1896 on top of the hill where the fortress had stood in earlier times. The area is known as Gardoš, a term derived from the old Slavonic word *gard* for a town or a fortress (*grad* in modern Serbian).

There were to be no more Hungarian or Austrian monuments here from the time that Serbian troops entered Zemun on 5 November 1918 and it became part of the new Kingdom of Serbs, Croats and Slovenes. The town's status again changed fundamentally. It was no longer an important border post but a quiet spot by the Danube, a favourite spot for lunch, away from the more hectic pace of Belgrade. The short journey could be made by boat, or by crossing the new King Alexander I Bridge spanning the Sava. It became an administrative part of the capital city in 1934, finally losing the autonomy it had enjoyed for almost two centuries. But Zemun did achieve the distinction of being home to the headquarters of the new Yugoslav air force. It provided the closest flat and solid ground to the capital, and the first civilian/military airfield was established nearby between 1929 and 1931, at the end of the street today called Tošin Bunar. In those days travellers could get to the airport quite easily from the centre of the old town by taking either a bus from Terazije or a tram from in front of the National Assembly.

The Second World War brought yet more changes for Zemun. It was occupied in April 1941 by German troops, and from October was under the jurisdiction of the Independent State of Croatia with its fascist Ustaše government. The Ustaše authorities conducted vicious policies against the non-Croat population, especially Jews, gypsies and Serbs, and Zemun lost a quarter of its 65,000 inhabitants. It was again a border town; the Kingdom of Yugoslavia was wiped away and Croatia and Serbia met at the point where the old Ottoman and Habsburg empires used to glare at one another. Following its liberation, it has continued its quiet life, relatively unburdened by demands from outside although remaining an administrative part of the capital.

Plans to integrate the two towns have been facilitated by road links but Zemun has retained something of its separate atmosphere. Some redevelopment and building work tool place after the war, but far more attention was given to founding New Belgrade, which has filled in the gap between the bank of the River Sava and the periphery of old Zemun. The older community's central district has the feel of an organic settlement that has evolved over time in tune with the demands of the people living there, whereas New Belgrade is an environment with solutions imposed by architects and administrators working on an initial blueprint. Zemun is something of an antidote for those who prefer their cities less planned and with life at a slightly reduced pace.

New Belgrade

New Belgrade (Novi Beograd) is the quarter occupying the area on the other bank of the River Sava from the old town, between Belgrade and Zemun. Before the Second World War this was mainly fields and meadows, a place to go for an excursion, perhaps for a picnic or for lunch in a country inn. There were plans to build here before the Second World War in order to unite Belgrade with Zemun. Bridges were constructed across the Sava and some work began, but the results were limited. Although it may no longer seem obvious, much of the land around Belgrade was wet and marshy and not conducive to large building projects without extensive drainage programmes. One of the earliest significant buildings on the opposite bank from Kalemegdan was Belgrade's first major exhibition site, the Old Exhibition Ground (Staro sajmište). It was completed in 1937 and can still be seen to the left of the Branko Bridge. Industrial fairs, concerts, exhibitions and some sporting fixtures were held here before the Second World War. It provided a venue for events which were of international significance, helping to promote Belgrade on the world scene as a city with facilities to attract outside investment.

When Belgrade was occupied the German authorities converted its buildings for use as a concentration camp. Many of the city's Jewish community were sent here, and then transported further afield or, indeed, met their end here. Some Serbs supported the occupying forces, but the overwhelming majority of ordinary Serbs were appalled by their anti-Semitic policies and helped individual Jewish families as they could. The almost total disappearance of the Jewish community is a very dark episode in the history of the city. Unfortunately, like many events of the Second World War in Belgrade, the fate of the Jews was not commemorated by the communist government. It fell under the general silence that tended to surround the city's war-time experience.

As in other areas, it has largely been the efforts of writers of fiction that have introduced the public to new interpretations of the past or presented events that the communists tried to consign to collective amnesia. The 1998 novel *Götz and Meyer* (Gec i Majer) by the Serbian-Jewish writer David Albahari deals directly with the topic of the Belgrade Jews in the war. In his version of events, the narrator of the work is a school teacher in contemporary Belgrade who becomes obsessed by what befell his family during the war. They were all Jews sent to the Old Exhibition

Ground from which not one returned alive. He has to do his own detective work, and discovers the awful method by which the Nazis killed their prisoners, constructing a special truck in which the fumes from the exhaust pipe were fed back into the enclosed wagon set behind the driver's cab. He tries to make his pupils from school empathize with the fate of the Jews, but they become hysterical. As he delves further into the past, so he begins to relive the trauma of the Holocaust. He even imagines that he sees the two drivers of the Nazi death-truck, the Götz and Meyer of the title, in Belgrade, giving their bodies a reality which history has otherwise forgotten. The closing image sees the narrator about to defend himself from what appears to be their attack as they enter his apartment. The Old Exhibition Ground has given up its secrets, but now they have to be faced by the current generation.

After the Second World War the communists had very ambitious plans to build a new city across the Sava and work began at the end of 1947. The inhospitable terrain required huge preparations to make it fit for construction and much was done by work brigades. These were groups of volunteer workers, students and others who gave their time and efforts to many of the large construction projects promoted by the new government in many areas of Yugoslavia. Such brigades were an important ideological institution, projecting the image of a country once divided by sectarian violence during the occupation but now united behind the Communist Party of Yugoslavia. Participation was also a way of taking part in the new system, bringing rewards both for those who truly believed in the ideals of communism and others who recognized it more selfishly as a starting point for a career in the new political structure. The brigades also attracted people from abroad, often members of the youth wings of various socialist parties in Western Europe. Many found themselves working on the project for New Belgrade.

The new district was planned according to socialist principles. One of the men responsible for drawing up the scheme was Milorad Macura (1914-89). He pointed out that in capitalist societies towns are not built on the basis of a rational programme, but in such a way that out of the amorphous conglomerate of structures making up the residential areas some buildings "enjoy all the privileges of a proper site, while others put up with all its deficiencies". New Belgrade was to be designed in order to avoid this kind of class differentiation. The apartment blocks were built in a regular and symmetrical order, while care and attention was given to providing suitable green areas between them for recreation. Pedestrians and motor traffic were divided in order to maximize the cleanliness of the environment. Provision was made for easy and effective access to transport facilities to other parts of Belgrade. Schools, shops and other urban facilities were included in the planning stages, but in the end there were not enough and many residents complain of the lack of amenities. All in all, New Belgrade has the air of a regulated and not an organic environment.

One of Belgrade's writers, Mihailo Pantić, has written a collection of short stories, *New Belgrade Stories* (Novobeogradske priče, 1994), set among the tower blocks across the Sava, and in one of them evokes with a few brush-strokes the opinion of many: "You have almost geometric perfection, that town without a real or even imagined centre, without a square and without a church, consisting only of residential quarters, which cannot be connected in any way into a single whole, but in the sharp air of early dawn shimmers like a slimy multi-celled colony thrown up on the riverbank."

New Belgrade is the residential district of the city most associated with communism. Since it was intended to be the Communist Party's showcase of socialist planning, a number of prestige projects were placed here. The Palace of the Federation (Palata federacije), the main government building on the federal level, was built between 1947 and 1961. It is a large complex with offices for the civil service surrounded by parkland close to the river between Mihailo Pupin and Nikola Tesla boulevards. A building of 26 storeys, then the tallest in Belgrade, was completed nearby in 1964 to house various political organizations, including the central committee of the League of Communists of Yugoslavia. It later became headquarters for the Socialist Party of Serbia when led by President Slobodan Milošević during the 1990s, and was thus a target for NATO missiles in 1999. After the bombardment the building was renovated, reduced by a few storeys that had suffered most damage and sold to a private developer. It is now known as the Confluence Business Centre (Poslovni centar "Ušće"). A new exhibition venue, the Sava Centre (Centar "Sava"), was constructed in 1977 close to the graceful Gazelle Bridge and used for concerts, film premieres, conferences and other events. The Hotel Beograd Intercontinental was added as part of the complex in 1979. The Hotel

Hyatt Regency was completed ten years later by the road leading onto Branko Bridge in a bold architectural style. The Museum of Modern Art (Muzej savremene umetnosti) can be seen directly across the Sava from Kalemegdan almost by the water's edge. The museum, opened in 1965, is set in a large grassed area and houses a collection charting the development of Yugoslav painting, sculpture and graphic arts from 1900 to the present.

This part of Belgrade has many different faces. What was intended to be the new Yugoslavia's representation of a collective utopia has become for many a wasteland of sub-standard housing that cannot cope with the pressures put on it in the years since the Second World War. The population of Belgrade has grown beyond all original expectations, and this part of town has become a vast dormitory district whose inhabitants commute each day to work over the Sava, return home from work and go again to the old town for entertainment in the evening. The bridges cannot handle the volume of traffic and they have become notorious bottlenecks. At the same time, New Belgrade contains examples of strikingly modern architectural design and in recent years some parts have become desirable residential addresses. Older buildings have been renovated and some demolished to make way for more solid constructions, especially in the area around the recent Belgrade Arena. These developments are on the road linking the old town with the airport, convenient for today's business community and close to the new business park developed in the vicinity. Well-heeled incomers are hence providing a stimulus for change, which has led to the first hypermarkets opening in this part of town.

New Belgrade is experiencing a renaissance, but not in the direction that Macura and his colleagues intended in the post-war period, not least because the expectations of the people of Belgrade in the twenty-first century have moved on significantly from those of 1945.

POPULAR MUSIC AND YOUTH CULTURE

As capital of socialist Yugoslavia, Belgrade was regarded as a Mecca for young people from Eastern Europe who wanted to taste the fruits of the decadent West. It was much easier to travel from Poland, Czechoslovakia and Hungary to Yugoslavia than to capitalist countries. The authorities in other countries with communist governments regarded Yugoslavia with suspicion. It was a mono-party state like them, but with some undesirable features—one of which was a vibrant youth culture. Youth movements representing different fashions in clothes and music such as rockers, hippies and later punks walked the streets, created their rebellious anthems and gathered in their favourite haunts like nowhere else in Eastern Europe.

The regime considered that a policy towards the arts in general that tolerated diversity would be more astute than repression, as Sabrina Ramet remarks in her book *Balkan Babel*: "Hence, although almost from the beginning the party's cultural commissars were sensitive to rock's potential for stirring rebellious sentiments, they opted for cooptation rather than repression. Astutely, they made it worthwhile for rock musicians to cooperate. The result was a pronounced sycophantic streak in Yugoslav rock beginning at an early stage."

Ramet offers an early example of such sycophancy: "The group *Indeksi*, for example—prominent in the mid-1960s—penned a song 'Yugoslavia,' which included the lines, 'We knew that the sun was shining on us, because we have Tito for our marshal!'" Other examples include the veteran Đorđe Balašević's songs "Count on us" (1978) and "Three Times I saw Tito" (1981), although he has not performed them since the break-up of Yugoslavia.

Teenagers had more of an opportunity to be who they wanted, choose a style of make-up and stand out from the crowd. Uniformity was not enforced on a population wanting to experiment and produce something as a mark of their generation. Belgrade had its own bands and music which really came to the fore in the late 1970s and early 1980s. Writing of this period in his book *The Culture of Power in Serbia*, Eric Gordy comments,

> Increasingly open to the West since the middle 1960s and still relatively prosperous, Belgrade youth generated a rock and roll culture that, at least in the minds of local fans, was on a par with the pop scenes of Western Europe. In 1981, the British music magazine *New Musical Express* listed the Belgrade art students' club *Akademija* as one of the finest music clubs in Europe. It also rated Belgrade's punk-pop group *Električni orgazam* as one of the finest bands in Europe.

Gordy captures more of the atmosphere of those years and the increasingly critical stance of musicians and singers when he turns to another group founded at the end of the 1970s, Riblja čorba, and its founder Bora Đorđević. He writes of them:

> Bora Đorđević achieved tremendous popularity with the band *Riblja čorba* (literally, Fish chowder, although the name also contains an implicit obscene connotation) in the first several years of the band's existence, mostly through his comic songs, which were principally about his own drunkenness and oafishness. At the same time, several of *Riblja čorba*'s early songs became anthems of anti-Communist rebelliousness."

Their song "I Won't Live in Block 65" is about the reality of life in New Belgrade, while "Member of the Mafia" is a thinly veiled attack on the communists: "What's a piece of paper to me, where it's written that I'm a member of the mafia."

One of the influential bands from that time was Partibrejkers, who are still performing over 25 years later. They have an official website now where their music is described in the following terms:

> Musically they are some kind of punk version of early 70s Stones style. Blues or better rhythm and blues influences are very strong. There are a lot of bands in ex-Yugoslav countries who sing that way. Try to imagine The Rolling Stones from the early 70s playing punk. It's not exactly the sound that the New York Dolls had—it's rawer and faster and more bluesy.

The bands and their fans were Yugoslavs and international in their orientation, so it is no surprise that most of them reacted against the chauvinist euphoria of the late 1980s. There were some notable exceptions, such as Bora Đorđević, who gave their services to nationalist regimes. On the Partibrejkers' website one of their fans refers to this period, "But there was big shit going on in Yugoslavia. Garage punk was in some way our protest against nationalistic politics." Bands from Belgrade, Zagreb, Sarajevo, Ljubljana and other major towns travelled and performed to large crowds in all parts of the country. They began touring again as soon as hostilities were over and it was possible to travel. The reception given to groups from other towns, now capital cities of different countries, shows no sign of animosity or hostility. If young people like the music it seems unimportant where the performers come from or if they speak in a slightly different dialect. Perhaps the indifference of youth to playing the card of identity politics produced an ambiguous and dangerous passivity during the wars in former Yugoslavia, but it may now be one of the most positive factors in bringing about reconciliation.

The 1990s saw the rise of a neo-folk brand of music known as "turbofolk", which combined the oriental rhythms of traditional folk music with a strong disco beat. Intended to appeal to young people, it evoked nostalgia for a false past of national heroics and the simple virtues of a patriarchal code, while promising the contradictory shallow rewards of success today with fast cars and money. On the surface it offered an authentic Serbian alternative to the decadent internationalism of rock and roll.

Belgrade became divided as loyalties in populist politics and popular music cut across each other. Turbofolk in Serbia was associated by default with village life and rural identities, but it slid into Belgrade via the social phenomenon of the urban peasant. The population of the city increased fast after the war from about 400,000 in 1951 to just over 1,400,000 in 1981, with newcomers arriving from the villages and small towns around Yugoslavia. Many families retained strong ties with their original homes fostering a ready environment in which to receive the electronic neo-folk melodies accompanied by kitsch parades of glamorous girls. The music was despised by those who preferred the anarchic defiance of punk or rock and roll. But the internationalist side was rapidly marginalized.

The market for popular music was relatively small and fairly easily controlled, a topic that Gordy discusses in some depth:

> Visibly staking out a cultural position that carries clear political implications—for urban culture, for the decadence of the West, against folk nostalgia and nationalism—Belgrade rock and roll narrowed its own cultural space. As the scene took its cultural importance and cultural mission seriously, the borders of the rock and roll genre hardened. With production and distribution of recordings nearly impossible and press runs down to a minimum, media access also minimal, and only a few performance venues, most of them small, commercial success in rock and roll was out of the question.

Pop music was caught up in the nationalist policies of the Milošević government. It has also proven to be one of the factors that connect people from all over the cultural space of former Yugoslavia. The Serbian entry won the 2007 Eurovision song contest largely because of votes from neighbouring countries recently at war. Plans are to host the 2008 competition in the Arena building in New Belgrade.

FOOTBALL AND NATIONALISM

Belgrade has many sporting venues and has hosted a variety of international events. At the beginning of the Second World War King Peter sponsored the Belgrade Grand Prix held on 3 September 1939. It was won by the famous Italian driver Tazio Nuvolari. The race had the dubious distinction of taking place just two days after Germany invaded Poland and was the only Grand Prix to be staged during the war. It was watched by some 100,000 spectators, almost a quarter of the city's population at the time. There has been no Belgrade Grand Prix since then as the communists considered the sport a bourgeois amusement.

In Velmar-Janković's novel *Dungeon* the narrator, Milica Pavlović, compares the number of those watching the race with those, like her, attending the opening of an exhibition by the painter Sava Šumanović:

> There were two main events. The more important one, judging by the number of spectators, was the international automobile and motorbike race round Kalemegdan Park; the lesser one, attracting a small attendance, was the opening of the exhibition of Sava Šumanović, in the New University building, on Prince's Square. (If I'm not mistaken, that is now the Philological Faculty building, on Students' Square.) Thirty-three racing cars were to take part in the race, six international aces of the track led by the famous Nuvolari (at least I think that's what that Italian was called: I didn't read the headlines referring to the international motor car races again) and 66 motorbikes; after a gap of eleven years, Sava Šumanović was exhibiting more than 400 oils, watercolours, drawings, sketches in the seven large rooms of the New University.

Since the second half of the twentieth century other sports have been more popular than motor racing in Belgrade: basketball, water polo and football. The national teams for Yugoslavia and later Serbia have been very successful in the first two disciplines. In basketball the Yugoslav team took the gold medal at the 1980 Olympic Games. They have been world champions five times, three as socialist Yugoslavia and twice as the Federal Republic of Yugoslavia in 1998 and 2001, and have won gold eight times in the European Championships, most recently in 1995, 1997 and 2001. Some Serbian players have moved to the United States and had very successful playing careers there including Vlade Divac and Predrag Stojaković.

The national water polo team has also enjoyed international success taking in total eight Olympic medals; three gold, four silver and one bronze. Only Hungary has won more medals in this sport. The team beat the USSR in the final of the 1968 Olympics, then in 1984 and 1988 beat the United States. The Partizan Water Polo Club has been European champions six times, most recently in 2006, and once took the Super Champions cup. Games are watched with great passion and a win at international level is generally followed by a cavalcade of cars through the city centre, with horns blaring, drivers and passengers cheering and waving scarves from windows.

The main football clubs in Belgrade are Partizan and Red Star (Crvena zvezda), although they are more correctly names of sporting associations covering a number of disciplines. Red Star was founded on 4 March 1945 and played its first match that day against a team from one of the Partisan battalions. Its second game was held a week later against some British soldiers serving with the military mission. Red Star won. In 1958 they played in the final of the European Cup. Their opponents were Manchester United who flew to Belgrade to play in Red Star's stadium. The result was a 3-3 draw, but Manchester won the tie 5-4 on aggregate. Their departure was delayed because one of the United players, Johnny Berry, could not find his passport. Their plane stopped for refuelling at Munich as scheduled, but on take-off there was an accident and the plane crashed with many dead and injured. Eight United players were amongst the fatalities resulting from the tragedy. Red Star is the only Serbian club to have won a UEFA competition, taking the European Cup in 1991 against Marseille in Bari. The same year they won the Intercontinental Cup in Tokyo.

Red Star's first supporters came from the elite area of town around Dedinje and Senjak, not far from their stadium. They were generally children of the pre-war bourgeoisie but were later joined by others from more modest backgrounds who eventually formed the first organized supporters' clubs. During the late 1980s they began to call themselves *Delije*, a Turkish word that in this context roughly equates to the Heroes. The fans travelled everywhere to see their team, singing and waving flags inside the stadium, while gaining a reputation for drinking and violence inside and outside the ground. With the rise of nationalism in Yugoslavia during the 1980s, their chants became increasingly pro-Serbian and chauvinistic whenever Red Star played a team from one of the other republics.

On 13 May 1990 an estimated 3,000 fans made their way to Croatia to watch their team against Dinamo Zagreb. Intense rivalry was common practice, but this match came shortly after the first multi-party elections in Croatia that elected a government in favour of independence. The meeting between fans from Zagreb and Belgrade was tense and violence flared up. The subsequent riot is regarded by some as the first sign that the ordinary people of Yugoslavia could no longer live together and that the future of the state was untenable.

Red Star fans were linked to the paramilitary formations which fought in Croatia and Bosnia, and in particular with Arkan's Tigers. One of their chants certainly became popular amongst the nationalists *Serbia to Tokyo* (*Srbija do Tokija*), first heard when Red Star took the World Club Championship in 1991. Its initial meaning simply indicated that the Serbian team was playing in Tokyo, but its later connotation was a celebration of territorial aggrandisement. It is open to debate whether the support of football hooligans for Serbian paramilitaries was the result of a plot to engage a large number of aggressive young men in the nationalist cause, or whether these aggressive young men gravitated towards a centre of violence.

Red Star's local rivals are the Partizan Football Club, founded on 4 October 1945, and named in honour of the resistance movement led by the communists. It was initially formed by the Yugoslav People's Army (Jugoslovenska narodna armija or JNA) and their ground used to be called the Stadium JNA but is now named after the club.

The stadium hosted an important annual event in former Yugoslavia. Each year a baton was taken around all republics by a relay of runners. The tradition began in 1945 in honour of Tito's birthday on 25 May and from the mid-1950s was incorporated in the celebrations for the Day of Youth on that date. The end of the relay was marked in a ceremony when the baton would be handed to the president in the Stadium JNA. The baton began its journey each year from a different republic, but after Tito's death some voices were raised against the event calling it a spectacle organized by the League of Communists in honour of itself with no real meaning for national solidarity as claimed.

Vesna Goldsworthy recalls the way in which the ceremony was continued in her autobiography *Chernobyl Strawberries*:

> For a while Yugoslavs continued to celebrate the day in the traditional manner, with torches lit from eternal flames relayed around the country by handsome athletes, young workers and bright students, in a well-rehearsed marathon which was the first item on the new bulletins throughout the spring. The longer it was since his demise, the more there was to celebrate. Like the widow of a murdered Sicilian Mafia don, the country clung to his memory in an incongruous mixture of mourning and *décolletage*, as if knowing that a collective nervous breakdown would follow once the ritual was no longer observed.

In the late 1980s, as in the other republics, Slovenia experienced its "awakening of the people". Slovene nationalist opinion was making its voice heard on a number of topics. Sabrina Ramet comments on the Slovene case: "This process can be dated to the publication by the Slovenian journal *Nova revija* (in February 1987) of a collection of articles devoted to the 'Slovenian national program', which included, *inter alia*, a protest against the second-class status of the Slovenian language in Yugoslavia." The complaints escalated and soon the republic was in dispute with the federal authorities in Belgrade on the constitutional right of republics to secede from the federation. In 1987 the baton for the Day of Youth should have begun its journey from the top of Slovenia's highest mountain, but in an act of dissent it never left. There was clearly a symbolic chain linking this event, the public memory of Tito and the Yugoslav ideal; at least when one disappeared so did the rest.

Partizan Football Club beat Manchester United in the semi-final of the 1966 European Cup but lost 2-1 in the final against Real Madrid. In 1989 they met Celtic, winning in the first leg played in Mostar 2-1, but losing 5-4 in Scotland, although Partizan won the tie because of the rule on away goals. They have a striking internal record with 130 Partizan players selected for the national team, one of whom, Savo Milošević, was capped more times than any other with a total of 101 appearances before he retired from international football in 2006.

Affectionately called the Black and Whites on account of their strip, Partizan hold the record for national championships since the break-up of Yugoslavia and remained unbeaten during the 2004-05 season. They were expelled from the 2007-08 UEFA Cup qualifying stages and given a hefty fine after fighting broke out between their supporters and fans of the opposing team when playing in Mostar, Bosnia Herzegovina. Their stadium in Belgrade is close to Red Star's home ground, the local derby always being a potential flash point for violence in the city.

Their fans are called *Grobari* (Gravediggers) for which there are two possible origins. One is that the name refers to Humska Street, where their home ground stands, *humka* being a word for burial mound. The other possibility is that it was used by their rivals from Red Star because the black and white colours of the team apparently resemble outfits worn by the city's gravediggers. These fans regularly followed the team to away matches in other Yugoslav republics and abroad where their reputation for violence matched Red Star's. In September 2005 the fans publicly stated their dissatisfaction with two of the club's officials, Nenad Bjeković and Žarko Zečević, for allegedly lining their own pockets by misappropriating club funds. They demanded their resignation and called a boycott of future matches. The boycott lasted until 2007 when changes were announced to the board of directors. During the boycott even the traditional derby with Red Star was poorly attended.

Ivan Čolović includes a short study of football hooliganism in his book *The Politics of Symbol in Serbia*. He draws a parallel between the fans' aggression and the mentality of war. He writes:

> The story of the collapse of Yugoslavia, in a frenzy of hatred and war, in honour of the gods of ethnic nationalism and pre-modern militarism may also be described as a story of the evolution of violence in Yugoslav sport, especially among hooligan football supporters, and of the gradual transference of that violence, at the end of the 1980s and beginning of the '90s, on to the terrain of inter-ethnic conflicts and "greater nation" politics, and thence on to the battlefield.

He describes how in the fervour of the 1980s football supporters carried flags and other paraphernalia proclaiming their ethnic identity in order to associate their team with the national cause. Their behaviour and sentiments ran in parallel with speeches and emblems from public meetings at the time, although expressed without the fans' pornographic obscenities:

> From the mid-1980s, the supporters' folklore in Serbia (songs, slogans, placards, flags, coats of arms, etc.), was dominated by the theme of ethnic identity, until then sporadic and proscribed. And at the same time that theme began to appear in political communication and propaganda, especially at the populist mass political rallies which gave the tone to political life in Serbia and Montenegro in the course of 1988 and 1989. And the supporters wanted, above all, to present themselves as belonging to "their nation", Star and Partizan supporters as Serbs, and at the same time to see opposing clubs as representatives of different nations, inimical to them.

Hooliganism on this level, a social evil in times of peace, helped to make the national differences simpler to understand and easier to justify violence eliding the reality of war with mass entertainment.

Red Star and Partizan may be the biggest and most popular football clubs in Belgrade but they are not the oldest. One of the oldest in Serbia is the city's Obilić Football Club, founded in 1924 and named after the legendary folk hero who killed the sultan at the Battle of Kosovo. The club had some success before the Second World War and continued to play even during the war years. But the two giants established under communist direction after the war dominated the leagues, leaving Obilić a poor relative only managing to make its way into the Yugoslav Third Division in the 1980s.

The end of the state of Yugoslavia was also the end of the big leagues as they subdivided into national divisions. Smaller clubs moved up the ladder and in the 1994-95 season Obilić reached the final of the Yugoslav Cup, which they lost to Red Star. In June 1996 Željko Ražnatović, or Arkan the paramilitary leader, took over the club. Under his lead the club went from strength to strength and in 1998 became Yugoslav league champion. It was the first time that the title had been taken by a team other than Red Star or Partizan since the break-up of Yugoslavia. But when UEFA threatened to ban the club from participation in European matches because of Arkan's criminal connections he passed his control to his wife, Svetlana Ražnatović, the turbofolk performer known as Ceca, in July 1998. She ran Obilić for a short period before she too stepped down, but took up the reins again in August 2000 in what may have been a tribute to her husband after his murder in January of that year. The club has not managed to follow up its earlier success and has sunk back into the mediocrity from which it came.

NATO's Bombs

After sanctions against the Federal Republic of Yugoslavia were lifted in 1995 daily life began to improve and a degree of normality returned to the streets of Belgrade. Yet it was not long before another crisis interrupted the re-integration of the country into the international community. The Albanians in the southern province of Kosovo were dissatisfied with rule from Belgrade and for a number of years lived in a state-within-a-state, eventually deciding to seek independence. The Kosovo Liberation Army attacked police and security installations, intimidating the non-Albanian population. The Serbian authorities responded with force, and in the estimation of some foreign governments their response was disproportionate and innocent civilians were killed.

NATO convened a meeting between Albanian and Serbian representatives on neutral territory in France in early 1999. The Serbian side rejected NATO's request to station troops in the region on the grounds that it was tantamount to a surrender of state sovereignty. NATO then threatened a military strike if the attacks on civilians did not stop. The conflict in Kosovo, in fact, escalated and NATO forces began their air attack on 24 March 1999 at about 8.00pm local time.

It was thought on both sides that the bombing of the country would only last a few days; either the Serbs would admit defeat or the NATO partners would not be able to maintain solidarity in the face of growing pressure to halt military operations. In the event, bombing continued almost daily for 78 days. The possibilities of a land invasion were aired in the media but it did not happen.

It was a most peculiar conflict, particularly from a Belgrade perspective. The government of Slobodan Milošević had never been popular in the city and did not do well in elections there. The nucleus of all opposition parties and groups was centred in Belgrade, with large anti-government demonstrations in 1991 and again in 1996-97. Many of those opposed to Milošević believed that they had the political backing of the democratic countries of Europe and North America. But, now the western military alliance was dropping explosive devices from the skies and firing missiles at them. Javier Solana, NATO's secretary-general, announced,

> We have no quarrel with the people of Yugoslavia who for too long have been isolated in Europe because of the policies of their government. Our actions are directed against the repressive policy of the Yugoslav leadership. We must stop violence and bring an end to the humanitarian catastrophe now taking place in Kosovo. We have a moral duty to do so.

The first targets were military, then those with both civilian and military uses such as bridges, factories, communications and power supplies.

In her book *The Diary of a Political Idiot: Normal Life in Belgrade* (2000) Jasmina Tesanović provides testimony of what many ordinary citizens thought and felt in those days. Her entry for 4 April 1999 records her reaction to NATO's repeated views about Serbs: "The wire is finally visible around our cage. We're bad wild Serbs from the fourteenth century, disguised in jeans, speaking English, but still aliens." This feeling of being excluded from the liberal, tolerant world outside hurt at first, then became confusing. Tesanović was receiving her news from the city itself, and not only from state television but also from CNN, BBC and Sky News. In a bizarre sequence bombs from the West were followed by news analysis of their impact from the same source.

One of the first effects of the campaign was to unite the population, since, whatever their internal differences, the air attacks were a direct threat to human life on the ground. By night sirens would sound a warning, the planes would be heard and sometimes seen, traces of anti-aircraft fire would rise to the sky, bomb blasts would follow, and then the wailing of emergency services. People at first took shelter below ground but later, realizing that it offered little protection from modern high explosives, they stayed at home. By day there was a mixture of carnival and anxiety. Daily concerts were held on Republic Square. People tried to make sure that there was always enough food at home, and phoned round to find out if family and friends were all safe. Tesanović comments on how the unthinkable became the norm: "Step by step, down, down, every day crossing a new border of horror, yesterday's fear, today's habit." Later, she continues:

> Yesterday was a beautiful day, with no electricity, no water. People had despair in their eyes, as if they had no idea what to do with themselves. It's not just the bombs, it's this pointless passing of time which destroys us. There are problems with the children, the small ones cry all the time, the big ones are angrier and more spoiled than ever.

The effects of the bombing can still be seen at some places on Belgrade's streets. Buildings associated with the army, police or government lining Knez Miloš Street were hit and, while many have been reconstructed, a few ruins still stand as memorials. There was fear that the NATO bombers would try to destroy the bridges in Belgrade, as they attacked all the bridges over the Danube in the northern town of Novi Sad and elsewhere. Bridges were assumed to be legitimate military targets as communication facilities that could be used by the Serbian army. But, these facilities in Belgrade were left intact.

There was some opposition to NATO's policy, evident in the many demonstrations that took place in cities around the world. The mistakes when civilians were bombed instead of military installations caused an international outcry. The Chinese Embassy in New Belgrade was struck with some lives lost, explained by NATO as the result of using out-of-date maps. In the early hours of 23 April NATO aircraft attacked the television studio at Tašmajdan, causing extensive damage and killing the technicians and others working inside at the time. A commemorative stone has been placed in the park nearby. It is inscribed with the names of those who perished and at the top it bears the one word *Zašto* (Why).

WAR FILMS
Many novels have been written and films made relating to wars in which Serbia has been involved during the twentieth century. The same can be said for any other culture, as wars evoke strong feelings and have an impact on our lives like few other events. They are central to the collective memory

of a society, giving a sense of destiny and greater purpose to the community. They act as markers in an otherwise undifferentiated passage of historical time by which a people can divide up its legacy as either pre-war or post-war. Novels and films about war also perform important functions in relation to the social imaginary. They help to form a specific shape of the war through which the conflict will enter the national imagination and leave a testimony of that experience. This shape is an important part of commemoration and mourning, of national or community re-building, memorializing victories and defeats, heroism and destruction.

Stories and films began to appear almost before the bombing was over. They share certain elements of the conflict, providing a recognizable set of details that immediately tell an audience the place and time of events. These motifs go further, giving form to that conflict and helping it to ease its way into the mythic structure of the national narrative. One of the first films to include the war as its main theme is *Wounded Land* (Ranjena zemlja, dir. Dragoslav Lazić, 1999), which contains images that are not uncommon in depictions of bombing as it affects a civilian town, but which are also specific to this particular war as experienced in Belgrade. The first sign of an impending attack is given by air-raid sirens, followed by columns of people lining up to go into an underground shelter. It could be a scene from the Blitz in London, except that the entrance to the shelter is next to the apartment block in which the families live and was constructed at the same time for such an eventuality. People make the best of their predicament with humour and resignation, while barbed comments and jokes are made at the expense of the British and American political leaders who support the NATO campaign. Most of those in the shelter are women, children and older men—brothers and other young men are away fighting the enemy. The mention of certain targets hit by NATO, such as the Chinese Embassy, is a reminder of the specific Belgrade scenario. Most films refer particularly to the attack on the television studio and typically include newsreel footage of the damage inflicted. The use of archive footage could be almost classed as a motif in itself. One of the strangest scenes shows people not only sitting through the bombing, but also watching it reported both on Serbian and western television stations. This mixing of first-hand and reported experience introduces a note of distance into critical moments, almost asking whether the bombing took place here or somewhere else. Another motif is a general fascination with the colour of the night sky illuminated by semi-circular bursts of orange on the horizon and the firework display sent up by anti-aircraft fire from the ground. This image is influenced by the spectacle of war as broadcast on television. Such scenes are sometimes observed from the tops of tall buildings by ordinary people treating the event as a performance, sitting in deck-chairs and watching through binoculars.

An altogether more complex portrayal of the war and its effects is given in the film *Land of Truth, Love and Freedom* (Zemlja istine, ljubavi i slobode, dir. Milutin Petrović, 2000). The focus of the main story falls on a patient in a mental hospital. He is a young man by the name of Boris, who worked as a film editor for Serbian television until traumatized by the NATO attack on the studio where he was working. He is taken to a doctor who begins a therapy session by showing him ink spots and asking for his immediate reaction to what he sees. The patient takes control of the session and from his professional expertise as a film editor makes up another story by selecting the ink spots and using them as story boards.

His story reflects the reality of 1990s Belgrade under sanctions. Two hitmen are hired to kill someone else. On completing their task, one of the assassins, Đorđe, goes on a rampage, killing his partner and then turning on other people. In the final scene of this film-within-a-film, Đorđe is visiting Belgrade zoo where he meets his former accomplice's widow, Mirela. They begin to talk and the two of them walk off together down a path in the zoo, as if a romantic episode between them is about to unfold. This embedded narrative alternates with scenes from 1999, presenting NATO's military campaign as part of the historical process in which Yugoslavia disappeared and Belgrade was subjected to sanctions. At the end the film returns to Boris in the hospital. He is standing by a wall in which a hole suddenly appears, through which he makes his escape into another world full of light. He has survived the pains and trauma of history, and is now prepared for a new story to begin.

Today's Belgrade

When hostilities came to an end in June 1999 President Milošević tried to present the conflict's outcome as a victory that he had engineered. If anyone believed him at the time, they did not a year later. At presidential elections in September 2000 the electorate voted against him. He tried once more to steal the votes, pretending that he had not lost and that there would have to be a second ballot as no candidate had won more than fifty per cent of the vote. The opposition, led by candidate Vojislav Koštunica, called for mass demonstrations on 5 October. This time the Belgrade crowds were joined by large numbers from outside the city. Police tried to block roads into Belgrade, while security forces attempted to contain the demonstrators, even resorting to the use of tear-gas. These attempts failed and a revolution unfolded on the streets. The main media offices, some police stations and finally the National Assembly building on King Alexander Boulevard were taken over by angry protesters. The army made it clear that it would not intervene.

The president recognized defeat on 6 October and stepped down. Belgrade, and the rest of the country, was jubilant that Milošević had finally been forced to resign. The following year he was arrested at his home and in June 2001 sent to The Hague to face charges at the International War Crimes Tribunal. He died in prison on 5 March 2006—leading to claims by some that he committed suicide and by others that he was poisoned. The government refused all requests that he be given a state funeral and his body was buried in his home town of Požarevac.

Koštunica became president and, shortly after, Zoran Đinđić (1952-2003), another of the main opposition leaders, became prime minister of Serbia's new coalition government. Đinđić was popular, especially in Belgrade, but he also earned many enemies for himself and it was clear that the gangland culture that had appeared in the city during the 1990s was not completely eradicated. He announced that he would act against organized crime and corrupt officials in the civil service. Taken together, these forces represented a powerful consortium and he was assassinated on 12 March 2003 by a sniper as he left the main government building. He was leaving through the back of the building, which stands on the corner of Knez Miloš and Nemanja Streets, on his way to get into his official car when the gunman fired. The shot came from an upper storey of one of the houses at the top of Admiral Guépratte Street, from a window with a clear view of the area below. It soon came to light that the plot involved former and current members of the state security services, Belgrade's criminal community and senior government officials.

Đinđić was eventually succeeded as prime minister by Koštunica, who has continued to lead a shaky coalition of more or less democratic parties with the Radical Party in opposition. Boris Tadić took over the leadership of the Democratic Party in 2004 and was elected president of Serbia in the same year. A new election for the office of president was held at the beginning of 2008 following constitutional changes after Montenegro's independence. Tadić's main rival was the leader of the Radicals, Tomislav Nikolić. One of the main issues concerned relations with the EU as it was suspected that the EU would support a Kosovan declaration of independence which Russia had opposed in the UN Security Council. Nikolić advocated closer ties with Russia, but the electorate by a narrow majority supported Tadić's more pro-western sentiments and he took the presidency for another term.

Belgrade went through a state of emergency in 1999, almost did so again in 2000, and then once more in 2003. Its status also went through changes in the same period when Montenegro voiced its unhappiness at its relationship with Serbia in the framework of the Federal Republic of Yugoslavia. So, on 4 February 2003 the Federal Assembly finally approved a new constitutional charter officially renaming the country as the State Union of Serbia and Montenegro. The term Yugoslavia was finally dead and would no longer be in use on maps and in atlases.

It was only a matter of time before Montenegro sought to go its own way. The country continued to be known under this unwieldy title until the referendum held on 21 May 2006 in Montenegro on secession from the state union. The vote was carried by a narrow margin and Montenegro became an independent state. Tito's Yugoslavia was now divided into six sovereign states, the culmination of a process which began fifteen or more years earlier.

Over the last one hundred years Belgrade has been the capital city of the Kingdom of Serbia, the Kingdom of Yugoslavia, Serbia under German occupation, the Socialist Federal Republic of Yugoslavia, the Federal Republic of Yugoslavia, Serbia and Montenegro, and now the Republic of Serbia. It still faces some political and diplomatic issues, particularly with respect to the future of Kosovo. The city rarely looks back over its various incarnations, although some of its older citizens have lived in as many as six or seven different countries, on a street with three of four different names, without ever having moved from the apartment in which they have spent the greater part of their lives.

It is a city with a vibrant atmosphere, perhaps because of all these sudden and dramatic changes. Investment is arriving in Belgrade, infrastructure is being improved, and foreign visitors are returning in large numbers. It has festivals of music, film and theatre throughout the year and a lively artistic life of its own. Literary circles organize readings and discussions between writers and critics. It gives the impression of a place that is not waiting for all problems to be settled before taking the bit between its teeth and setting off again, thinking of the future and what can still be accomplished rather than what has gone before.

CITY OF CONTRASTS

Belgrade has experienced many drastic transformations of such a nature that they have barely allowed the town and its inhabitants to define their own identity before another disruption brings new challenges and new identities. It seems to possess holes and lacunae in its history that hinder those who seek a pattern of development to explain its evolution from one period to the next.

Belgrade was taken by Karađorđe and given its first taste of urban development by Miloš Obrenović. It was visited by the European Enlightenment in the shape of Dositej Obradović and given its language by Vuk Karadžić. The city's political culture has been formed at the meeting point of different civilizations. It lies in a border region between East and West, the Balkans and Europe. It is situated at the point where two rivers meet below the fortress that has sheltered Roman, Byzantine, Bulgarian, Hungarian, Ottoman and Serbian troops. Taken over by the Partisans in the 1940s and subjected to communist ideology, it was over time restored to something approaching normalcy. In the 1990s Belgrade succumbed again to an alien force, one which applied its criminal rules to the life of the city.

It has been severely damaged in the two world wars of the twentieth century, only on each occasion to rise again and become successful at the head of the Kingdom of Yugoslavia and Tito's Yugoslavia. Its urban contours give a visual reminder of these meeting points. It has two large Orthodox churches, one of them wrapped in a western architectural design, the other topped by a more characteristic cupola. The centre of the old town is a complex jigsaw of traditional Balkan style, the classical monumentalism of European architecture, Modernist fusions and Postmodernist experiment. New Belgrade contains all possible examples of contemporary urban design and planning.

Extremes of history, geography, politics and culture have combined to form the city and its image. Constantly moving, never quite settled, the Belgrade of the imagination is imbued with a ghostly presence, a spectral form real but difficult to pin down. It is made up of doubled and redoubled identities, reflections of the discontinuous lines of its past and the memories of its many origins. It is a city that gives its artists the opportunity to fill in the gaps, to repair the holes left by accidents of history and geography. The story of Belgrade is a dramatic narrative, and its storytellers offer a glimpse of its elusive unity.

Appendix

SERBIAN LANGUAGE

Serbian is no more or less difficult than any other foreign language for speakers of English to learn. It is one of the members of the Slavonic family of languages which can be found across much of Eastern Europe. They are sub-divided into three groups: the East Slavonic group (Byelorussian, Russian, Ukrainian), the West Slavonic (Czech, Polish, Slovak, Sorbian) and the South Slavonic (Bulgarian, Croatian, Macedonian, Serbian, Slovene). Some would add Bosnian and Montenegrin to this list of South Slavonic languages but these terms have not yet acquired the greater currency of the others. Until recently the languages spoken across Serbia, Croatia, Bosnia and Montenegro were considered one, called Serbo-Croatian. Nowadays, many native speakers regard them as quite separate linguistic units, like badges of different nationalities and cultural traditions. They remain very close and are mutually comprehensible; Serbs, Croats and Bosnians have no need for an interpreter to speak to one another. Language or dialect differences, as in the United Kingdom, identify where people are from rather than their ethnic group.

There is one factor which distinguishes Serbian from the other Slavonic languages. Walking down the streets of Belgrade, or any other Serbian town, the visitor will immediately see examples of writing in both Latin and Cyrillic letters all around. The Latin alphabet is like the one used in English and the Serbian Cyrillic alphabet is similar to the one in Russian. Of the two alphabets Cyrillic was developed for writing first, with the Latin script introduced as Serbian culture moved closer to the West. There is no strict rule to say which alphabet should be used on which occasion, while for individual use it is a matter of personal choice. Some newspapers are printed in Cyrillic and some in the Latin alphabet: billboards, labels on goods in shops, even graffiti may be in one or the other script. Of course, they are not mixed in the same word or text. In order to find your way around town and read street signs and other information you need to be able to recognize both alphabets. However, it is quite straightforward to convert from one to the other using the table given below. Both the Latin and the Cyrillic alphabets contain 30 letters to represent the same 30 sounds. The Latin alphabet is given in the first row with its Cyrillic equivalent underneath:

1	2	3	4	5	6	7	8	9	10
A a	B b	C c	Č č	Ć ć	D d	Dž dž	Đ đ	E e	F f
А а	Б б	Ц ц	Ч ч	Ћ ћ	Д д	Џ џ	Ђ ђ	Е е	Ф ф

11	12	13	14	15	16	17	18	19	20
G g	H h	I i	J j	K k	L l	Lj lj	M m	N n	Nj nj
Г г	Х х	И и	Ј ј	К к	Л л	Љ љ	М м	Н н	Њ њ

21	22	23	24	25	26	27	28	29	30
O o	P p	R r	S s	Š š	T t	U u	V v	Z z	Ž ž
О о	П п	Р р	С с	Ш ш	Т т	У у	В в	З з	Ж ж

Spelling and pronunciation are very easy in Serbian since words are written according to phonetic principles. Each letter represents one sound and each word is spelt as it is pronounced.

The following notes are intended to help provide a basic guide to pronunciation by dividing the letters of the Latin alphabet which differ in their sounds from English into three groups.

I   Vowels tend to be shorter than in English:

- a   as in c*a*t
- e   as in f*e*ll
- i   as the *ea* in l*ea*n
- o   as in kn*o*t
- u   as the *oo* in m*oo*n

II   These letters have only one distinct sound:

- c   pronounced like the *ts* at the end of ca*ts* (never like a *k* or *s*)
- g   pronounced like the *g* at the beginning of *g*oat (never as in lar*g*e)
- h   pronounced in the throat like the sound at the end of Scottish loc*h*
- j   pronounced like the *y* at the beginning of *y*ou
- lj   pronounced like the *ll* in the middle of mi*ll*ion
- nj   pronounced like the *ni* in the middle of on*i*on
- r   pronounced with a trill, not in the throat as in French

III   The last group of letters is formed with the help of accents above the letter but they represent sounds which are similar to ones in English:

č   pronounced like the *ch* in *ch*ild
ć   pronounced like the *t* in *t*une
dž pronounced like the *j* in *j*udge
đ   pronounced like the *d* in *d*ew
š   pronounced like the *sh* in *sh*oe
ž   pronounced like the *s* in the middle of plea*s*ure
The letters Đ and đ in the Latin alphabet are sometimes written as Dj
and dj respectively.

NAMES OF STREETS

In order to make it easier to identify street names when walking in town
I append here a list of those featured in the book with their Serbian form
in both Latin and Cyrillic script:

Admiral Guépratte Street	ULICA ADMIRALA GEPRATA УЛИЦА АДМИРАЛА ГЕПРАТА
Andrić Crescent	ANDRIĆEV VENAC АНДРИЋЕВ ВЕНАЦ
Balkan Street	BALKANSKA ULICA БАЛКАНСКА УЛИЦА
Belgrade Street	BEOGRADSKA ULICA БЕОГРАДСКА УЛИЦА
Botić Street	BOTIĆEVA ULICA БОТИЋЕВА УЛИЦА
Branko Bridge	BRANKOV MOST БРАНКОВ МОСТ
Brothers Jugović Street	ULICA BRAĆE JUGOVIĆA УЛИЦА БРАЋЕ ЈУГОВИЋА
Crown Street	KRUNSKA ULICA КРУНСКА УЛИЦА
Flower Square	CVETNI TRG ЦВЕТНИ ТРГ
France Street	FRANCUSKA ULICA ФРАНЦУСКА УЛИЦА

Gavrilo Princip Street	ULICA GAVRILA PRINCIPA УЛИЦА ГАВРИЛА ПРИНЦИПА
Gospodar Jevrem Street	GOSPODAR JEVREMOVA ULICA ГОСПОДАР ЈЕВРЕМОВА УЛИЦА
Gračanica Street	GRAČANIČKA ULICA ГРАЧАНИЧКА УЛИЦА
Hilandar Street	HILANDARSKA ULICA ХИЛАНДАРСКА УЛИЦА
Jewish Street	JEVREJSKA ULICA ЈЕВРЕЈСКА УЛИЦА
Karađorđe Street	KARAĐORĐEVA ULICA КАРАЂОРЂЕВА УЛИЦА
King Alexander Boulevard	BULEVAR KRALJA ALEKSANDRA БУЛЕВАР КРАЉА АЛЕКСАНДРА
King Milan Street	ULICA KRALJA MILANA УЛИЦА КРАЉА МИЛАНА
King Peter I Street	ULICA KRALJA PETRA I УЛИЦА КРАЉА ПЕТРА I
Knez Alexander Karađorđević Boulevard	BULEVAR KNEZA ALEKSANDRA KARAĐORĐEVIĆA БУЛЕВАР КНЕЗА АЛЕКСАНДРА КАРАЂОРЂЕВИЋА
Knez Mihailo Street	ULICA KNEZA MIHAILA УЛИЦА КНЕЗА МИХАИЛА
Knez Miloš Street	ULICA KNEZA MILOŠA УЛИЦА КНЕЗА МИЛОША
Kosančić Crescent	KOSANČIĆEV VENAC КОСАНЧИЋЕВ ВЕНАЦ
Kosovo Street	KOSOVSKA ULICA КОСОВСКА УЛИЦА
Liberation Boulevard	BULEVAR OSLOBOĐENJA БУЛЕВАР ОСЛОБОЂЕЊА

Macedonia Street	MAKEDONSKA ULICA МАКЕДОНСКА УЛИЦА
Mackenzie Street	MAKENZIJEVA ULICA МАКЕНЗИЈЕВА УЛИЦА
Mihailo Pupin Boulevard	BULEVAR MIHAILA PUPINA БУЛЕВАР МИХАИЛА ПУПИНА
Nemanja Street	NEMANJINA ULICA НЕМАЊИНА УЛИЦА
Nikola Pašić Square	TRG NIKOLE PAŠIĆA ТРГ НИКОЛЕ ПАШИЋА
Nikola Tesla Boulevard	BULEVAR NIKOLE TESLE БУЛЕВАР НИКОЛЕ ТЕСЛЕ
Njegoš Street	NJEGOŠEVA ULICA ЊЕГОШЕВА УЛИЦА
Obilić Crescent	OBILIĆEV VENAC ОБИЛИЋЕВ ВЕНАЦ
Prince Marko Street	ULICA KRALJEVIĆA MARKA УЛИЦА КРАЉЕВИЋА МАРКА
Queen Natalija Street	ULICA KRALJICE NATALIJE УЛИЦА КРАЉИЦЕ НАТАЛИЈЕ
Republic Square	TRG REPUBLIKE ТРГ РЕПУБЛИКЕ
Skadar Street	SKADARSKA ULICA СКАДАРСКА УЛИЦА
Slavija Square	TRG SLAVIJA ТРГ СЛАВИЈА
Student Square	STUDENTSKI TRG СТУДЕНТСКИ ТРГ
Sveta Gora Street	SVETOGORSKA ULICA СВЕТОГОРСКА УЛИЦА
Tadeusz Kościuszko Street	ULICA TADEUŠA KOŠĆUŠKA УЛИЦА ТАДЕУША КОШЋУШКА

Takovo Street	TAKOVSKA ULICA **ТАКОВСКА УЛИЦА**
Terazije	TERAZIJE **ТЕРАЗИЈЕ**
Tsar Dušan Street	ULICA CARA DUŠANA **УЛИЦА ЦАРА ДУШАНА**
Tsar Uroš Street	ULICA CARA UROŠA **УЛИЦА ЦАРА УРОША**
Užice Street	UŽIČKA ULICA **УЖИЧКА УЛИЦА**
Vasa Čarapić Street	ULICA VASE ČARAPIĆA **УЛИЦА ВАСЕ ЧАРАПИЋА**
Višnjić Street	VIŠNJIĆEVA ULICA **ВИШЊИЋЕВА УЛИЦА**
Vojvoda Mišić Boulevard	BULEVAR VOJVODE MIŠIĆA **БУЛЕВАР ВОЈВОДЕ МИШИЋА**
Vojvoda Putnik Boulevard	BULEVAR VOJVODE PUTNIKA **БУЛЕВАР ВОЈВОДЕ ПУТНИКА**
Zadar Street	ZADARSKA ULICA **ЗАДАРСКА УЛИЦА**

Further Reading

The sections below contain the titles of the more important sources used in writing this book. All quotations from Serbian/Croatian original sources have been translated by the author, except where a translation is given below in which case quotations have been taken from the published translation.

BELGRADE (IN SERBIAN)

Antonić, Zdravko et al (eds), *Istorija Beograda*. Belgrade: Balkanološki institut SANU, Izdavačka kuća Draganić, 1995

Bogunović, Slobodan-Giša, *Arhitektonska enciklopedija Beograda XIX i XX veka*, 3 volumes. Belgrade: Beogradska knjiga, 2005

Crnjanski, Miloš, *Beograd*. Belgrade: Narodna knjiga, 1999 (Translation of French publication *Belgrade*. Belgrade: Bureau central de presse, 1936)

Čubrilović, Vasa et al (eds), *Istorija Beograda*, 3 volumes. Belrgade: Prosveta, 1974

Glumac, Slobodan, *Belgrade*. Belgrade: Jugoslovenska revija, 1989

Nušić, Branislav Đ., "Beogradske kafane", in *Sabrana dela Branislava Nušića*, vol XXII. Belgrade: Geca Kon, 1935, pp.125-183

Prodanović, Mileta, *Stariji i lepši Beograd*. Belgrade: Stubovi kulture, 2001

Radulović, Jovan et al (eds), *Ulice i trgovi Beograda*, 2 volumes. Belgrade: Biblioteka grada Beograda, 2004

Vujović, Branko, *Beograd u prošlosti i sadašnjosti*. Belgrade: Draganić, 1994

Vujović, Sreten, *Grad u senci rata: Ogeldi o gradu, siromaštvu i sukobima*. Novi Sad: Prometej; Belgrade: Institut za sociologiju Filozofskog fakulteta, 1997

TRAVELLERS AND OBSERVERS (IN SERBIAN)

Crnjanski, Miloš, "Posleratna književnost: literarna sećanja", in *Izabrana dela*, vol XII. Belgrade: Nolit, 1983, pp.63-92

Damjanović, Ratomir et al (eds), *Serbia: Srpski narod, srpska zemlja, srpska duhovnost u delima stranih autora*. Belgrade: Itaka, 1996

Lamartin, Alfons de, *Spisi o Srbima* (Lamartine, Alphonse de, *Les écrits sur les Serbes*). Belgrade: Utopija, 2006 (Bilingual edition of Lamartine's writings on Serbia)

Lukić, Sveta, *Bivši Beograd*. Belgrade: Draganić, 1995

Makavejev, Dušan, "Memorandum Kosančićevog venca 7", in Predrag Palavestra (ed), *Spomenica Slobodana Selenića: Povodom sedamdesetogodišnjice rođenja*. Belgrade: Srpska akademija nauka i umetnosti, 2004, pp.29-32

Pavlović, Mihailo (ed), *Du regarde au texte: Anthologie de textes français sur le pays et les peuples Yougoslaves (Od pogleda do teksta: Antologija francuskih tekstova o jugoslovenskim krajevima i narodima)*. Belgrade: Narodna knjiga, 1983 (Bilingual extracts by French travel writers to the region)

Ribnikar, Jara, *Muzej 4. jul 1941*. Belgrade: Muzej grada Beograda, 1977

Savić, Pavle *et al* (eds), *Beograd u sećanjima 1900-1918*. Belgrade: Srpska književna zadruga, 1977

Savić, Pavle *et al* (eds), *Beograd u sećanjima 1919-1929*. Belgrade: Srpska književna zadruga, 1980

Sekulić, Isidora, *Zapisi o mome narodu*, in *Sabrana dela Isidore Sekulić*, vol III. Belgrade: Vuk Karadžić, 1977

HISTORY OF SERBIA AND REGION (IN SERBIAN)

Knežević, Aleksandar and Tufegdžić, Vojislav, *Kriminal koji je izmenio Srbiju*. Belgrade: Radio B-92, 1995

Marković, Predrag J., *Trajnost i promena: Društvena istorija socijalističke i postsocijalističke svakodnevnice u Jugoslaviji i Srbiji*. Belgrade: Službeni glasnik, 2007

Samardžić, Radovan (ed), *Istorija srpskog naroda*, 3rd edition, 10 volumes. Belgrade: Srpska književna zadruga, 2000

Stojanović, Dubravka, *Srbija i demokratija 1903-1914: Istorijska studija o "zlatnom dobu srpske demokratije"*. Belgrade: Čigoja štampa, 2003

LITERARY AND CRITICAL HISTORIES (IN SERBIAN/CROATIAN)

Central Committee of the League of Communists of Croatia, Report on cultural production known as *Bijela knjiga* (*The White Book*), 1984 (Copy of the original typescript was circulated via the Association of Writers of Serbia)

Deretić, Jovan, *Istorija srpske književnosti*. Belgrade: Nolit, 1983

Palavestra, Predrag, *Kritička književnost: Alternativa postmodernizma*. Belgrade: Vuk Karadžić, 1983

Popović, Pavle, *Jugoslovenska književnost*. Cambridge: Cambridge University Press, 1918

Further Reading

Skerlić, Jovan, *Istorija nove srpske književnosti*. Belgrade: S. B. Cvijanović; Zadužbina I. M. Kolarca, 1914

TRAVELLERS AND OBSERVERS (IN ENGLISH)
Yovitchitch is the anglicized spelling of Lena Jovičić's surname.

De Windt, Harry, *Through Savage Europe: being the narrative of a Journey (undertaken as special correspondent of the "Westminster Gazette") throughout the Balkan states and European Russia*. London: T. Fisher Unwin, 1907

Durrell, Lawrence, *Spirit of Place: Mediterranean Writings*. London: Faber and Faber, 1969

Goldsworthy, Vesna, *Chernobyl Strawberries: A Memoir*. London: Atlantic Books, 2006

Le Queux, William Tufnell (published anonymously), *An Observer in the Near East*. London: Eveleigh Nash, 1907

Maclean, Fitzroy, *Eastern Approaches*. London: Penguin, 1991

Montagu, Lady Mary Wortley, *Turkish Embassy Letters*. London: William Pickering, 1993

Reed, John, *The War in Eastern Europe: Travels through the Balkans in 1915*. London: Orion, 1994

Tesanović, Jasmina, *The Diary of a Political Idiot: Normal Life in Belgrade*. San Francisco: Midnight Editions, 2000

Thompson, Mark, *A Paper House: the Ending of Yugoslavia*. London: Vintage, 1992

West, Rebecca, *Black Lamb and Grey Falcon: the Record of a Journey through Yugoslavia in 1937*, 2 volumes. London: Macmillan, 1943

Yovitchitch, Lena A., *Yugoslavia*. London: A. & C. Black, 1928

Yovitchitch, Lena A., *Pages from Here and There in Serbia*. Belgrade: S. B. Cvijanovich, 1926

HISTORY OF SERBIA AND REGION (IN ENGLISH)
Beloff, Nora, *Tito's Flawed Legacy: Yugoslavia and the West: 1939-84*. London: Victor Gollanz, 1985

Djilas, Milovan, *Tito: The Story from Inside*. London: Weidenfeld and Nicolson, 1981

Djokić, Dejan (ed), *Yugoslavism: Histories of a Failed Idea 1918-1992*. London: Hurst, 2003

Dragović-Soso, Jasna, *"Saviours of the Nation": Serbia's Intellectual Opposition and the Revival of Nationalism.* London: Hurst, 2002

Drulović, Milojko, *Self-Management on Trial.* Nottingham: Spokesman Books, 1978

Glenny, Misha, *The Balkans 1804-1999: Nationalism, War and the Great Powers.* London: Granta Books, 2000

Jelavich, Barbara, *History of the Balkans,* 2 volumes. Cambridge: Cambridge University Press, 1984

Judah, Tim, *The Serbs: History, Myth and the Destruction of Yugoslavia.* New Haven and London: Yale University Press, 1997

Judah, Tim, *Kosovo: War and Revenge.* New Haven and London: Yale University Press, 2000

Maclean, Fitzroy, *Tito: A Pictorial Biography.* London: Macmillan, 1980

Markovich, Slobodan G., *British Perceptions of Serbia and the Balkans, 1903-1906.* Paris: Dialogue, 2000

Palairet, Michael, "God's Property Developer: Francis Mackenzie of Gairloch in Serbia (1876-95)", in Peter Henry *et al* (eds), *Scotland and the Slavs: Selected Papers from the Glasgow-90 East-West Forum.* Nottingham: Astra Press, 1993, pp.87-113

Pavlowitch, Stevan K., *The Improbable Survivor: Yugoslavia and its Problems 1918-1988.* London: Hurst, 1988

Pavlowitch, Stevan K., *Serbia: The History of an Idea.* New York: New York University Press, 2002

Popov, Nebojša (ed), *The Road to War in Serbia: Trauma and Catharsis.* Budapest: Central European University Press, 2000

Selenić, Slobodan, "History and Politics as Fate: A Comment on the Mainstream Contemporary Serbian Novel", in Predrag Palavestra (ed), *Responsibility of Contemporary Science and Intelligentsia.* Belgrade: Serbian Academy of Arts and Sciences, 1992, pp.227-31

Singleton, Fred, *A Short History of the Yugoslav Peoples.* Cambridge: Cambridge University Press, 1985

Škrivanić, Gavro A., "Roman Roads and Settlements in the Balkans", in Francis W. Carter (ed), *An Historical Geography of the Balkans.* London: Academic Press, 1977, pp.115-45

Thomas, Robert, *Serbia under Milošević: Politics in the 1990s.* London: Hurst, London, 1999

Todorov, Nikolai, *The Balkan City 1400-1900.* Seattle: University of

Washington Press, 1983

Woodward, Susan L., *Balkan Tragedy: Chaos and Dissolution after the Cold War.* Washington D. C.: Brookings Institute, 1995

On Cultural Production in Serbia and the Region (in English)

Barac, Antun, *A History of Yugoslav Literature.* Ann Arbor: Michigan Slavic Publications, 1973

Blagojević, Ljiljana, *Modernism in Serbia: The Elusive Margins of Belgrade Architecture, 1919-1941.* Cambridge Mass.: MIT Press, 2003

Čolović, Ivan, *The Politics of Symbol in Serbia: Essays in Political Anthropology.* London: Hurst, 2002

Eekman, Thomas, *Thirty Years of Yugoslav Literature (1945-1975).* Ann Arbor: Michigan Slavic Publications, 1978

Gocić, Goran, *Notes from the Underground: The Cinema of Emir Kusturica.* London and New York: Wallflower Press, 2001

Gordy, Eric D., *The Culture of Power in Serbia: Nationalism and the Destruction of Alternatives.* Pennsylvania: Pennsylvania State University Press, 1999

Goulding, Daniel J., *Liberated Cinema: The Yugoslav Experience, 1945-2001,* 2nd edition. Bloomington and Indianapolis: Indiana University Press, 2002

Hawkesworth, Celia, *Voices in the Shadows: Women and Verbal Art in Serbia and Bosnia.* Budapest: Central European University Press, 2000

Iordanova, Dina, *Cinema of Flames: Balkan Film, Culture and the Media.* London: British Film Institute, 2001

Ivić, Pavle (ed), *The History of Serbian Culture.* Middlesex: Porthill Publishers, 1995

Lord, Albert B., *The Singer of Tales,* 2nd edition. Cambridge Mass.: Harvard University Press, 2001

Lukić, Sveta, *Contemporary Yugoslav Literature: A Sociopolitical Approach.* Urbana: University of Illinois Press, 1972

Norris, David A., *In the Wake of the Balkan Myth: Questions of Identity and Modernity.* London: Macmillan, 1999

Palavestra, Predrag, *History of the Serbian PEN (A Personal View: 1926-2006) Reconstruction and Testimony:* Belgrade: Serbian PEN Center, 2006

Ramet, Sabrina P., *Balkan Babel: the Disintegration of Yugoslavia from the Death of Tito to Ethnic War,* 2nd edition. Boulder: Westview Press, 1996

Wachtel, Andrew B., *Making a Nation, Breaking a Nation: Literature and*

Cultural Politics in Yugoslavia. Stanford: Stanford University Press, 1998
Wilson, Duncan, *The Life and Times of Vuk Stefanović Karadžić 1787-1864*.
Ann Arbor: University of Michigan Press, 1986

LITERATURE IN TRANSLATION
Many other works of Serbian literature are translated into English, but do not present Belgrade in the manner which is the subject of this book. To read more see: Mihailovich, Vasa D., and Matejic, Mateja, *A Comprehensive Bibliography of Yugoslav Literature in English 1593-1980*. Columbus: Slavica Publishers, 1984, with supplementary volumes. Milos Tsernianski is the anglicized spelling of Miloš Crnjanski.

Albahari, David, *Götz and Meyer*. London: Harvill Press, 2004
Andrić, Ivo, *The Woman from Sarajevo*. London: Calder and Boyars, 1966
Arsenijević, Vladimir, *In the Hold*. London: Harvill Press, 1996
Davičo, Oscar, *The Poem*. London: Lincolns-Prager, 1959
Josić Višnjić, Miroslav, *Belgrade Diary*. Belgrade: Poligraf, 2002
Kiš, Danilo, *The Encyclopaedia of the Dead*. London: Faber and Faber, 1990
Lazarević, Laza, "The First Morning Service with Father", in Svetozar Koljević (trans and ed), *Yugoslav Short Stories*. London: Oxford University Press, 1966, pp.1-18
Locke, Geoffrey N. W. (trans), *The Serbian Epic Ballads: An Anthology*. London: Association of Serbian Writers Abroad, 2002
Mihailović, Dragoslav, *When Pumpkins Blossomed*. New York: Harcourt Brace Jovanovich, 1971
Nušić, Branislav, *Three Comedies: The Bereaved Family, "Dr", Mrs. Minister*. London: Association of Serbian Writers Abroad, 2001
Obradović, Dositej, *The Life and Adventures of Dimitrije Obradović: who as a monk was given the name Dositej, written and published by himself*. Berkley and Los Angeles: University of California Press, 1953
Pavlović, Miodrag, *Links*. Toronto: Exile Editions, 1989
Pekić, Borislav, *The Houses of Belgrade*. New York: Harcourt Brace Jovanovich, 1978
Popa, Vasko, *Collected Poems*. London: Anvil Press Poetry, 1997
Selenić, Slobodan, *Premeditated Murder*. London: Harvill Press 1996
Selenić, Slobodan, *Fathers and Forefathers*. London: Harvill Press, 2003
Tsernianski, Milos, *Migrations*. New York: Harcourt Brace, 1994

Velmar-Janković, Svetlana, *Dungeon*. Belgrade: Dereta, 1996

LANGUAGE TEXTBOOK
Ribnikar, Vladislava and Norris, David, *Teach Yourself Serbian*. London: Hodder Headline, 2003

WEB RESOURCES
www.beograd.org.yu (Belgrade City)
www.belgradetourism.org.yu (Belgrade Tourist Organization)
www.serbia-tourism.org (Serbian Tourist Organization)
www.rastko.org.yu (website of Serbian cultural project)

GUIDEBOOKS
Ćorović, Ljubica, *Belgrade Tourist Guide*. Belgrade: Kreativni centar, 2003
Dulović, Vladimir, *Serbia in Your Hands: Travel Guide*. Belgrade: Komshe, 2006
Mitchell, Laurance, *Serbia: The Bradt Travel Guide*. Chalfont St. Peter: Bradt, 2005
Mitchell, Laurence, *Belgrade: The Bradt City Guide*. Chalfont St. Peter: Bradt, 2005

Index of Literary & Historical Names

Index of Places & Landmarks